OSINT Foundations: The Beginner's Guide to Open-Source Intelligence

Algoryth Ryker

Uncover the Secrets Hidden in Plain Sight

In the digital age, information is the most powerful weapon, and Open-Source Intelligence (OSINT) is the key to unlocking it. Every second, countless pieces of data are generated, stored, and shared across the internet—on websites, social media platforms, forums, and hidden databases. For those with the right knowledge, these digital footprints offer unparalleled insights into individuals, corporations, cyber threats, and world events.

But how do you transform raw, scattered information into actionable intelligence?

"OSINT Foundations" is your gateway into the world of intelligence gathering, teaching you how to systematically search, collect, analyze, and verify information from publicly available sources. Whether you're an investigator, cybersecurity analyst, journalist, law enforcement officer, business researcher, or an inquisitive mind, this book will provide you with the essential skills to navigate and harness the vast world of open-source intelligence.

What You Will Learn

1. The Essence of OSINT – What, Why, and How

Before diving into the techniques, it's essential to understand what OSINT is and how it differs from traditional intelligence gathering. This book will explore the historical evolution of OSINT, its role in cybersecurity, law enforcement, corporate research, and ethical hacking, and why it has become an indispensable tool in today's interconnected world.

You'll also gain insight into the OSINT workflow—from data collection and verification to analysis and reporting—laying the foundation for structured, efficient investigations.

2. Legal and Ethical Boundaries – The Thin Line Between Research and Intrusion

One of the biggest challenges in OSINT is staying within legal and ethical boundaries. With data privacy laws like GDPR and CCPA evolving worldwide, understanding what is legal, ethical, and responsible is crucial.

This chapter will guide you through the fine line between public data collection and privacy invasion, discuss legal OSINT practices vs. illegal hacking, and explore responsible disclosure protocols when you discover sensitive information. Real-world case studies will highlight ethical dilemmas and best practices for responsible OSINT investigations.

3. The OSINT Mindset – Analyst vs. Investigator

Being an OSINT practitioner isn't just about using tools—it's about thinking critically and strategically. This chapter will help you develop a methodical approach to intelligence gathering, sharpen your ability to detect biases, and train you to think like an adversary.

You'll explore:

- The difference between an OSINT analyst and an investigator
- How cognitive biases affect intelligence gathering
- The Red Team approach to OSINT (thinking like a hacker or threat actor)
- How to approach OSINT from a threat intelligence perspective

4. The Essential OSINT Toolkit – Free & Paid Resources

The right tools can make or break an OSINT investigation. This book provides a deep dive into the most powerful OSINT resources available, including:

- Search engines optimized for intelligence gathering
- People search engines & data aggregators
- Metadata and image analysis tools
- Social media monitoring platforms
- Browser extensions and plugins that enhance OSINT investigations

By the end of this section, you'll have a well-organized arsenal of tools to conduct investigations efficiently and securely.

5. Google Dorking – Hacking Search Engines for Hidden Data

Did you know that Google holds far more information than what appears on the first few pages of results? With advanced search operators, known as Google Dorking, you can uncover hidden web pages, find sensitive documents, and retrieve information that most people don't realize exists.

This chapter teaches you:

- How to use Google search operators effectively
- How to find exposed databases and unprotected files
- How to uncover forgotten or deleted content on the web
- How to search metadata and file types for intelligence

6. Social Media OSINT – Tracking Digital Footprints

Social media is one of the richest sources of intelligence, providing real-time insights into individuals, organizations, and global events. However, most information isn't easily accessible—unless you know where to look.

You'll learn:

- How to extract hidden data from Facebook, Twitter, Instagram, LinkedIn, and more
- How to track digital footprints using social media analysis tools
- How to archive and monitor social media activity over time
- How to use social media OSINT for crisis intelligence and threat analysis

7. Website & Domain Investigations – Looking Behind the Curtain

Who owns a website? Where is it hosted? Has it been involved in cyberattacks or fraud?

This chapter covers techniques for investigating domains and websites, including:

- Using WHOIS lookups to trace website ownership
- Analyzing website metadata and tracking codes
- Investigating hosting infrastructure and IP addresses
- Detecting fake or malicious websites

8. Image & Video Verification – Exposing Fakes and Finding Truth

The rise of deepfakes and manipulated media has made verification a critical skill in OSINT. In this section, you'll discover:

- Reverse image search techniques to track photos across the web
- How to extract metadata from photos and videos
- How to use shadows, landmarks, and weather to geolocate images
- How to detect AI-generated images and deepfake videos

9. Geolocation & Mapping – Finding People and Places

Maps and satellite imagery provide invaluable clues in investigations. You'll learn:

- How to extract geolocation data from social media and images

- How to use Google Maps, Street View, and satellite imagery for OSINT
- How to analyze terrain, landmarks, and environmental clues

10. Reporting & Documentation – Turning Data into Actionable Intelligence

Collecting intelligence is only half the battle—presenting it clearly and effectively is just as important. This chapter teaches you:

- How to structure OSINT reports for different audiences (law enforcement, corporate, cybersecurity, etc.)
- Best practices for writing non-biased, fact-based intelligence reports
- How to redact and protect sensitive OSINT findings

11. OPSEC for OSINT Practitioners – Protecting Yourself While Investigating

OSINT investigations can expose your digital footprint as well. This chapter covers operational security (OPSEC) best practices, including:

- How to avoid leaving digital traces while conducting OSINT
- Using VPNs, proxies, and secure browsers
- How to detect and defend against counter-OSINT and online threats

12. Hands-On OSINT – Real-World Investigations

The best way to master OSINT is through practice. This book includes step-by-step exercises where you'll:

- Conduct an OSINT investigation on a person
- Verify the authenticity of a viral news story
- Track an email address using OSINT techniques
- Investigate a suspicious website or domain

Become an OSINT Investigator

Whether you're looking to improve your research skills, conduct in-depth investigations, or protect yourself from misinformation, "OSINT Foundations" equips you with the knowledge and tools to uncover the truth in an era of digital deception.

Are you ready to become an OSINT investigator?

Let's dive in.

1. Introduction to OSINT: What, Why & How

Open-Source Intelligence (OSINT) is the art of gathering, analyzing, and interpreting publicly available information to extract valuable insights. In an age where data flows freely across digital landscapes, OSINT has become an essential skill for analysts, investigators, journalists, and cybersecurity professionals. But what exactly is OSINT, and why is it so powerful? This chapter lays the foundation by defining OSINT, exploring its significance in various fields, and breaking down the methodologies used to conduct effective intelligence gathering. Whether you're a curious beginner or an aspiring analyst, understanding the what, why, and how of OSINT is the first step toward mastering the craft of digital intelligence.

1.1 What is Open-Source Intelligence?

Open-Source Intelligence (OSINT) refers to the process of collecting, analyzing, and utilizing publicly available information to generate intelligence that can be used for decision-making, security assessments, investigations, or competitive analysis. Unlike classified intelligence, OSINT relies solely on information that is accessible to the general public through various sources, including the internet, media outlets, public records, and academic publications.

The rise of OSINT has been driven by the digital age, where an abundance of information is readily available online. Governments, businesses, journalists, and independent researchers increasingly use OSINT to uncover trends, identify risks, and gain insights into various topics. OSINT is widely used in cybersecurity, law enforcement, military operations, corporate security, and journalism, among other fields.

Origins and Evolution of OSINT

While the concept of OSINT has gained widespread recognition in the 21st century, it has been in practice for centuries. Historically, open-source intelligence was derived from newspapers, books, radio broadcasts, and public records. Governments and military organizations have long utilized publicly available information to assess geopolitical developments, monitor adversaries, and predict potential threats.

During World War II, OSINT played a crucial role in intelligence gathering. The British and American governments analyzed foreign radio broadcasts and newspapers to extract valuable insights about enemy movements and propaganda strategies. After the war, intelligence agencies continued refining their OSINT methods, incorporating new technologies as they became available.

The emergence of the internet revolutionized OSINT, making information more accessible than ever before. Social media, online forums, blogs, and news websites provide real-time updates on global events, enabling intelligence analysts to track developments as they happen. The availability of satellite imagery, databases, and leaked documents further enhances OSINT's capabilities. Today, OSINT is an indispensable tool for governments, corporations, and individuals seeking to stay informed and make data-driven decisions.

Key Components of OSINT

OSINT encompasses a wide range of sources and methodologies. The main components of OSINT include:

Publicly Available Information (PAI): This includes newspapers, magazines, books, government reports, academic research, and corporate filings. Publicly available records such as court documents, patents, and business registrations also fall under this category.

Internet and Social Media Intelligence (SOCMINT): Social media platforms such as Twitter, Facebook, LinkedIn, and TikTok serve as valuable sources of intelligence. Analysts monitor trends, discussions, and user-generated content to assess public sentiment and identify emerging threats.

Geospatial Intelligence (GEOINT): Satellite imagery, geographic information systems (GIS), and mapping tools help analysts visualize and interpret geographical data. This is particularly useful for monitoring natural disasters, conflict zones, and infrastructure developments.

Cyber Threat Intelligence (CTI): OSINT is widely used in cybersecurity to track cyber threats, data breaches, and malicious activities. Analysts monitor hacker forums, dark web marketplaces, and data leaks to identify potential risks.

Technical Intelligence (TECHINT): Information about emerging technologies, scientific advancements, and industrial trends can be gathered from patents, research papers, and technical publications.

Human Intelligence from Open Sources (HUMINT-OS): This involves gathering insights from industry experts, whistleblowers, and public forums where individuals share knowledge and experiences.

Dark Web Intelligence: While the dark web is not easily accessible, it contains a wealth of information related to cybercrime, illicit trade, and underground activities. OSINT tools can analyze marketplaces, forums, and encrypted communication channels to extract intelligence.

The Role of OSINT in Different Sectors

OSINT is used in various industries, each benefiting from publicly available data in unique ways:

Government and Military: Intelligence agencies use OSINT to monitor political developments, track extremist activities, and assess potential security threats. Military analysts utilize OSINT to understand enemy tactics, troop movements, and geopolitical strategies.

Law Enforcement: Police and security agencies leverage OSINT to investigate crimes, track fugitives, and analyze social media for evidence. OSINT tools help in identifying criminal networks, cyber threats, and fraudulent activities.

Cybersecurity: Cybersecurity professionals use OSINT to detect vulnerabilities, track data breaches, and identify phishing campaigns. Threat intelligence teams analyze hacker forums and data dumps to prevent cyberattacks.

Corporate Intelligence: Businesses employ OSINT to monitor competitors, assess market trends, and identify potential business risks. Companies also use OSINT to conduct background checks on employees and partners.

Journalism and Media: Investigative journalists use OSINT to uncover corruption, track misinformation, and verify facts. Many high-profile investigative reports rely on OSINT techniques such as analyzing leaked documents and tracking financial records.

Humanitarian and Crisis Response: OSINT plays a crucial role in disaster response and humanitarian efforts. Organizations use satellite imagery and social media reports to assess damage, coordinate relief efforts, and monitor conflict zones.

OSINT Tools and Techniques

A wide range of tools and techniques are used in OSINT gathering, including:

- **Search Engines and Advanced Queries**: Google Dorking, for example, helps analysts find hidden or overlooked information on websites.
- **Social Media Monitoring Tools**: Tools like Maltego, Social Mention, and TweetDeck track social media activities and trends.
- **WHOIS and Domain Analysis**: Services such as WHOIS lookup help identify domain ownership and website origins.
- **Metadata Extraction**: Tools like ExifTool analyze metadata from images and documents to determine origins and modifications.
- **Dark Web Monitoring**: OSINT tools such as TOR and SpiderFoot scan the dark web for intelligence on illicit activities.
- **Geospatial Analysis**: Google Earth, Sentinel Hub, and OpenStreetMap provide geospatial intelligence for situational awareness.

Ethical and Legal Considerations in OSINT

Although OSINT relies on publicly available data, ethical and legal considerations must be taken into account. Analysts must adhere to privacy laws, data protection regulations, and ethical guidelines when collecting and analyzing information. Some of the key concerns include:

- **Privacy and Surveillance**: OSINT should not be used to infringe on individuals' privacy or engage in mass surveillance without legal authorization.
- **Data Accuracy and Verification**: False or misleading information can spread easily, making it crucial to verify sources and cross-check data.
- **Responsible Use of OSINT**: Organizations and individuals must use OSINT for legitimate purposes and avoid malicious activities such as stalking or doxxing.
- **Legal Boundaries**: Different countries have varying laws on data collection and intelligence gathering. Analysts must ensure compliance with local and international regulations.

The Future of OSINT

As technology continues to evolve, OSINT will become an even more powerful tool for intelligence gathering. Artificial intelligence (AI) and machine learning are being integrated into OSINT workflows to automate data analysis and enhance predictive capabilities. Advances in big data analytics, blockchain intelligence, and quantum computing will further expand OSINT's potential.

Additionally, the increasing use of encryption and privacy-focused technologies may present new challenges for OSINT practitioners. As digital platforms introduce stronger security measures, analysts will need to adapt their techniques to maintain access to critical information.

Despite these challenges, OSINT will remain a cornerstone of modern intelligence, providing valuable insights to governments, businesses, and individuals. As long as information remains publicly accessible, OSINT will continue to shape decision-making processes across multiple domains.

Open-Source Intelligence (OSINT) is a powerful method of gathering and analyzing publicly available information. It plays a vital role in government, law enforcement, cybersecurity, journalism, and corporate intelligence. While OSINT presents numerous opportunities, it also comes with ethical and legal responsibilities. As technology advances, OSINT will continue to evolve, offering even greater capabilities for intelligence gathering and analysis.

1.2 The Evolution of OSINT: Past to Present

Open-Source Intelligence (OSINT) has undergone a significant transformation over the centuries, evolving from traditional information gathering methods to a sophisticated, technology-driven discipline. As the availability of information has expanded, so too have the tools and techniques used to collect, analyze, and utilize publicly accessible data. This chapter explores the historical development of OSINT, tracing its roots from ancient times to the modern digital era.

1.2.1 Early History of OSINT: Before the 20th Century

The concept of gathering intelligence from publicly available sources dates back to ancient civilizations. While OSINT as a formalized discipline did not exist, governments, military leaders, and scholars have always relied on public information to make strategic decisions.

- **Ancient Times**: In ancient China, military strategist Sun Tzu, in The Art of War, emphasized the importance of intelligence gathering, including information from public sources such as local rumors, market activity, and traveler reports. Similarly, the Roman Empire extensively used public records, speeches, and correspondence to monitor political and military affairs across its vast territories.

- **Medieval Period**: During the Middle Ages, monarchs and military commanders relied on merchants, travelers, and diplomats to gather information about foreign lands and potential threats. Open sources like letters, religious texts, and trade records provided valuable insights.
- **Renaissance and Enlightenment Era**: The invention of the printing press in the 15th century revolutionized access to information. Governments and intelligence agencies began collecting and analyzing published books, newspapers, and academic works to gain strategic advantages.

These early forms of OSINT laid the groundwork for more structured intelligence practices in later centuries.

1.2.2 OSINT in the 20th Century: The Rise of Mass Media and Government Intelligence

The 20th century saw a significant shift in OSINT methods, driven by technological advancements and global conflicts. With the rise of mass communication, intelligence agencies increasingly relied on publicly available sources to track political developments, military movements, and public sentiment.

World War I and World War II: The Formalization of OSINT

- **During World War I**, governments began systematically monitoring newspapers, radio broadcasts, and diplomatic communications for intelligence. The British Room 40 intelligence unit, for example, analyzed intercepted German messages alongside public information to assess enemy strategies.
- **World War II** marked the true institutionalization of OSINT. The British Political Warfare Executive (PWE) and the American Office of Strategic Services (OSS) monitored global radio transmissions, propaganda materials, and public speeches to extract intelligence on Axis powers.
- **The U.S. Foreign Broadcast Monitoring Service (FBMS),** later renamed the Open Source Center (OSC), analyzed international radio broadcasts to assess enemy intentions.

The Cold War: Expansion of OSINT Techniques

- **The Cold War** (1947-1991) intensified the need for intelligence gathering, leading to an expansion of OSINT methodologies.

- Governments closely monitored Soviet and Western media, academic publications, and radio transmissions to understand ideological shifts and technological advancements.
- The U.S. Central Intelligence Agency (CIA) and the KGB analyzed public economic data, scientific journals, and political speeches to track each other's capabilities and strategies.

During this period, OSINT was often overshadowed by classified intelligence methods (HUMINT, SIGINT, etc.), but it remained a critical tool for strategic analysis.

1.2.3 The Digital Revolution: OSINT in the Late 20th and Early 21st Century

The advent of the internet and digital communication fundamentally transformed OSINT, making information more accessible and abundant than ever before.

The Rise of the Internet and Online Information (1990s - 2000s)

- The 1990s saw the rise of digital databases, government websites, and online news sources, greatly expanding the scope of OSINT.
- Intelligence agencies began leveraging online forums, corporate records, and academic publications to extract insights.
- The emergence of Google (founded in 1998) and other search engines revolutionized information discovery, allowing analysts to find publicly available data more efficiently.

The Social Media Boom and OSINT's Expansion (2010s - Present)

- The 2010s witnessed an explosion of user-generated content on platforms like Facebook, Twitter, YouTube, Instagram, and TikTok.
- OSINT analysts could now track real-time events, public sentiment, and individual activities through social media.
- The Arab Spring (2010-2012) demonstrated the power of social media as an OSINT source, with governments, journalists, and activists using platforms to monitor and influence uprisings.
- The Russia-Ukraine conflict (2014 and ongoing) showcased OSINT's role in tracking military movements, verifying information, and exposing propaganda.

Geospatial and Cyber OSINT

- The availability of satellite imagery (Google Earth, Sentinel Hub) enabled OSINT practitioners to analyze geographic and military developments.
- The rise of cyber OSINT led to the monitoring of hacker forums, data leaks, and cyber threats using tools like Shodan and Maltego.

Today, OSINT is no longer limited to governments and intelligence agencies—it is widely used by cybersecurity experts, journalists, private investigators, businesses, and even hobbyists.

1.2.4 The Future of OSINT: Trends and Challenges

As technology continues to evolve, the future of OSINT will be shaped by new developments, opportunities, and challenges.

Emerging Trends in OSINT

- **Artificial Intelligence and Machine Learning (AI/ML):** AI-powered OSINT tools can process vast amounts of data, identify patterns, and automate intelligence gathering.
- **Blockchain Intelligence**: OSINT practitioners are increasingly using blockchain analysis to track cryptocurrency transactions and financial fraud.
- **Deepfake and Misinformation Detection**: With the rise of synthetic media, OSINT tools are evolving to detect fake images, videos, and manipulated content.
- **Dark Web Intelligence**: Analysts continue to refine methods for monitoring hidden websites and encrypted communications for threat intelligence.

Challenges Facing OSINT

- **Privacy Regulations**: Stricter data protection laws (e.g., GDPR) may limit access to certain types of publicly available information.
- **Misinformation and Disinformation**: The rapid spread of false information makes it difficult for OSINT analysts to verify sources.
- **Encryption and Anonymization**: The increasing use of encryption and privacy tools may restrict access to critical intelligence sources.
- **Ethical Concerns**: The fine line between ethical OSINT practices and potential privacy violations remains a key issue.

Despite these challenges, OSINT will continue to be a vital component of intelligence operations, business decision-making, and investigative research.

The evolution of OSINT from ancient intelligence gathering to modern digital analysis highlights its enduring importance. From printed newspapers to social media, from radio broadcasts to satellite imagery, OSINT has adapted to every technological shift. Today, OSINT is more powerful than ever, but it also faces new challenges, including misinformation, privacy concerns, and cyber threats. As the digital landscape continues to evolve, so too will the techniques and tools of OSINT, ensuring its relevance in an increasingly data-driven world.

1.3 OSINT vs. Traditional Intelligence Gathering

Intelligence gathering is a crucial component of decision-making for governments, law enforcement, businesses, and security agencies. Traditionally, intelligence collection relied on classified and covert methods to obtain strategic information. However, the rise of Open-Source Intelligence (OSINT) has revolutionized the field, making intelligence gathering more accessible and efficient. This chapter explores the differences between OSINT and traditional intelligence gathering, examining their methodologies, advantages, limitations, and roles in modern intelligence operations.

1.3.1 Defining OSINT and Traditional Intelligence

What is OSINT?

Open-Source Intelligence (OSINT) is intelligence derived from publicly available information. It involves collecting, analyzing, and interpreting data from sources that anyone can access, such as:

- News articles, blogs, and media reports
- Social media platforms (Facebook, Twitter, LinkedIn, etc.)
- Government publications and legal records
- Academic papers and technical documents
- Satellite imagery and geospatial data
- Cybersecurity reports and hacker forums

OSINT provides valuable insights in real time and is widely used in cybersecurity, law enforcement, corporate security, and journalism.

What is Traditional Intelligence?

Traditional intelligence refers to classified or covert methods of intelligence collection. It involves gathering sensitive or restricted information through:

- Human Intelligence (**HUMINT**): Information collected from spies, informants, or undercover agents.
- Signals Intelligence (**SIGINT**): Interception of electronic communications, such as phone calls, emails, or radio signals.
- Imagery Intelligence (**IMINT**): Intelligence gathered through classified satellite and aerial reconnaissance.
- Geospatial Intelligence (**GEOINT**): Analysis of geographic and environmental data for strategic purposes.
- Measurement and Signature Intelligence (**MASINT**): Detection of unique signatures from radar, infrared, or nuclear emissions.

Traditional intelligence methods are primarily used by military, intelligence agencies, and national security organizations.

1.3.2 Key Differences Between OSINT and Traditional Intelligence

Feature	OSINT (Open-Source Intelligence)	Traditional Intelligence
Source of Information	Publicly available sources (news, social media, public records, etc.)	Classified and covert sources (espionage, intercepted communications, surveillance)
Accessibility	Available to anyone, including governments, businesses, and individuals	Restricted to authorized agencies with legal permissions
Collection Methods	Uses search engines, social media monitoring, data scraping, and geospatial analysis	Uses espionage, wiretapping, satellite imagery, and cyber intrusion
Speed & Timeliness	Real-time data collection (e.g., live social media updates)	Often delayed due to operational risks and data processing
Cost & Resources	Generally low-cost, leveraging free or paid online tools	High cost due to specialized equipment, field agents, and operational security
Legal & Ethical Constraints	Must comply with data protection laws but generally legal	Often requires government authorization and operates under strict legal frameworks
Verification & Reliability	Vulnerable to misinformation, bias, and manipulation	More reliable due to classified sources but can be subject to deception
Use Cases	Cybersecurity, market research, crisis monitoring, criminal investigations	Military operations, counterterrorism, national security, espionage

While both OSINT and traditional intelligence have unique strengths, they are often used together to create a comprehensive intelligence picture.

1.3.3 Advantages and Limitations of OSINT

Advantages of OSINT

- **Cost-Effective**: OSINT does not require expensive surveillance equipment or covert operations. Most data is freely available or acquired at a low cost.
- **Rapid Information Flow**: OSINT provides real-time intelligence, especially through social media and live reporting.
- **Legally Accessible**: Since OSINT relies on public sources, it does not violate privacy laws or require special permissions.
- **Wide Coverage**: OSINT allows access to diverse sources across multiple sectors, languages, and regions.
- **Useful for Cyber Threat Intelligence**: OSINT tools can detect security vulnerabilities, leaked credentials, and cybercriminal activities on dark web forums.

Limitations of OSINT

- **Misinformation and Bias**: The internet is flooded with fake news, propaganda, and misleading content that can distort intelligence assessments.
- **Verification Challenges**: Analysts must cross-check multiple sources to ensure accuracy and reliability.
- **Data Overload**: The vast amount of publicly available information can make analysis time-consuming and complex.
- **Limited in Scope**: Some intelligence (e.g., military secrets, classified documents) is inaccessible through OSINT.

1.3.4 Advantages and Limitations of Traditional Intelligence

Advantages of Traditional Intelligence

- **High Reliability**: Classified intelligence is often gathered through secure and verified methods, reducing the risk of misinformation.
- **Access to Restricted Information**: Unlike OSINT, traditional intelligence can uncover hidden or secret data crucial for national security.
- **Strong Operational Security**: Intelligence agencies implement strict procedures to protect sources and methods.

- **Tactical and Strategic Value**: Traditional intelligence is essential for counterterrorism, espionage, and military operations.

Limitations of Traditional Intelligence

- **High Costs**: Covert operations require significant financial investment in technology, human resources, and security.
- **Time-Intensive**: Collecting and analyzing classified intelligence can be slow due to verification and bureaucratic processes.
- **Legal and Ethical Constraints**: Many intelligence-gathering techniques require government authorization and can raise ethical concerns about surveillance and privacy.
- **Potential for Intelligence Failures**: If misinterpreted or compromised, traditional intelligence can lead to strategic miscalculations (e.g., the failure to predict 9/11 attacks).

1.3.5 The Integration of OSINT and Traditional Intelligence

Modern intelligence operations increasingly rely on a combination of OSINT and traditional intelligence methods. Intelligence agencies use OSINT as an initial information-gathering tool before deploying classified techniques for deeper analysis.

Examples of OSINT and Traditional Intelligence Integration:

- **Counterterrorism**: OSINT helps track extremist propaganda online, while SIGINT intercepts communications between terrorist groups.
- **Cybersecurity**: OSINT identifies leaked credentials and vulnerabilities, while HUMINT infiltrates cybercriminal networks.
- **Military Strategy**: OSINT monitors troop movements via social media, while IMINT provides classified satellite imagery for verification.
- **Law Enforcement**: OSINT gathers background information on suspects, while traditional surveillance methods track criminal activities.

By combining both approaches, intelligence agencies enhance their ability to detect threats, verify information, and improve decision-making.

1.3.6 The Future of Intelligence Gathering

As technology advances, both OSINT and traditional intelligence methods will continue to evolve. Some key trends include:

- **AI-Powered OSINT**: Artificial Intelligence (AI) will automate data collection and analysis, improving the accuracy of OSINT.
- **Blockchain and Cryptocurrency Intelligence**: OSINT will play a major role in tracking financial transactions on decentralized platforms.
- **Quantum Cryptography**: Advances in quantum computing may challenge traditional intelligence methods by making encrypted data harder to access.
- **Privacy and Regulation**: Stricter laws on data protection (e.g., GDPR) may impact OSINT collection practices.
- **Hybrid Intelligence Models**: Intelligence agencies will increasingly integrate OSINT with traditional methods for a more comprehensive intelligence approach.

While OSINT and traditional intelligence gathering differ in methodology, cost, and accessibility, both are essential for modern intelligence operations. OSINT provides rapid, low-cost insights from publicly available sources, while traditional intelligence offers deeper, more classified data for critical decision-making. In today's complex security landscape, the best intelligence strategies combine both approaches, leveraging the strengths of each to ensure a well-rounded, effective intelligence framework. As technology and global challenges evolve, intelligence gathering will continue to adapt, ensuring that both OSINT and traditional methods remain indispensable tools in the field of security and decision-making.

1.4 Common Uses of OSINT (Cybersecurity, Law Enforcement, Business, etc.)

Open-Source Intelligence (OSINT) has become an essential tool across multiple industries, enabling organizations to gather, analyze, and act on publicly available data. While OSINT was historically associated with government intelligence and military applications, its uses have expanded into cybersecurity, law enforcement, corporate security, journalism, and more. This chapter explores the most common applications of OSINT and how different sectors leverage it for strategic and operational decision-making.

1.4.1 OSINT in Cybersecurity

Cybersecurity is one of the most prominent fields that heavily relies on OSINT to detect threats, analyze vulnerabilities, and respond to cyberattacks. Security analysts and ethical hackers use OSINT to gather intelligence on cybercriminal activities, exposed data, and network vulnerabilities.

Key Applications of OSINT in Cybersecurity:

Threat Intelligence & Dark Web Monitoring:

- OSINT tools help track data breaches, leaked credentials, and cybercriminal discussions on dark web forums.
- Cybersecurity firms monitor hacker activities to anticipate potential threats before they escalate.

Phishing and Social Engineering Prevention:

- OSINT is used to analyze fraudulent websites, email addresses, and phishing campaigns.
- Security teams gather intelligence on how attackers target employees via social media.

Attack Surface Mapping:

- OSINT tools like Shodan and Censys help security teams identify exposed servers, open ports, and misconfigured databases.
- Organizations use OSINT to assess their digital footprint and prevent unauthorized access.

Incident Response & Forensics:

- After a cyberattack, OSINT helps investigate the source of the breach, attacker tactics, and the extent of data exposure.
- Analysts use OSINT to correlate IP addresses, malware hashes, and social media discussions related to an attack.

OSINT Tools Used in Cybersecurity:

- **Shodan**: Identifies internet-exposed devices and vulnerabilities.
- **VirusTotal**: Analyzes malware and suspicious URLs.
- **Have I Been Pwned**: Detects leaked email credentials from data breaches.
- **SpiderFoot**: Automates OSINT gathering for cybersecurity investigations.

1.4.2 OSINT in Law Enforcement and Criminal Investigations

Law enforcement agencies leverage OSINT for criminal investigations, surveillance, and intelligence gathering. By analyzing publicly available information, investigators can uncover leads, track suspects, and prevent criminal activities.

Key Applications of OSINT in Law Enforcement:

Crime Investigation & Suspect Profiling:

- OSINT helps police gather information about suspects through social media, forums, and public records.
- Investigators analyze online footprints to connect suspects to criminal activities.

Missing Persons and Human Trafficking Cases:

- OSINT tools help track missing persons by monitoring social media activity and online classified ads.
- Investigators use geolocation analysis and image recognition to identify victims or traffickers.

Terrorism and Extremism Monitoring:

- Law enforcement agencies track extremist groups and individuals spreading propaganda online.
- OSINT is used to detect radicalization efforts and potential threats before they materialize.

Financial Crimes and Fraud Detection:

- Investigators analyze cryptocurrency transactions, leaked financial documents, and fraudulent business activities using OSINT.
- Dark web monitoring helps detect stolen credit card data and money laundering schemes.

OSINT Tools Used in Law Enforcement:

- **Maltego**: Graph-based intelligence analysis for criminal investigations.
- **Social Links**: Extracts data from social media for intelligence gathering.

- **CheckUsernames**: Identifies accounts linked to usernames across multiple platforms.
- **PimEyes**: A facial recognition tool for identifying individuals online.

1.4.3 OSINT in Business and Competitive Intelligence

Companies use OSINT for market research, risk assessment, brand reputation management, and competitor analysis. By monitoring public data sources, businesses can make informed strategic decisions.

Key Applications of OSINT in Business:

Competitive Intelligence:

- Companies analyze competitor strategies, product launches, and customer sentiment through news articles, social media, and financial reports.
- OSINT tools track pricing changes, mergers, and acquisitions in real time.

Risk and Fraud Detection:

- Businesses monitor employees, vendors, and third-party partners for potential fraud or reputational risks.
- OSINT helps identify fake companies, counterfeit products, and intellectual property theft.

Brand Reputation Management:

- Companies track online reviews, social media discussions, and news articles to protect their brand image.
- OSINT tools help detect fake reviews, misinformation campaigns, and negative PR trends.

Cybersecurity Risk Assessment:

- Organizations assess their digital exposure by scanning for leaked credentials, exposed databases, and phishing domains.
- OSINT helps identify impersonation attempts and fraudulent brand use.

OSINT Tools Used in Business Intelligence:

- **Google Alerts**: Monitors mentions of a brand, company, or competitor.
- **SEMrush**: Provides SEO and digital marketing intelligence.
- **Brandwatch**: Tracks brand reputation and social media sentiment.
- **ZoomInfo**: Gathers business intelligence on companies and executives.

1.4.4 OSINT in Journalism and Media

Investigative journalists rely on OSINT to fact-check information, verify sources, and uncover hidden truths. By analyzing online data, journalists can expose corruption, criminal networks, and misinformation.

Key Applications of OSINT in Journalism:

Fact-Checking and Misinformation Detection:

- Journalists use OSINT to verify images, videos, and news stories circulating on social media.
- Tools like Google Reverse Image Search help debunk fake news.

Investigative Reporting:

- OSINT helps uncover corruption, money laundering, and organized crime activities.
- Journalists analyze leaked documents, financial records, and government data to support investigations.

Geolocation and Video Analysis:

- Investigators use geospatial tools to verify the location and authenticity of images and videos.
- OSINT is used to track war zones, protests, and human rights violations.

Whistleblower Protection and Source Verification:

OSINT helps journalists authenticate anonymous sources while ensuring their privacy and security.

OSINT Tools Used in Journalism:

- **Google Reverse Image Search**: Verifies the authenticity of images.

- **Bellingcat Toolkit**: A collection of OSINT tools for journalists.
- **Wayback Machine**: Retrieves archived versions of deleted web pages.
- **TweetDeck**: Monitors breaking news and trends on Twitter.

1.4.5 OSINT in Military and National Security

Military and national security agencies use OSINT for intelligence gathering, strategic planning, and counterterrorism efforts.

Key Applications of OSINT in Military and National Security:

Situational Awareness and Threat Monitoring:

- OSINT helps track geopolitical developments, military movements, and potential threats.
- Analysts monitor foreign news, satellite imagery, and social media for intelligence insights.

Counterterrorism and Extremism Analysis:

- Security agencies track extremist content and recruitment efforts online.
- OSINT helps identify and disrupt terrorist networks.

Geospatial and Satellite Intelligence:

- Publicly available satellite imagery is used to track troop deployments, military exercises, and conflicts.

Cyber Warfare and Digital Espionage:

- Governments use OSINT to analyze cyber threats, detect disinformation campaigns, and protect national infrastructure.

OSINT Tools Used in National Security:

- **Google Earth**: Provides geospatial intelligence and satellite imagery.
- **Palantir**: Advanced data analytics for intelligence gathering.
- **ShadowDragon**: Monitors digital footprints and online activity.

OSINT is a powerful intelligence-gathering method with widespread applications across cybersecurity, law enforcement, business, journalism, and national security. Its ability to provide real-time, cost-effective, and legally accessible insights makes it an indispensable tool in today's data-driven world. However, users must also be aware of misinformation risks, ethical concerns, and legal constraints while leveraging OSINT. As technology advances, OSINT will continue to evolve, offering even more sophisticated methods for intelligence gathering and analysis.

1.5 The OSINT Workflow: From Collection to Analysis

Open-Source Intelligence (OSINT) involves a structured process that transforms publicly available data into actionable intelligence. The OSINT workflow consists of multiple stages, ensuring that raw information is collected, verified, analyzed, and transformed into useful insights. This chapter explores each phase of the OSINT workflow, detailing the methodologies, tools, and best practices used in intelligence gathering and analysis.

1.5.1 Understanding the OSINT Workflow

The OSINT workflow follows a systematic approach, often modeled on traditional intelligence cycles. The key stages include:

- **Planning and Requirements Definition** – Identifying intelligence needs and objectives.
- **Data Collection** – Gathering relevant information from open sources.
- **Processing and Organization** – Structuring and filtering collected data.
- **Analysis and Correlation** – Extracting meaningful insights from data.
- **Dissemination and Reporting** – Presenting findings to decision-makers.
- **Feedback and Refinement** – Evaluating and improving intelligence efforts.

Each phase plays a crucial role in ensuring the accuracy, reliability, and usability of OSINT data.

1.5.2 Phase 1: Planning and Requirements Definition

Defining Intelligence Goals

Before beginning OSINT collection, analysts must define their objectives:

- What specific information is needed?

- Who is the target (e.g., an individual, organization, or event)?
- What are the key indicators of interest?

Scoping the Research

- Identify relevant data sources (news, social media, government databases, etc.).
- Determine the timeframe for analysis (real-time monitoring vs. historical research).
- Consider ethical and legal constraints, ensuring compliance with data privacy laws.

Choosing OSINT Tools & Techniques

Different investigations require different tools and methodologies. For example:

- **Social Media Intelligence (SOCMINT)**: Tools like Maltego, TweetDeck.
- **Cyber Threat Intelligence**: Tools like Shodan, VirusTotal.
- **Geospatial Intelligence (GEOINT)**: Google Earth, Sentinel Hub.

1.5.3 Phase 2: Data Collection

OSINT data collection involves extracting information from diverse sources. This can be done manually or through automated tools.

Types of OSINT Sources:

Publicly Available Data:

- News articles, blogs, and reports.
- Government records and legal documents.
- Academic research papers.

Social Media Intelligence (SOCMINT):

- Monitoring platforms like Twitter, Facebook, LinkedIn, and TikTok.
- Analyzing user interactions, geolocation tags, and shared content.

Technical and Cyber Intelligence:

- Searching for exposed credentials or vulnerabilities.
- Using tools like Shodan (for scanning internet-exposed devices).

Dark Web Intelligence:

- Monitoring hacker forums, marketplaces, and illicit activities.
- Using Tor, dark web monitoring services.

Geospatial Intelligence (GEOINT):

- Satellite imagery, maps, and geographic data.
- Tracking infrastructure developments, conflict zones, and weather patterns.

Automated Data Collection Techniques

- **Web Scraping**: Extracting data from websites using Python scripts or tools like Scrapy, BeautifulSoup.
- **APIs & Data Feeds**: Leveraging APIs from platforms like Twitter, Google Maps for structured data retrieval.
- **Google Dorking**: Using advanced Google search queries to uncover hidden files, databases.

1.5.4 Phase 3: Processing and Organization

Once data is collected, it needs to be cleaned, structured, and stored efficiently.

Key Steps in Data Processing:

- **Filtering & De-duplication**: Removing redundant or irrelevant data.
- **Metadata Extraction**: Identifying timestamps, locations, authorship.
- **Language Translation**: Translating foreign-language content using AI tools like Google Translate.
- **Structuring Data**: Storing information in databases, spreadsheets, or intelligence dashboards.

Common OSINT Processing Tools:

- **MITRE ATT&CK Framework** – Cyber threat analysis.
- **ExifTool** – Extracting metadata from images, videos.
- **Hunchly** – Archiving and organizing web-based investigations.

1.5.5 Phase 4: Analysis and Correlation

After processing, OSINT analysts must interpret the data, identifying patterns, anomalies, and key insights.

Key Analytical Methods:

Link Analysis (Graph-Based Intelligence):

- Visualizing relationships between people, organizations, and events.
- **Tools**: Maltego, i2 Analyst's Notebook.

Sentiment and Trend Analysis:

- Assessing public opinion on social media.
- Identifying misinformation or propaganda campaigns.

Temporal Analysis:

- Understanding event sequences and timelines.
- Correlating multiple data points for deeper insights.

Geospatial Analysis:

- Mapping movements, locations of interest using satellite imagery.

Case Study: OSINT in Cyber Threat Analysis

An OSINT analyst detects chatter about a potential data breach on a hacker forum. By correlating leaked credentials with real-time threat feeds, they identify a compromised company and alert its security team.

1.5.6 Phase 5: Dissemination and Reporting

Creating an OSINT Report

An intelligence report should be structured to provide clear, actionable insights. It typically includes:

- **Executive Summary**: Key findings and conclusions.
- **Data Sources & Evidence**: Supporting documentation.
- **Risk Assessment**: Potential threats and impact.

- **Recommendations**: Suggested actions or preventive measures.

Presentation Formats:

- Written reports (PDFs, Word documents).
- Infographics and data visualizations.
- Real-time dashboards for continuous monitoring.

Ensuring Secure Sharing:

- Use encrypted communication channels.
- Maintain confidentiality when handling sensitive OSINT data.

1.5.7 Phase 6: Feedback and Refinement

After intelligence is disseminated, feedback is gathered from stakeholders to improve future OSINT efforts.

Continuous Improvement:

- Evaluate accuracy and impact of previous intelligence reports.
- Adjust collection methods based on changing threats.
- Adopt new tools and methodologies as technology evolves.

Ethical and Legal Considerations in OSINT

- Avoid violating privacy laws (e.g., GDPR, CCPA).
- Respect terms of service for data collection.
- Ensure OSINT activities do not lead to misinformation or unintended harm.

The OSINT workflow is a structured, iterative process that transforms publicly available data into valuable intelligence. From initial planning to final reporting, each phase plays a critical role in ensuring accurate, reliable, and ethical intelligence gathering. As technology continues to advance, OSINT methodologies will evolve, making intelligence more efficient and impactful across various industries, including cybersecurity, law enforcement, business intelligence, and national security.

1.6 Challenges & Limitations of OSINT

Open-Source Intelligence (OSINT) is a powerful method for gathering and analyzing publicly available information. However, despite its many advantages, OSINT comes with significant challenges and limitations. These issues stem from data reliability, ethical concerns, legal restrictions, technological barriers, and the overwhelming volume of information available. In this chapter, we will explore the key challenges associated with OSINT and how professionals can mitigate these obstacles.

1.6.1 Data Overload and Information Filtering

One of the primary challenges in OSINT is the sheer volume of data available. The internet generates vast amounts of information daily, including news articles, social media posts, blogs, government reports, and leaked documents.

Key Issues:

- **Too Much Data**: Analysts often struggle to sift through massive datasets to find relevant intelligence.
- **Misinformation and Disinformation**: The internet is filled with false or misleading information, requiring careful verification.
- **Duplicate and Redundant Data**: Multiple sources may report the same information, making it difficult to identify original content.

Mitigation Strategies:

- Use automated data collection and filtering tools (e.g., Maltego, OSINT Framework).
- Implement machine learning models to detect patterns and filter out irrelevant data.
- Prioritize trusted sources and cross-verify information before analysis.

1.6.2 Reliability and Accuracy of Information

Because OSINT relies on publicly available data, verifying the credibility of sources is a major challenge. False information, manipulated content, and rumors can mislead analysts and lead to incorrect conclusions.

Key Issues:

- **Unverified Social Media Posts**: Anyone can post information online, making it difficult to determine authenticity.

- **Deepfakes and Digital Manipulation**: Advances in AI-generated content make it harder to distinguish real from fake.
- **Bias in News and Reporting**: Media outlets and sources may have political or ideological biases.

Mitigation Strategies:

- Use fact-checking tools like Snopes, Google Fact Check Explorer, and Reverse Image Search.
- Cross-reference multiple sources to confirm the accuracy of information.
- Apply metadata analysis tools (e.g., ExifTool) to verify images and videos.

1.6.3 Legal and Ethical Considerations

While OSINT involves collecting publicly available data, legal and ethical concerns still arise regarding privacy, surveillance, and data usage.

Key Issues:

- **Data Privacy Laws**: Regulations like the General Data Protection Regulation (GDPR) in Europe and the California Consumer Privacy Act (CCPA) impose restrictions on data collection and use.
- **Ethical Boundaries:** OSINT analysts must consider whether gathering and using certain information is morally justifiable, even if legal.
- **Corporate Espionage Risks**: Businesses using OSINT for competitive intelligence must ensure they do not violate ethical guidelines.

Mitigation Strategies:

- Adhere to legal frameworks like GDPR, CCPA, and national data protection laws.
- Follow ethical guidelines for responsible OSINT collection, such as those outlined by organizations like Bellingcat and OSINTCurious.
- Avoid hacking, unauthorized access, or deception to obtain information.

1.6.4 Data Access Restrictions and Paywalls

Not all useful information is freely available. Many valuable databases, research articles, and reports are locked behind paywalls or restricted-access websites.

Key Issues:

- **Subscription-Only Content**: News outlets and academic journals often require paid access.
- **Government and Corporate Restrictions**: Some public records are restricted to certain individuals or require formal requests (e.g., FOIA requests).
- **Geoblocking**: Some content is restricted based on geographic location.

Mitigation Strategies:

- Use Open Access databases and repositories (e.g., arXiv, DOAJ for academic research).
- Request data through formal channels, such as Freedom of Information Act (FOIA) requests.
- Utilize VPNs or proxies when ethical and legal to bypass geographic restrictions.

1.6.5 Rapidly Changing Information Landscape

The digital environment evolves quickly, making OSINT a constantly moving target. Platforms change policies, websites disappear, and new technologies emerge.

Key Issues:

- **Frequent Algorithm Changes**: Social media platforms modify their algorithms and privacy settings, affecting data availability.
- **Content Removal and Deletions**: Users delete posts, accounts, or entire platforms shut down.
- **Emerging Technologies**: AI, blockchain, and encrypted communication apps make it harder to track online activity.

Mitigation Strategies:

- Use tools like Wayback Machine (Internet Archive) to access deleted content.
- Continuously update OSINT methodologies to adapt to new digital trends.
- Maintain a diverse set of data sources to avoid over-reliance on a single platform.

1.6.6 Security and Counter-OSINT Measures

As OSINT becomes more widely used, adversaries have also developed countermeasures to evade detection and tracking.

Key Issues:

- **Use of Anonymization Tools**: Criminals and bad actors use VPNs, Tor, and encrypted messaging to avoid surveillance.
- **Misinformation Campaigns**: Governments, organizations, or individuals may deliberately spread false information to mislead OSINT analysts.
- **Cybersecurity Threats**: OSINT investigators risk exposure to malware, phishing, and tracking when collecting data from untrusted sources.

Mitigation Strategies:

- Use secure browsing environments like virtual machines (VMs) or dedicated OSINT workstations.
- Apply operational security (OPSEC) measures, such as masking your digital footprint while conducting investigations.
- Train analysts to recognize deception techniques and disinformation tactics.

1.6.7 OSINT Tool Limitations and Technical Challenges

Although numerous OSINT tools exist, each has its limitations. Some tools may not provide complete or real-time data, and others require advanced technical knowledge to operate effectively.

Key Issues:

- **Tool Limitations**: Some OSINT tools have restricted functionality, requiring multiple tools for comprehensive intelligence gathering.
- **False Positives and False Negatives**: Automated tools may misinterpret data, leading to incorrect conclusions.
- **Technical Skill Requirements**: Effective OSINT analysis often requires expertise in scripting, database management, and network security.

Mitigation Strategies:

- Combine multiple OSINT tools to cross-verify results.
- Regularly update and test tools to ensure accuracy and reliability.
- Invest in training and continuous learning for OSINT professionals.

1.6.8 Ethical Dilemmas in OSINT Investigations

Ethical concerns are a recurring challenge in OSINT investigations, particularly when handling sensitive data.

Key Issues:

- **Surveillance vs. Privacy**: Monitoring individuals online, even with publicly available data, raises ethical questions.
- **Potential for Misuse**: OSINT data can be exploited for malicious purposes, such as stalking, harassment, or cyber-attacks.
- **Bias in Analysis**: Analysts may unintentionally introduce personal or cultural biases into their interpretations.

Mitigation Strategies:

- Establish clear ethical guidelines for OSINT investigations.
- Avoid intrusive data collection methods that violate privacy rights.
- Ensure diverse perspectives in OSINT analysis to reduce bias.

While OSINT offers immense value for cybersecurity, law enforcement, business intelligence, and journalism, it comes with significant challenges. Analysts must navigate issues related to data accuracy, legal restrictions, ethical concerns, and technological barriers. By employing best practices, utilizing verification techniques, and adapting to the evolving digital landscape, OSINT professionals can mitigate these challenges and maximize the effectiveness of their intelligence efforts.

As the field of OSINT continues to grow, addressing these limitations will be essential to maintaining ethical, legal, and effective intelligence-gathering practices.

2. Legal & Ethical Considerations in OSINT

While OSINT relies on publicly available information, navigating the legal and ethical boundaries of intelligence gathering is crucial. Understanding the laws governing data collection, privacy rights, and digital investigations helps ensure compliance and prevents unintended legal consequences. Beyond legality, ethical considerations shape responsible OSINT practices—distinguishing between intelligence and intrusion. This chapter explores key legal frameworks, best practices for ethical intelligence gathering, and the fine line between open-source research and privacy violations. By maintaining integrity and adhering to ethical guidelines, OSINT practitioners can harness intelligence without compromising legality or ethical standards.

2.1 Understanding Data Privacy Laws (GDPR, CCPA, etc.)

Data privacy laws are essential in regulating how personal information is collected, stored, and used by organizations and individuals. These laws aim to protect users' rights, ensure transparency, and hold businesses accountable for data misuse. As Open-Source Intelligence (OSINT) professionals and organizations rely on publicly available data, understanding legal frameworks such as the General Data Protection Regulation (GDPR) and the California Consumer Privacy Act (CCPA) is crucial to maintaining ethical and legal compliance.

This chapter explores the fundamental principles of data privacy laws, key regulations, their impact on OSINT, and best practices for lawful intelligence gathering.

2.1.1 The Importance of Data Privacy Laws

With the rise of digital technology, data privacy has become a global concern. Governments worldwide have enacted laws to:

- Protect individuals' personal information from misuse and unauthorized access.
- Ensure transparency in data collection, processing, and storage.
- Provide individuals with control over their personal data.
- Hold businesses accountable for data breaches and non-compliance.

For OSINT professionals, compliance with these laws is essential to avoid legal consequences while conducting investigations.

2.1.2 General Data Protection Regulation (GDPR)

The General Data Protection Regulation (GDPR) is a comprehensive data privacy law enacted by the European Union (EU) in 2018. It applies to all organizations that process the personal data of EU citizens, regardless of where the company is based.

Key Principles of GDPR:

- **Lawfulness, Fairness, and Transparency**: Organizations must process data legally and transparently.
- **Purpose Limitation**: Data should only be collected for a specified purpose.
- **Data Minimization**: Only necessary data should be collected and stored.
- **Accuracy**: Personal data must be kept accurate and up to date.
- **Storage Limitation**: Data should not be kept longer than necessary.
- **Integrity and Confidentiality**: Data must be secured against unauthorized access and breaches.

GDPR Rights for Individuals:

- **Right to Access**: Individuals can request copies of their data.
- **Right to Rectification**: Users can correct inaccurate information.
- **Right to Erasure ("Right to be Forgotten")**: Individuals can request deletion of their data under certain conditions.
- **Right to Restrict Processing**: Users can limit how their data is used.
- **Right to Data Portability**: Individuals can transfer their data to another service provider.
- **Right to Object**: Users can refuse data processing for certain purposes.

GDPR and OSINT:

- Analysts must ensure they are not collecting or processing personal data unlawfully.
- Scraping or storing personal information from EU-based websites could lead to legal violations.
- OSINT practitioners should avoid sharing or distributing sensitive personal data obtained without consent.

Example: If an investigator collects and stores social media data from EU users without their explicit consent, this could violate GDPR rules.

2.1.3 California Consumer Privacy Act (CCPA)

The California Consumer Privacy Act (CCPA) was enacted in 2020 and applies to businesses that collect data from California residents. It grants individuals more control over their personal information.

Key Provisions of CCPA:

- **Right to Know**: Consumers can request details on what personal data is collected and why.
- **Right to Delete**: Consumers can request businesses to delete their personal information.
- **Right to Opt-Out**: Individuals can refuse the sale of their personal data.
- **Right to Non-Discrimination**: Businesses cannot penalize users for exercising their privacy rights.

CCPA vs. GDPR: Key Differences

Feature	GDPR	CCPA
Scope	Protects all EU residents	Protects California residents
Data Subjects' Rights	Broad and detailed rights, including the right to be forgotten	Limited to data access, deletion, and opt-out rights
Consent Requirement	Requires explicit consent for data collection	Implies consent but allows opting out
Fines for Non-Compliance	Up to 4% of global revenue or €20 million	$2,500 per violation (or $7,500 for intentional violations)

CCPA and OSINT Considerations:

- OSINT practitioners must ensure that collected data does not violate CCPA restrictions.
- Selling or sharing personal data of California residents without their permission could lead to legal consequences.
- Automated data collection methods (e.g., web scraping) must respect privacy settings and opt-out preferences.

Example: A cybersecurity firm scraping personal data from a California-based website without user consent may face CCPA penalties.

2.1.4 Other Notable Data Privacy Laws

Apart from GDPR and CCPA, several countries have implemented their own data privacy regulations:

Brazil – General Data Protection Law (LGPD)

- Similar to GDPR, Brazil's Lei Geral de Proteção de Dados (LGPD) regulates personal data collection and processing.
- Grants individuals rights to access, correct, and delete their data.

Canada – Personal Information Protection and Electronic Documents Act (PIPEDA)

- Requires businesses to obtain user consent before collecting or sharing personal data.
- Applies to organizations engaged in commercial activities.

United States – Various State Laws

- Aside from CCPA, states like Virginia and Colorado have passed their own privacy laws.
- The proposed American Data Privacy Protection Act (ADPPA) aims to establish nationwide privacy rules.

China – Personal Information Protection Law (PIPL)

- Introduced in 2021, PIPL is China's equivalent of GDPR.
- Strictly regulates how companies handle personal data, with heavy penalties for violations.

2.1.5 How Data Privacy Laws Affect OSINT Investigations

Legal Risks for OSINT Practitioners:

- Collecting personal data without consent could violate GDPR or CCPA.
- Storing scraped data without encryption or proper security may lead to compliance issues.
- Sharing or selling personal information obtained from open sources could be illegal.
- Failing to respect "right to be forgotten" requests can result in penalties.

Best Practices for OSINT Compliance:

- Use publicly available, non-personal data whenever possible.
- Anonymize or redact personal information if it's not essential for the investigation.
- Follow ethical guidelines when using OSINT tools to ensure responsible intelligence gathering.
- Stay updated on privacy laws as they continue to evolve.

Tools to Ensure Compliance:

- **Data anonymization software** (e.g., Blur, ProtonMail).
- **Privacy-focused search engines** (e.g., DuckDuckGo).
- **Legal compliance checkers** (e.g., OneTrust, TrustArc).

Understanding data privacy laws is crucial for anyone engaged in OSINT. GDPR, CCPA, and other global regulations impose strict requirements on data collection, processing, and storage. OSINT professionals must navigate these laws carefully to avoid legal risks while conducting ethical intelligence gathering. By following best practices and respecting individual privacy rights, OSINT investigators can ensure compliance and maintain credibility in their field.

2.2 Legal vs. Illegal OSINT Practices

Open-Source Intelligence (OSINT) involves collecting and analyzing publicly available information to support investigations, cybersecurity, law enforcement, and business intelligence. However, while OSINT is a powerful tool, there is a fine line between legal and illegal practices. Understanding this boundary is critical to ensuring compliance with data privacy laws, ethical guidelines, and professional standards.

This chapter explores the differences between legal and illegal OSINT practices, key laws governing intelligence gathering, and best practices to ensure lawful investigations.

2.2.1 What Constitutes Legal OSINT?

Legal OSINT refers to intelligence gathering that adheres to laws, ethical standards, and terms of service of online platforms. It involves collecting information from publicly accessible sources without violating privacy laws or engaging in unauthorized access.

Sources of Legal OSINT:

- **Public Websites & Blogs**: News sites, company websites, forums, and personal blogs.
- **Social Media (Public Posts):** Information shared openly on platforms like Twitter, Facebook, and LinkedIn.
- **Government Records**: Public databases, court records, patents, and FOIA (Freedom of Information Act) requests.
- **Academic and Research Databases**: Open-access papers, industry reports, and whitepapers.
- **Search Engines & Web Archives**: Google, Bing, DuckDuckGo, and the Internet Archive (Wayback Machine).

Examples of Legal OSINT Practices:

✓ Searching for publicly available job postings to analyze industry hiring trends.

✓ Gathering business intelligence from corporate reports and financial filings.

✓ Monitoring public social media discussions related to cybersecurity threats.

✓ Using WHOIS databases to check domain ownership details for cybersecurity investigations.

Legal OSINT respects user privacy, follows platform terms of service, and does not involve deception, hacking, or unauthorized data access.

2.2.2 What Makes OSINT Illegal?

OSINT becomes illegal when it violates privacy laws, breaches computer systems, accesses restricted data without permission, or involves deception and fraud.

Common Illegal OSINT Practices:

🚫 **Unauthorized Access ("Hacking")**

- Accessing private databases, password-protected accounts, or systems without permission.
- Using brute-force attacks or exploiting vulnerabilities to gain access.
- Bypassing paywalls or encrypted data storage without authorization.

⊘ Violation of Data Privacy Laws

- Collecting and storing personal data without consent (violates GDPR, CCPA, and other regulations).
- Scraping social media posts marked as private or intended for a restricted audience.
- Selling or distributing personal data obtained through OSINT investigations.

⊘ Impersonation & Deception

- Creating fake accounts to gain access to restricted information.
- Using phishing techniques to trick individuals into revealing private data.
- Pretending to be someone else to extract sensitive details (social engineering).

⊘ Publishing or Distributing Sensitive Data

- Doxxing (publishing personal information like home addresses, phone numbers, or financial details).
- Sharing classified government or corporate documents obtained illegally.
- Selling personally identifiable information (PII) on the dark web.

Examples of Illegal OSINT Activities:

✗ Scraping private social media profiles without consent.

✗ Using hacking tools to gain access to confidential databases.

✗ Selling stolen credentials or personal data from data breaches.

✗ Impersonating an official to gain unauthorized access to restricted documents.

Engaging in such activities can lead to criminal prosecution, hefty fines, and permanent bans from online platforms.

2.2.3 Key Laws Governing OSINT Practices

Several laws regulate OSINT practices worldwide, ensuring that intelligence gathering respects privacy, cybersecurity, and ethical standards.

1. General Data Protection Regulation (GDPR) – Europe

- Prohibits the collection, storage, and processing of personal data without user consent.
- Grants individuals the "Right to be Forgotten," requiring data removal upon request.
- Imposes severe penalties for violations (up to €20 million or 4% of global revenue).

2. California Consumer Privacy Act (CCPA) – USA

- Gives California residents control over their personal data.
- Prohibits selling or sharing consumer data without permission.
- Allows consumers to request data deletion from companies.

3. Computer Fraud and Abuse Act (CFAA) – USA

- Criminalizes unauthorized access to computer systems.
- Covers hacking, credential theft, and data breaches.
- Violators face prison sentences and financial penalties.

4. Personal Information Protection and Electronic Documents Act (PIPEDA) – Canada

- Governs how businesses collect and use personal data.
- Requires organizations to obtain user consent before gathering personal information.

5. UK Computer Misuse Act (CMA) – United Kingdom

- Makes it illegal to access data without permission or use hacking techniques.
- Covers cybercrimes such as phishing, malware distribution, and data theft.

6. Freedom of Information Act (FOIA) – USA & Other Countries

- Allows individuals to request government records, except classified or restricted data.
- Useful for legal OSINT investigations in journalism, research, and corporate analysis.
- Understanding these laws is essential for OSINT professionals to avoid engaging in illegal activities.

2.2.4 Ethical Considerations in OSINT

Beyond legal requirements, OSINT investigators must follow ethical guidelines to ensure responsible intelligence gathering.

Ethical OSINT Principles:

✅ **Transparency**: Clearly state the purpose of intelligence collection.

✅ **Respect for Privacy**: Avoid unnecessary collection of personal information.

✅ **Data Security**: Protect and securely store collected information.

✅ **Non-Malicious Intent**: Avoid using OSINT for harassment, stalking, or illegal activities.

✅ **Verification**: Always verify the accuracy of information before publishing or reporting.

Organizations like Bellingcat, OSINTCurious, and the Global Investigative Journalism Network provide ethical frameworks for OSINT professionals.

2.2.5 Best Practices for Staying Legal in OSINT Investigations

To ensure compliance with data privacy laws and ethical guidelines, OSINT professionals should adopt the following best practices:

◆ **Use Only Publicly Available Data**

- Stick to open websites, public records, and authorized databases.
- Avoid accessing restricted content through deceptive means.

◆ **Respect Privacy and Terms of Service**

- Check website terms before scraping or collecting data.
- Do not collect or distribute personally identifiable information (PII) without consent.

◆ **Verify Information from Multiple Sources**

- Cross-check data to avoid spreading misinformation.
- Use fact-checking tools like Google Fact Check Explorer and Snopes.

◆ **Obtain Proper Authorization When Necessary**

- For restricted data, obtain proper legal permissions or FOIA approvals.
- Seek consent when dealing with sensitive personal data.

◆ **Stay Updated on Global Privacy Laws**

- Data protection regulations evolve constantly—OSINT practitioners must stay informed.
- Follow cybersecurity and legal advisories to ensure compliance.
- By following these principles, OSINT professionals can conduct investigations legally, ethically, and effectively.

The distinction between legal and illegal OSINT is crucial for intelligence professionals, journalists, cybersecurity analysts, and law enforcement officers. While OSINT offers valuable insights, violating privacy laws, using hacking techniques, or engaging in unethical practices can lead to serious legal consequences.

By adhering to legal frameworks, respecting privacy, and following ethical guidelines, OSINT professionals can ensure responsible intelligence gathering that benefits society without infringing on individual rights.

2.3 The Ethics of OSINT Investigations

Ethical considerations play a crucial role in Open-Source Intelligence (OSINT) investigations. While OSINT involves gathering publicly available information, the way this information is collected, analyzed, and used can raise significant ethical concerns. Ethical OSINT practices ensure that intelligence gathering respects privacy, avoids harm, and maintains integrity.

This chapter explores the ethical principles of OSINT, common ethical dilemmas, guidelines for responsible investigations, and best practices for balancing security needs with privacy rights.

2.3.1 Why Ethics Matter in OSINT

OSINT provides valuable insights for cybersecurity, law enforcement, journalism, and corporate intelligence, but improper use can lead to:

- **Privacy violations** (e.g., doxxing or intrusive surveillance).
- **Misinformation and bias** (e.g., spreading false data or misinterpreting sources).
- **Legal consequences** (e.g., breaching data protection laws).

- **Harm to individuals or organizations** (e.g., targeting individuals unfairly).

An ethical OSINT approach ensures that investigations are conducted responsibly, lawfully, and fairly while minimizing risks to individuals and society.

2.3.2 Ethical Principles in OSINT

Ethical OSINT investigations follow a set of guiding principles that help professionals act responsibly.

1. Legality

✓ Follow all applicable laws governing data privacy, cybersecurity, and intelligence gathering.

✓ Respect platform terms of service (e.g., avoiding unauthorized data scraping).

✓ Do not access restricted data without proper authorization.

2. Privacy & Consent

✓ Respect individuals' right to privacy—do not collect unnecessary personal information.

✓ Avoid collecting or sharing sensitive personal data (e.g., home addresses, financial details).

✓ Obtain consent where required (especially for interviews, private data, or sensitive content).

3. Accuracy & Reliability

✓ Verify all information before using it—cross-check multiple sources.

✓ Avoid spreading misinformation or biased analysis.

✓ Clearly distinguish between facts, assumptions, and speculation.

4. Non-Malicious Intent

✓ Use OSINT for ethical purposes (e.g., security, law enforcement, research).

✓ Do not use OSINT for harassment, blackmail, or unauthorized surveillance.

✓ Avoid weaponizing intelligence against individuals or organizations.

5. Transparency & Accountability

✓ Be open about methods and sources (when legally possible).

✓ Document research processes to ensure credibility and accountability.

✓ Follow organizational ethical codes when conducting investigations.

These principles help OSINT professionals balance security, intelligence needs, and ethical considerations while avoiding harmful practices.

2.3.3 Common Ethical Dilemmas in OSINT

Ethical OSINT investigations often involve complex dilemmas. Here are some of the most common challenges:

1. Privacy vs. Security

- **Example**: A law enforcement agency investigates online threats but must avoid violating suspects' privacy rights.
- **Solution**: Focus on public data and lawful requests while ensuring proper legal oversight.

2. Doxxing and Personal Data Exposure

- **Example**: A journalist uncovers corruption and wants to expose a public figure's personal details.
- **Solution**: Avoid publishing home addresses, family information, or personal identifiers that could lead to harm.

3. Bias in Data Collection & Analysis

- Example: An OSINT analyst relies on one-sided news sources, leading to misleading conclusions.
- Solution: Cross-check multiple sources and consider diverse perspectives to avoid bias.

4. Scraping & Terms of Service Violations

- **Example**: A cybersecurity firm scrapes social media data without user consent, violating platform rules.
- **Solution**: Use authorized APIs and comply with platform policies to avoid ethical and legal risks.

5. Dark Web & Ethical Boundaries

- **Example**: An investigator gathers intelligence on cybercriminal activities via the dark web.
- **Solution**: Ensure legal compliance and avoid direct engagement in illegal forums.

Navigating these dilemmas requires careful judgment, adherence to ethical principles, and consultation with legal experts when needed.

2.3.4 Ethical OSINT Guidelines for Different Fields

Different industries rely on OSINT for various purposes. Below are ethical guidelines for specific fields:

1. Cybersecurity & Threat Intelligence

- Only collect publicly available security threat indicators (e.g., IP addresses, malware signatures).
- Do not conduct unauthorized penetration testing or hacking.
- Report vulnerabilities responsibly (e.g., coordinated disclosure with affected parties).

2. Law Enforcement & Intelligence Agencies

- Follow due process and legal guidelines when collecting intelligence.
- Respect civil liberties and avoid mass surveillance or unjust profiling.
- Ensure investigations are proportionate and necessary to security threats.

3. Journalism & Investigative Reporting

- Verify information before publishing to prevent misinformation.
- Protect sources and respect confidentiality agreements.
- Avoid intrusive or unethical data collection methods.

4. Corporate & Business Intelligence

- Ensure fair competition and avoid using OSINT for industrial espionage.
- Follow data protection laws when gathering customer or employee information.
- Do not manipulate intelligence to mislead or harm competitors.

5. Non-Governmental Organizations (NGOs) & Human Rights Investigations

- Protect witnesses and vulnerable individuals when collecting evidence.
- Use OSINT to expose crimes and injustice responsibly.
- Verify sources thoroughly to avoid false accusations or disinformation.

Each industry must balance its ethical responsibilities with intelligence needs while ensuring compliance with legal standards.

2.3.5 Best Practices for Ethical OSINT Investigations

To maintain ethical integrity, OSINT practitioners should follow these best practices:

✅ **Set Clear Ethical Guidelines**: Develop and follow a professional code of ethics.

✅ **Limit Personal Data Collection**: Avoid gathering unnecessary or sensitive personal information.

✅ **Verify All Information**: Cross-check sources to prevent misinformation.

✅ **Respect Privacy Rights**: Do not engage in doxxing or unauthorized surveillance.

✅ **Ensure Transparency**: Where possible, disclose how data is collected and used.

✅ **Follow Laws & Terms of Service**: Ensure compliance with data privacy regulations and platform policies.

✅ **Secure Data Storage**: Protect collected information from misuse, leaks, or unauthorized access.

✅ **Use OSINT for Good:** Focus on security, research, and responsible investigations rather than malicious activities.

By adhering to these principles, OSINT professionals can conduct investigations that are ethical, legal, and beneficial to society.

The ethics of OSINT investigations require careful consideration of privacy, legality, and responsible intelligence practices. While OSINT can uncover valuable information, improper or unethical use can lead to privacy violations, legal risks, and reputational damage.

By following ethical principles, OSINT practitioners can conduct investigations responsibly, ensure fairness, and protect individuals from harm. Ethics should not be an afterthought but a core foundation of OSINT methodologies.

2.4 Responsible Disclosure: What to Do with Your Findings

When conducting Open-Source Intelligence (OSINT) investigations, professionals often uncover sensitive, critical, or even alarming information. Whether it's a security vulnerability, evidence of illegal activity, misinformation, or potential threats, handling these findings responsibly is crucial. Improper disclosure can lead to legal consequences, ethical breaches, or even harm to individuals and organizations.

This chapter explores the principles of responsible disclosure, the best practices for reporting findings, and how different industries should handle OSINT discoveries in a legal and ethical manner.

2.4.1 What is Responsible Disclosure?

Responsible disclosure refers to the ethical and structured process of reporting intelligence findings to the appropriate parties while minimizing risks of harm, exploitation, or legal violations.

Key Goals of Responsible Disclosure:

✅ Ensure the right people receive the information.

✅ Prevent unnecessary panic, exploitation, or misuse of the data.

✅ Protect privacy and security while maintaining legal compliance.

✅ Maintain transparency and accountability in the disclosure process.

Failure to handle OSINT findings responsibly can lead to privacy violations, public panic, reputational damage, or criminal liability.

2.4.2 Types of OSINT Findings Requiring Disclosure

Different types of intelligence findings require distinct approaches for responsible disclosure.

1. Cybersecurity Vulnerabilities

- Uncovered software vulnerabilities (e.g., security flaws, misconfigured databases).
- Exposed API keys, credentials, or sensitive corporate data.
- Leaked customer information or personally identifiable information (PII).

◆ Disclosure Process:

✓ Notify the affected company or website administrator privately.

✓ Follow industry best practices for vulnerability disclosure (e.g., Coordinated Vulnerability Disclosure (CVD)).

✓ If unresolved, report through official bug bounty programs or government cybersecurity agencies.

2. Criminal or Illicit Activity

- Evidence of fraud, human trafficking, cybercrime, or illegal transactions.
- Social media discussions indicating violence, terrorism, or threats.
- Dark web marketplaces selling stolen data, drugs, or weapons.

◆ Disclosure Process:

✓ Report findings to law enforcement or intelligence agencies.

✓ Avoid sharing details publicly to prevent tipping off criminals.

✓ Ensure proper chain of custody if the data is needed as legal evidence.

3. Disinformation & Fake News

- Misinformation campaigns influencing public opinion.
- Fake accounts spreading political propaganda or extremist ideologies.
- AI-generated deepfakes designed to mislead the public.

◆ Disclosure Process:

✓ Report disinformation to fact-checking organizations (e.g., Snopes, Google Fact Check).

✓ Notify social media platforms to remove false content.

✓ Educate the public through responsible journalism without amplifying falsehoods.

4. Insider Threats & Corporate Espionage

- Employees leaking confidential business data.
- Stolen intellectual property being sold or exposed online.
- Evidence of corporate fraud, bribery, or unethical business practices.

◆ **Disclosure Process:**

✓ Report findings internally through whistleblower channels or corporate legal teams.

✓ If unresolved, escalate to regulatory agencies or law enforcement.

✓ Protect whistleblower identity to prevent retaliation.

5. Personal Data Leaks (Doxxing, PII Exposure)

- Private individuals' home addresses, phone numbers, or financial details exposed online.
- Celebrities or public figures targeted with harassment campaigns.
- Stolen personal data from data breaches.

◆ **Disclosure Process:**

✓ Notify affected individuals privately (if safe to do so).

✓ Report data leaks to the website host, security teams, or privacy regulators.

✓ Avoid spreading or resharing leaked personal data.

2.4.3 Who Should You Report Your Findings To?

The appropriate recipient of an OSINT disclosure depends on the nature of the discovery.

Type of Finding	Report To
Cybersecurity Vulnerabilities	Company security team, CERTs, Bug Bounty platforms (e.g., HackerOne)
Criminal Activity	Law enforcement, FBI, Interpol, Europol
Disinformation & Misinformation	Fact-checking organizations, social media platforms
Corporate Espionage	Internal security teams, regulatory agencies
Personal Data Leaks	Affected individuals, website admins, data protection authorities

Always ensure confidentiality and avoid public disclosure unless necessary.

2.4.4 Best Practices for Responsible Disclosure

To handle OSINT findings ethically and legally, follow these best practices:

1. Follow the "Need to Know" Principle

- Only disclose findings to those who need to take action.
- Avoid unnecessary exposure that could lead to exploitation.

2. Ensure Accuracy Before Reporting

- Verify findings from multiple sources before making a report.
- Avoid spreading false alarms or exaggerated claims.

3. Use Secure Communication Channels

- Use encrypted emails (e.g., PGP, ProtonMail) or secure portals for sensitive disclosures.
- Avoid public forums for reporting critical security flaws.

4. Respect Privacy & Legal Compliance

- Do not share personal data irresponsibly.
- Follow data protection laws (GDPR, CCPA) when handling sensitive information.

5. Follow Established Disclosure Policies

- If dealing with cybersecurity flaws, follow Coordinated Vulnerability Disclosure (CVD).

- Check if the company has a bug bounty program before reporting vulnerabilities.

2.4.5 Ethical Considerations in Disclosure

Beyond legal compliance, ethical considerations play a major role in responsible disclosure.

1. Avoid Public "Name & Shame" Tactics

- Publicly exposing vulnerabilities without notifying the affected party can cause harm.
- Always give organizations time to fix issues before public disclosure.

2. Consider Potential Harm

- Could the disclosure endanger individuals (e.g., whistleblowers, activists)?
- Would exposing information cause public panic or economic damage?

3. Be Transparent & Accountable

- Document the steps taken to verify and report findings.
- Be ready to explain why and how the information was collected.

Responsible disclosure balances public safety, privacy rights, and security needs without causing harm or violating ethical boundaries.

Handling OSINT findings responsibly is as important as the intelligence-gathering process itself. Improper disclosure can lead to legal, ethical, and security risks, while responsible reporting ensures that findings are used constructively to protect individuals, organizations, and public safety.

By following best practices, OSINT professionals can maximize the benefits of intelligence gathering while minimizing risks and harm.

2.5 OPSEC for OSINT Investigators: Staying Legal & Safe

Operational Security (OPSEC) is a crucial aspect of Open-Source Intelligence (OSINT) investigations. While OSINT focuses on gathering publicly available information, the process itself can expose investigators to legal, ethical, and security risks. Without proper

OPSEC, OSINT professionals may unintentionally reveal their identity, compromise an investigation, or even violate laws.

This chapter explores the fundamentals of OPSEC for OSINT practitioners, covering risk mitigation, anonymity techniques, legal considerations, and best practices to ensure safety and compliance while conducting investigations.

2.5.1 Why OPSEC Matters in OSINT

OPSEC is essential for OSINT professionals for several reasons:

1. Protecting Investigator Identity

- Many OSINT investigations target cybercriminals, extremist groups, or fraudulent entities that might retaliate.
- Without OPSEC, adversaries can track and doxx investigators, leading to harassment or physical threats.

2. Avoiding Legal Violations

- Some data collection methods (e.g., scraping, accessing restricted content) may violate terms of service or laws.
- Poor OPSEC can unintentionally lead to unauthorized access or privacy breaches.

3. Preventing Digital Footprints in Investigations

- Using personal accounts, real IP addresses, or known devices can alert targets that they are being monitored.
- Proper OPSEC ensures covert data collection without compromising the investigation.

4. Ensuring Data Security

- Investigators deal with sensitive findings that must be stored and shared securely.
- Poor security practices can lead to data leaks, breaches, or unauthorized access.

By implementing strong OPSEC strategies, OSINT professionals can operate safely, legally, and effectively.

2.5.2 Key OPSEC Strategies for OSINT Investigators

OPSEC consists of multiple layers of security measures to protect OSINT professionals from exposure or legal risks.

1. Maintaining Anonymity Online

Use a Secure and Private Internet Connection

✅ Use a Virtual Private Network (VPN) to mask your real IP address.

✅ Consider using Tor Browser for additional anonymity when needed.

✅ Avoid using personal Wi-Fi connections—consider secure public or burner networks.

Separate Personal & OSINT Identities

✅ Create burner accounts for OSINT research instead of using personal social media.

✅ Use different email addresses and phone numbers for OSINT investigations.

✅ Avoid logging into personal accounts while conducting research.

Protect Your Device Fingerprint

✅ Use privacy-focused browsers (e.g., Firefox with hardened settings, Brave).

✅ Disable JavaScript and tracking scripts on investigative sessions.

✅ Use browser extensions like uBlock Origin, Privacy Badger, or NoScript to block trackers.

2. Secure Communications & Data Handling

Use Encrypted Communication Tools

✅ Use ProtonMail, Tutanota, or other encrypted email services.

✅ Use Signal, Element, or Wire for secure messaging.

✅ Avoid discussing investigations on insecure platforms (e.g., WhatsApp, Facebook Messenger).

Secure Data Storage

✓ Encrypt sensitive data using tools like VeraCrypt or BitLocker.

✓ Store findings on secure external drives or air-gapped systems.

✓ Use password managers (e.g., Bitwarden, KeePass) to store OSINT credentials safely.

Redact Sensitive Information

✓ Before sharing reports, sanitize metadata from documents and images (e.g., Exif metadata removal).

✓ Redact PII and sensitive findings from OSINT reports to avoid unintended leaks.

3. Avoiding Digital Traces in Investigations

Operational Browsing Hygiene

✓ Use incognito/private browsing mode for research.

✓ Rotate between different browser agents or VMs to avoid detection.

✓ Be cautious of honeypot sites that log visitor information.

Avoid Interacting with Targets Directly

✓ Never like, comment, or interact with target accounts on social media.

✓ Use screenshot tools instead of downloading content that might notify the target.

✓ Avoid logging into personal accounts while conducting OSINT research.

Use Virtual Machines (VMs) or Isolated Systems

✓ Set up a dedicated VM (e.g., VirtualBox, Qubes OS) for OSINT work.

✓ Use Tails OS or Whonix for high-security investigations.

✓ Do not mix OSINT research with personal browsing activities.

2.5.3 Legal Considerations for OSINT OPSEC

Even if OSINT involves public data, some collection techniques can still be legally risky. Investigators must understand where the legal lines are drawn to stay compliant.

1. Understanding Computer Crime Laws

- Accessing unauthorized data (even accidentally) can be illegal (e.g., hacking laws, unauthorized database access).
- Web scraping laws vary by country—some sites prohibit automated data extraction.
- Avoid circumventing paywalls, logins, or protected data without authorization.

2. Respecting Terms of Service (ToS)

- Many platforms (Facebook, Twitter, LinkedIn) have ToS that prohibit data scraping.
- Violating ToS might not always be illegal but can lead to account bans or legal action.
- If unsure, consult legal experts or cybersecurity policies before conducting investigations.

3. Following Data Protection Laws (GDPR, CCPA, etc.)

- Do not collect or store personal data unnecessarily.
- Avoid sharing PII (Personally Identifiable Information) unless legally required.
- Anonymize or redact sensitive data before publishing reports.

4. Law Enforcement & Government-Specific Rules

- Government OSINT analysts often have stricter rules regarding data retention.
- Intelligence agencies must follow laws on surveillance and privacy protection.
- Ethical considerations apply even when gathering data for national security purposes.

2.5.4 Common OPSEC Mistakes to Avoid

- Using personal social media accounts for OSINT investigations.
- Not using a VPN or anonymous browsing while conducting research.
- Clicking on suspicious links that might track or expose your identity.
- Engaging with target profiles (liking, commenting, following).

● Failing to sanitize metadata from screenshots, documents, or images.
● Using insecure storage or communication methods (e.g., storing sensitive data on Google Drive).
● Forgetting to rotate IP addresses when investigating multiple sources.

2.5.5 Best Practices for Staying Safe & Legal

✓ Use dedicated OSINT accounts and devices separate from personal use.

✓ Always use a VPN or Tor when researching sensitive subjects.

✓ Store and share data securely using encryption tools.

✓ Follow ethical guidelines and legal frameworks for data collection.

✓ Regularly update security tools and software to avoid vulnerabilities.

✓ If handling high-risk investigations, consider working in teams for added safety.

By maintaining strong OPSEC, OSINT investigators can conduct their work legally, ethically, and securely, minimizing risks while maximizing the effectiveness of their investigations.

OPSEC is a fundamental skill for OSINT practitioners. Without proper security measures, investigators can expose themselves to cyber threats, legal consequences, or operational failure. By applying strong anonymity techniques, secure communication practices, and legal awareness, OSINT professionals can ensure safe, ethical, and effective intelligence gathering.

2.6 Case Studies: Ethical OSINT Investigations vs. Misuse

Open-Source Intelligence (OSINT) can be a powerful tool for good when used ethically and responsibly. However, it can also be misused, leading to privacy violations, harassment, or even legal consequences. This chapter explores real-world case studies of OSINT being used ethically and effectively, as well as examples of its misuse, highlighting the importance of responsible practices.

2.6.1 Ethical OSINT Investigations: Case Studies

Ethical OSINT investigations prioritize privacy, legality, and responsible disclosure while gathering intelligence for legitimate purposes such as law enforcement, cybersecurity, journalism, and human rights advocacy.

Case Study #1: Tracking Human Trafficking Networks

Background:

Human trafficking remains a global crisis, with victims often lured through online recruitment. In 2020, an OSINT investigation by the Anti-Human Trafficking Intelligence Initiative (ATII) helped law enforcement agencies uncover a trafficking network operating via social media and online classified ads.

OSINT Techniques Used:

✓ **Social media monitoring**—analyzing suspicious job postings and recruitment messages.
✓ **Image analysis**—reverse image searches to track victims' photos across platforms.
✓ **Dark web research**—identifying forums where traffickers operated.
✓ **Geolocation tools**—cross-referencing images and metadata to find trafficking locations.

Outcome:

- Law enforcement successfully raided multiple locations, rescuing several victims.
- Several perpetrators were arrested, and trafficking websites were taken down.
- The investigation followed legal and ethical guidelines, ensuring victim confidentiality.

◆ **Key Lesson**: Ethical OSINT can save lives when used for legitimate investigations while respecting privacy laws.

Case Study #2: Exposing Corruption Through OSINT

Background:

Investigative journalists from Bellingcat, an independent OSINT research group, uncovered corruption involving public officials in multiple countries.

OSINT Techniques Used:

✅ **Analyzing leaked financial documents**—tracking suspicious offshore accounts.

✅ **Satellite imagery**—verifying luxury properties owned by corrupt officials.

✅ **Flight tracking data**—identifying officials' secretive travel movements.

✅ **Cross-referencing open data**—comparing public asset declarations with real holdings.

Outcome:

- Governments launched anti-corruption investigations, leading to arrests and policy changes.
- The journalists followed strict ethical and legal guidelines, ensuring transparency.
- The findings were publicly disclosed through responsible reporting.

◆ **Key Lesson**: OSINT is a valuable tool in journalism, provided it follows ethical and legal standards.

Case Study #3: Cybersecurity & Threat Intelligence

Background:

In 2021, an OSINT analyst discovered a misconfigured cloud database exposing millions of user records belonging to a healthcare provider.

OSINT Techniques Used:

✅ **Shodan and Censys scans**—to identify exposed databases.

✅ **Metadata analysis**—confirming the source of the leaked records.

✅ **Responsible disclosure**—privately notifying the healthcare company before public disclosure.

Outcome:

- The company secured the database before any malicious exploitation occurred.
- No patient data was leaked or sold, thanks to rapid responsible reporting.
- The researcher avoided legal issues by following responsible disclosure protocols.

◆ **Key Lesson**: Ethical cybersecurity investigations require responsible disclosure to prevent harm.

2.6.2 Misuse of OSINT: Case Studies

When OSINT is misused, it can lead to privacy violations, harassment, misinformation, or illegal activities. The following case studies highlight the dangers of unethical OSINT practices.

Case Study #4: Doxxing & Privacy Violations

Background:

During a political controversy, an OSINT enthusiast uncovered personal details of a public figure and shared them online, including their home address and family details.

OSINT Techniques Used (Unethically):

✗ **Social media scraping**—gathering personal details from old posts.
✗ **WHOIS lookup abuse**—revealing private domain registration data.
✗ **Reverse image search**—identifying family members and their locations.

Outcome:

- The public figure faced harassment, threats, and real-world dangers.
- Legal action was taken against the individual responsible for the doxxing.
- The case raised awareness about the dangers of weaponizing OSINT against individuals.

● **Key Lesson**: Using OSINT to expose personal details without consent is unethical and often illegal.

Case Study #5: Fake News & Disinformation

Background:

A social media influencer used OSINT techniques to create false narratives, misrepresenting data to support a conspiracy theory.

Unethical OSINT Techniques Used:

✗ **Selective image analysis**—using out-of-context photos to manipulate public opinion.

✗ **Fabricated geolocation**—misleading audiences with fake satellite imagery.

✗ **Data manipulation**—altering statistics to fit a false narrative.

Outcome:

- The misinformation campaign spread widely, leading to public panic.
- Fact-checking organizations debunked the false claims, but damage was already done.
- The influencer was banned from multiple platforms for spreading harmful misinformation.

● **Key Lesson**: OSINT must be used for truthful, evidence-based reporting, not to manipulate narratives.

Case Study #6: Corporate Espionage & Unethical OSINT Use

Background:

A competitor company hired OSINT investigators to spy on a rival firm's executives, using social engineering and data collection techniques.

Unethical OSINT Techniques Used:

✗ **Phishing attacks**—extracting sensitive business data from employees.

✗ **LinkedIn scraping**—targeting executives for insider information.

✗ **Dark web searches**—looking for leaked credentials to access internal systems.

Outcome:

- The company faced legal consequences after the unethical data collection was exposed.
- Employees involved in the OSINT operation were fired and blacklisted.
- The case highlighted the legal risks of using OSINT for corporate espionage.

● **Key Lesson**: OSINT should not be used for illegal competitive intelligence or corporate espionage.

2.6.3 Ethical vs. Unethical OSINT: A Comparison

Factor	Ethical OSINT	Unethical OSINT
Purpose	Law enforcement, cybersecurity, journalism, research	Doxxing, harassment, misinformation, espionage
Legality	Fully legal & compliant with laws	Often illegal or violating ToS
Privacy Respect	Protects sensitive data & PII	Exposes personal information without consent
Data Use	Factual, unbiased, responsible	Misleading, manipulative, harmful
Disclosure	Follows responsible reporting & ethics	Reckless or harmful disclosure

Ethical OSINT practices serve the greater good, helping law enforcement, journalists, and security professionals protect individuals and society. However, misuse of OSINT can lead to privacy violations, misinformation, or even criminal consequences.

By following legal guidelines, respecting privacy, and ensuring accuracy, OSINT professionals can use their skills responsibly and ethically, maximizing the benefits of open-source intelligence while minimizing risks and harm.

3. OSINT Mindset: Analyst vs. Investigator

Successful OSINT practitioners approach intelligence gathering with a strategic mindset, but the role they play influences how they think and operate. Analysts focus on identifying patterns, trends, and broader intelligence insights, while investigators pursue specific targets, uncovering hidden connections and tracing digital footprints. This chapter explores the key differences between an analyst's strategic approach and an investigator's tactical methodology, highlighting the mindset, skills, and workflows required for each. By understanding these perspectives, you can refine your approach to OSINT and develop the adaptability needed to excel in both roles.

3.1 The Difference Between an OSINT Analyst & an Investigator

Open-Source Intelligence (OSINT) plays a vital role in various fields, from cybersecurity to law enforcement. However, not all OSINT professionals have the same role. Two primary types of OSINT practitioners are OSINT analysts and OSINT investigators. While both rely on gathering and analyzing open-source data, their objectives, methodologies, and professional responsibilities differ.

This chapter explores the key differences between an OSINT analyst and an OSINT investigator, highlighting their distinct skills, workflows, and use cases.

3.1.1 Who is an OSINT Analyst?

An OSINT analyst is a professional responsible for gathering, processing, and interpreting open-source data to produce actionable intelligence. Analysts focus on data synthesis, pattern recognition, and threat assessments, often working in government, corporate, or intelligence sectors.

Primary Responsibilities of an OSINT Analyst

✓ Data Collection & Processing

- Gathering large datasets from news, social media, public records, and web sources.

- **Using automated tools** (e.g., Maltego, SpiderFoot) to aggregate and organize information.

✅ Threat & Risk Assessment

- Identifying trends, vulnerabilities, and security risks in the data.
- Analyzing cyber threats, geopolitical risks, or market trends.

✅ Report Writing & Intelligence Briefings

- Producing structured reports with findings for decision-makers.
- Visualizing data using graphs, charts, and mapping tools.

✅ Monitoring & Alerting

- Setting up continuous alerts for emerging threats (e.g., cybersecurity breaches, political unrest).
- Using OSINT dashboards for real-time intelligence updates.

✅ Collaboration with Teams

- Working closely with law enforcement, security teams, and business executives.
- Providing intelligence that helps organizations make informed decisions.

Typical Work Environments for OSINT Analysts

- Government intelligence agencies (e.g., CIA, MI6, Europol).
- Cybersecurity firms (threat intelligence teams).
- Corporate security departments.
- Research and journalism organizations.

📌 **Example**: A cybersecurity OSINT analyst monitors the dark web for leaked credentials and alerts companies to potential data breaches.

3.1.2 Who is an OSINT Investigator?

An OSINT investigator is someone who actively conducts intelligence-gathering operations to track individuals, organizations, or events for investigative purposes. Unlike analysts, who focus on data interpretation, investigators perform hands-on research and often engage in deep-dive investigations.

Primary Responsibilities of an OSINT Investigator

✓ **Conducting Investigations on Targets**

- Gathering intelligence on individuals, groups, or companies.
- Using social media investigations, geolocation tracking, and public records searches.

✓ **Identifying and Profiling Threat Actors**

- Investigating cybercriminals, fraudsters, missing persons, or extremists.
- Mapping connections between individuals using link analysis tools.

✓ **Covert Research & Identity Protection**

- Operating under strict OPSEC (Operational Security) protocols.
- Using burner accounts, VPNs, and anonymized browsing to avoid detection.

✓ **Evidence Collection & Documentation**

- Gathering screenshots, metadata, and OSINT records for legal or investigative purposes.
- Ensuring compliance with legal and ethical guidelines when handling sensitive data.

✓ **Field Investigations & Law Enforcement Support**

- Assisting in criminal investigations, corporate fraud detection, or missing person cases.
- Often working alongside private investigators, journalists, or law enforcement.

Typical Work Environments for OSINT Investigators

- Law enforcement agencies (e.g., FBI, Interpol).
- Private investigation firms.

- Cybercrime and fraud detection teams.
- Human rights and activist groups.

📌 **Example**: An OSINT investigator working for law enforcement tracks a cybercriminal's Bitcoin transactions to uncover illegal activities.

3.1.3 Key Differences Between OSINT Analysts & Investigators

Feature	OSINT Analyst	OSINT Investigator
Primary Role	Analyzes and interprets OSINT data.	Conducts deep-dive investigations and hands-on research.
Work Focus	Threat intelligence, risk assessment, cybersecurity.	Criminal cases, fraud investigations, missing persons.
Key Skills	Data analysis, reporting, visualization.	Covert research, identity protection, evidence collection.
Tools Used	Maltego, SpiderFoot, IBM i2 Analyst's Notebook.	Social media search tools, WHOIS lookups, dark web monitoring.
Data Handling	Processes and interprets data for decision-makers.	Collects and verifies evidence for legal or investigative use.
Privacy & OPSEC	Ensures compliance with data protection laws.	Maintains anonymity and secure research practices.
Employment Sector	Government, cybersecurity, corporate intelligence.	Law enforcement, private investigations, journalism.

3.1.4 Overlapping Skills & Collaboration Between Analysts & Investigators

While OSINT analysts and investigators have distinct roles, they often work together in various fields.

Common OSINT Skills Shared by Both Roles

✓ **Data Collection & Research** – Both analysts and investigators use open-source tools to gather intelligence.

✓ **Critical Thinking & Pattern Recognition** – Both require strong analytical skills to interpret data effectively.

✓ **Legal & Ethical Awareness** – Both must follow privacy laws (GDPR, CCPA) and ethical guidelines.

✓ **Threat Identification** – Whether assessing risks (analyst) or tracking a suspect (investigator), both focus on identifying threats.

How They Work Together

♦ **Example 1**: In a cybercrime case, an OSINT analyst might track hacker group activity, while an OSINT investigator traces the real-world identities of criminals.
♦ **Example 2:** In a corporate fraud investigation, an analyst reviews financial transactions, while an investigator follows up with covert research on key suspects.

3.1.5 Which Role is Right for You?

If you're considering a career in OSINT, think about your skills and interests:

💡 **You might be an OSINT Analyst if…**

✓☐ You enjoy data analysis and reporting.
✓☐ You prefer working with big datasets and intelligence tools.
✓☐ You like identifying patterns, trends, and risks.
✓☐ You want to work in corporate security, government, or cybersecurity.

🔍 **You might be an OSINT Investigator if…**

✓☐ You enjoy hands-on research and deep investigations.
✓☐ You like tracking down criminals, fraudsters, or missing persons.
✓☐ You have strong OPSEC skills and enjoy covert research.
✓☐ You want to work in law enforcement, private investigations, or journalism.

While OSINT analysts and OSINT investigators both use open-source intelligence, their roles, objectives, and methods differ significantly. Analysts focus on data interpretation and intelligence reporting, while investigators specialize in deep research and evidence collection.

Both roles are essential in today's digital world, working together to enhance cybersecurity, law enforcement, corporate security, and investigative journalism. By understanding these differences, aspiring OSINT professionals can choose a career path that aligns with their skills and interests.

3.2 Developing a Curious & Methodical Mindset

Open-Source Intelligence (OSINT) requires more than just technical skills—it demands a curious and methodical mindset. The ability to ask the right questions, think critically, and follow a structured investigative process is what separates skilled OSINT professionals from casual information seekers.

This chapter explores the importance of curiosity in OSINT investigations, how to develop a methodical approach, and practical techniques for enhancing logical thinking and analytical skills.

3.2.1 Why Curiosity is Essential in OSINT

Curiosity is the driving force behind successful OSINT investigations. It fuels an investigator's desire to dig deeper, verify information, and connect seemingly unrelated pieces of data. Without curiosity, an OSINT professional may overlook hidden clues or critical insights.

How Curiosity Enhances OSINT Investigations

🔍 **Finding Hidden Patterns** – A curious investigator looks beyond surface-level information, questioning why data exists and how it connects.

☐ **Asking the Right Questions** – The best OSINT investigations start with a question:

- Who is behind this online identity?
- Where was this image taken?
- What connections exist between these entities?

☐☐ **Exploring Alternative Sources** – A curious mind doesn't settle for the first source. Instead, it cross-references multiple datasets, platforms, and tools.

💡 **Creativity in Investigations** – Sometimes, OSINT requires thinking outside the box, such as analyzing metadata, timestamps, or linguistic clues to uncover insights.

📌 **Example**: In a cybercrime investigation, a curious OSINT investigator might analyze username patterns to link a hacker's alias to their real-world identity.

3.2.2 The Importance of a Methodical Approach

While curiosity helps generate leads, a structured and methodical approach ensures investigations are thorough, accurate, and legally sound. OSINT investigations can quickly become overwhelming, so a clear framework is essential.

The Key Components of a Methodical OSINT Process

🖋 1. Define the Investigation Goal

- What specific intelligence are you trying to gather?
- Are you investigating a person, organization, event, or trend?
- What is the expected outcome (e.g., risk assessment, profiling, evidence gathering)?

🔍 2. Identify Reliable Data Sources

- Select appropriate OSINT tools and databases.
- Consider social media platforms, public records, news archives, dark web sources.

📊 3. Collect & Organize Data Systematically

- Use structured note-taking methods (e.g., spreadsheets, case management tools).
- Track timestamps, URLs, metadata, and references to maintain credibility.

☐ 4. Verify & Cross-Reference Information

- Check for misinformation, fake profiles, and manipulated media.
- Use tools like Google Reverse Image Search, InVID, and metadata extractors to validate sources.

☐ 5. Analyze Data for Patterns & Connections

- Use link analysis tools (e.g., Maltego, Gephi) to visualize relationships.
- Identify common keywords, geolocation tags, and user behaviors.

🔊 6. Document Findings & Present Results

- Summarize key insights in clear, concise reports.
- Ensure findings are fact-based, legally compliant, and actionable.

📌 **Example**: When analyzing a phishing campaign, a methodical approach might involve:

- Identifying suspicious email domains.
- Cross-referencing them with known threat databases.
- Mapping connections between multiple phishing websites.
- Compiling the findings in a report for cybersecurity teams.

3.2.3 Techniques for Developing a Curious & Methodical Mindset

1. Practice Critical Thinking

- Always ask "Why?" "How?" and "What's missing?" when analyzing data.
- Challenge assumptions and consider alternative explanations.

2. Improve Pattern Recognition

- Train your brain to spot anomalies, trends, and recurring behaviors.
- Play investigative games like Capture the Flag (CTF) challenges or OSINT puzzles.

3. Learn from Real-World Case Studies

- Study past OSINT investigations, analyzing how professionals gathered and verified intelligence.
- Follow OSINT communities (e.g., Bellingcat, OSINTCurious, IntelTechniques).

4. Use Mind Maps & Visualizations

- Create relationship diagrams to track connections between entities.
- Tools like Maltego, Obsidian, and MISP help visualize complex networks.

5. Develop a Routine for OSINT Investigations

- Follow a structured workflow to maintain consistency.
- Keep an OSINT research log to track investigations over time.

6. Stay Legally & Ethically Informed

- Always verify the legality of data collection methods in your jurisdiction.
- Follow ethical guidelines to ensure privacy and responsible disclosure.

★ **Example**: A curious OSINT investigator researching a political misinformation campaign might notice repeated use of similar language in different posts—a sign of bot activity. A methodical approach would involve collecting timestamps, identifying key influencers, and mapping out a bot network.

3.2.4 Common Pitfalls to Avoid

📖 1. **Confirmation Bias** – Avoid focusing only on data that supports your pre-existing beliefs. Stay neutral and let the facts guide your conclusions.

📖 2. **Skipping Verification** – Always double-check sources to prevent spreading false or misleading information.

📖 3. **Information Overload** – OSINT can produce too much data. Use structured methods to filter relevant insights.

📖 4. **Ignoring OPSEC (Operational Security)** – Be cautious of your digital footprint while investigating sensitive topics. Use anonymized browsers, VPNs, and secure communication tools.

📖 5. **Ethical Violations** – Do not doxx, hack, or collect personally identifiable information (PII) unlawfully. Always operate within legal boundaries.

Developing a curious and methodical mindset is essential for OSINT analysts and investigators. Curiosity drives deeper exploration, while a structured approach ensures accuracy and reliability.

By continuously practicing critical thinking, data verification, and pattern recognition, OSINT professionals can enhance their investigative skills and produce valuable, ethical, and actionable intelligence.

3.3 The Importance of Source Verification & Bias Awareness

In Open-Source Intelligence (OSINT), the accuracy and reliability of information are paramount. OSINT professionals must verify their sources rigorously and remain aware of potential biases that could distort their findings. Misinformation, disinformation, and biased reporting can all impact investigations, leading to incorrect conclusions, flawed risk assessments, and even legal consequences.

This chapter explores the importance of verifying sources, techniques for cross-referencing data, and strategies for recognizing and mitigating bias in OSINT investigations.

3.3.1 Why Source Verification Matters in OSINT

OSINT investigations rely on publicly available data, which varies in credibility, accuracy, and authenticity. Verifying sources ensures that intelligence is based on fact rather than speculation, manipulation, or deception.

Key Risks of Unverified Sources

⚠️ **Spreading Misinformation** – False or misleading information can damage reputations and cause incorrect conclusions.

⚠️ **Legal & Ethical Issues** – Acting on unverified data could violate privacy laws or result in false accusations.

⚠️ **Deception & Disinformation** – Threat actors often spread fake news, deepfakes, and manipulated media to mislead investigators.

⚠️ **Wasted Resources** – Pursuing incorrect leads wastes time and effort, reducing investigative efficiency.

📌 **Example**: A journalist conducting an OSINT investigation into a political candidate might come across fake social media posts created to damage their reputation. Without proper verification, they risk publishing false claims.

3.3.2 How to Verify OSINT Sources

To ensure the accuracy of collected intelligence, OSINT professionals follow a structured verification process.

Step 1: Identify the Original Source

- Trace information back to the original author, publication, or website.

- Check for official sources (government records, academic studies, established media).
- Be cautious of second-hand reports or screenshots that lack context.

Step 2: Cross-Reference Information

- Compare data across multiple independent sources.
- Use fact-checking tools like Snopes, FactCheck.org, and PolitiFact.
- Confirm details using official databases, WHOIS lookups, and government records.

Step 3: Verify the Date & Context

- Ensure that the information is current and relevant to the investigation.
- Watch out for old events being recycled as "breaking news".
- Use Google Reverse Image Search to check if photos are reused from past events.

Step 4: Analyze the Credibility of the Source

- Who published the information? Are they a reputable organization or an anonymous user?
- Does the source have a history of spreading false or biased information?
- Are they affiliated with any political, corporate, or ideological groups?

Step 5: Examine for Manipulation or Bias

- Check if images, videos, or documents have been altered, cropped, or selectively edited.
- Use forensic tools like InVID (for video verification), FotoForensics (for image analysis), and Metadata2Go (for file metadata checks).

📌 **Example**: During a cybercrime investigation, an OSINT investigator finds leaked credentials on a dark web forum. To verify, they cross-reference the data with breach notification services (like Have I Been Pwned) and confirm the legitimacy of the breach.

3.3.3 Understanding & Mitigating Bias in OSINT

Bias in OSINT investigations can distort findings, leading to inaccurate or misleading conclusions. Bias can be intentional (propaganda, disinformation) or unintentional (personal cognitive bias, media framing).

Types of Bias in OSINT Investigations

⊞ **Media Bias** – Different media outlets present the same event with different perspectives. Example: Coverage of protests may be framed as "peaceful demonstrations" or "riots," depending on the source.

☐ **Confirmation Bias** – Investigators may favor information that aligns with their pre-existing beliefs and ignore contradictory evidence.

☐ **Cultural & Political Bias** – Certain regions or governments control narratives by restricting or manipulating available information.

🎭 **Psychological Bias** – The way information is presented (word choice, emotional appeal) can influence perceptions and decision-making.

💻 **Algorithmic Bias** – Search engines and social media platforms prioritize content based on user preferences, potentially creating an echo chamber of like-minded perspectives.

📌 **Example**: An OSINT analyst researching online extremism might encounter biased think tank reports or politically motivated studies. Without considering bias, their analysis could be skewed.

3.3.4 How to Detect & Reduce Bias in OSINT

🔍 1. Cross-Check Conflicting Sources

- Compare multiple reports, ideally from different political, geographical, or ideological backgrounds.
- Be cautious of sources that only present one perspective.

🎭 2. Recognize Your Own Bias

- Regularly question your own assumptions and interpretations.
- Engage with different perspectives to challenge your thinking.

☐ 3. Use Neutral & Fact-Based Sources

- Prioritize official records, peer-reviewed studies, and independent investigations.

- Be cautious of sources with highly emotional or politically charged language.

4. Apply Structured Analysis Techniques

- Use structured analytic techniques (SATs) like Analysis of Competing Hypotheses (ACH) to avoid cognitive bias.
- Ask: What evidence contradicts my conclusion?

⚠ 5. Be Skeptical of Viral Content

- If something seems too sensational or extreme, verify it before trusting it.
- Use forensic tools to check for deepfakes, edited videos, and fabricated news articles.

📌 **Example**: An OSINT investigator tracking military conflicts might notice satellite images circulating on social media. Instead of assuming they are real, they use geolocation tools like Google Earth or Sentinel Hub to confirm the authenticity of the images.

3.3.5 Tools for Source Verification & Bias Detection

Source Verification Tools

☑ **Google Reverse Image Search** – Check if an image has been used before.

☑ **InVID** – Analyze video authenticity and metadata.

☑ **Wayback Machine** – View archived versions of altered or deleted web pages.

☑ **WHOIS Lookup** – Investigate domain ownership and history.

☑ **OSINT Framework** – A collection of tools for verifying different types of OSINT data.

Bias Awareness & Fact-Checking Tools

☑ **AllSides** – Shows how different media outlets cover the same news story.

☑ **Snopes** – Debunks viral misinformation and hoaxes.

☑ **Politifact & FactCheck.org** – Verify political statements and claims.

☑ **Media Bias Fact Check** – Analyzes news sources for potential bias.

📌 **Example**: A researcher examining disinformation campaigns might use AllSides to compare left-leaning, right-leaning, and centrist news coverage of the same event.

Verifying sources and recognizing bias are critical skills for OSINT professionals. Unchecked information can lead to false conclusions, legal risks, and reputational damage.

By applying structured verification methods, cross-referencing sources, and using specialized tools, OSINT investigators can ensure that their findings are accurate, unbiased, and actionable.

The best OSINT practitioners are both skeptical and open-minded, always questioning the reliability of their data while considering multiple perspectives.

3.4 Thinking Like an Adversary: Red Team OSINT Approaches

In the world of Open-Source Intelligence (OSINT), thinking like an adversary is a crucial skill for uncovering vulnerabilities, assessing threats, and improving security. The Red Team approach—a methodology used by ethical hackers, penetration testers, and security professionals—focuses on simulating real-world attacks to identify weaknesses before malicious actors exploit them.

This chapter explores how OSINT professionals can adopt a Red Team mindset, leverage adversarial tactics for cybersecurity, law enforcement, and corporate security, and improve defensive strategies by understanding the attacker's perspective.

3.4.1 What is Red Team OSINT?

Red Team OSINT involves using the same techniques as adversaries to test security measures, uncover sensitive information, and simulate real-world attacks. Unlike traditional OSINT, which focuses on intelligence gathering, Red Team OSINT is proactive, identifying and exploiting vulnerabilities to strengthen defenses.

Red Team vs. Blue Team in OSINT

● **Red Team (Attackers)** – Simulate adversaries to expose weaknesses.
◓ **Blue Team (Defenders)** – Protect and respond to threats based on intelligence.
☐ **Purple Team (Collaborative Approach)** – Red and Blue Teams work together to enhance security.

✦ **Example**: A cybersecurity Red Team might use OSINT techniques to find an employee's leaked credentials on the dark web, then attempt to gain unauthorized access to their company's internal systems.

3.4.2 How Adversaries Use OSINT for Attacks

Malicious actors rely on OSINT to gather intelligence on targets, exploit weaknesses, and execute cyber, physical, or psychological attacks. Understanding their tactics helps security professionals stay ahead.

Common OSINT-Based Attack Vectors

💡 **Social Engineering & Phishing** – Harvesting personal data to craft convincing phishing emails, phone scams, or impersonation attacks.

🔍 **Doxxing & Personal Exposure** – Collecting and publishing sensitive personal information to intimidate or harm individuals.

📡 **Reconnaissance for Cyber Attacks** – Mapping an organization's infrastructure, identifying exposed services, and finding exploitable vulnerabilities.

🚪 **Physical Security Exploits** – Identifying weak access points, employee routines, or unsecured locations for unauthorized entry.

✦ **Example**: A hacker planning a spear-phishing attack might use OSINT to collect an employee's email patterns and personal interests from LinkedIn and Twitter to craft a highly convincing fake email.

3.4.3 Red Team OSINT Methodology

A structured approach helps Red Teams simulate real-world attack scenarios while maintaining ethical and legal boundaries.

Step 1: Define the Target & Objectives

- Identify the organization, individual, or system being tested.
- Set clear engagement rules to avoid legal violations.
- Determine the goal (e.g., assess phishing susceptibility, find leaked credentials, test physical security).

Step 2: Passive Reconnaissance (Stealth OSINT Gathering)

- Collect publicly available data without directly interacting with the target.
- Search social media, company websites, WHOIS records, and data breaches.
- Use tools like theHarvester, Recon-ng, and SpiderFoot.

Step 3: Active Reconnaissance (Engaging the Target)

- Interact with the target's systems, employees, or networks.
- Probe for misconfigured cloud storage, exposed login pages, or weak passwords.
- Use techniques like OSINT-based pretexting or fake social media personas.

Step 4: Analyzing & Exploiting Vulnerabilities

- Identify exploitable weaknesses based on collected intelligence.
- Simulate phishing, impersonation, or social engineering scenarios.
- Map connections using Maltego or Gephi to uncover hidden relationships.

Step 5: Reporting & Mitigation Recommendations

- Document findings clearly and professionally.
- Provide actionable security recommendations to strengthen defenses.
- Ensure that intelligence is handled ethically and legally.

📌 **Example**: A Red Team OSINT investigator might identify an employee's personal Gmail address from a data breach, then check if it's reused on the company's VPN login page, revealing a potential security risk.

3.4.4 Essential Red Team OSINT Tools & Techniques

🔎 **Reconnaissance & Data Collection**

✓ **OSINT Framework** – A directory of OSINT tools for various investigations.
✓ **theHarvester** – Gathers emails, subdomains, and IPs from public sources.
✓ **Shodan & Censys** – Scans the internet for exposed devices and services.
✓ **Google Dorking** – Uses advanced search operators to uncover hidden data.

🦹 **Social Engineering & Threat Mapping**

✓ **LinkedIn & Facebook Graph Search** – Maps employee relationships.
✓ **Sherlock** – Identifies usernames across social media platforms.

✅ **Social-Engineer Toolkit (SET)** – Automates social engineering attacks (for testing).

☐☐ **Dark Web & Breach Intelligence**

✅ **Have I Been Pwned** – Checks for leaked credentials.
✅ **DeHashed** – Searches for compromised emails and passwords.
✅ **Tor & Dark Web Marketplaces** – Monitors threat actor discussions.

📌 **Example**: A Red Team OSINT expert might use Shodan to identify a company's exposed remote desktop login, then verify if credentials have been leaked in past breaches.

3.4.5 Defensive Countermeasures Against OSINT Attacks

By understanding how adversaries operate, organizations can harden their security posture and reduce their OSINT footprint.

1. Reduce the OSINT Attack Surface

🚫 **Limit publicly available data** – Remove sensitive employee details from LinkedIn and social media.
🔐 **Secure domain records** – Use WHOIS privacy protection.
☐ **Educate employees** – Train staff to recognize social engineering tactics.

2. Implement Technical Security Controls

🔑 **Use strong authentication** – Enforce MFA and password managers.
🛡 **Monitor exposed services** – Regularly scan internet-facing assets using Shodan or Censys.
☐ **Deploy security awareness programs** – Simulate phishing tests and OSINT-based threat assessments.

📌 **Example**: A company might conduct an internal Red Team OSINT assessment to identify what an attacker could learn about them, then take steps to remove unnecessary exposure.

3.4.6 Ethical Considerations in Red Team OSINT

While Red Team OSINT simulates real-world attacks, ethical boundaries must always be maintained.

✅ **Obtain Proper Authorization** – Always have legal permission before conducting security assessments.

✅ **Follow Ethical Guidelines** – Never harm, manipulate, or publish private information.

✅ **Avoid Gray Areas** – Do not engage in unauthorized penetration testing or social engineering without consent.

📌 **Example**: An ethical Red Team OSINT investigator conducting a phishing assessment should inform stakeholders, obtain consent, and report findings responsibly.

Adopting a Red Team OSINT mindset helps security professionals anticipate real-world attack strategies and improve defenses. By thinking like an adversary, OSINT practitioners can proactively identify vulnerabilities, strengthen security, and protect against emerging threats.

By combining OSINT reconnaissance, social engineering tactics, and ethical hacking principles, Red Team OSINT provides critical insights that empower organizations to stay one step ahead of attackers.

3.5 The Cognitive Biases That Affect OSINT Investigations

In Open-Source Intelligence (OSINT), cognitive biases can skew analysis, distort conclusions, and impact decision-making. These biases are subconscious tendencies that affect how we interpret information, often leading to errors in judgment, flawed assessments, and inaccurate intelligence reports.

To be effective, OSINT investigators must identify, understand, and mitigate these biases. This chapter explores common cognitive biases, their impact on OSINT, and strategies to minimize their influence.

3.5.1 What Are Cognitive Biases?

Cognitive biases are systematic thinking errors that affect how people process information. They are often influenced by emotions, personal experiences, or external pressures and can lead to faulty assumptions, overconfidence, and poor decision-making.

In OSINT, these biases can cause investigators to:

- Misinterpret data due to preconceived notions.
- Overlook key evidence that contradicts existing beliefs.
- Rely on unreliable sources without proper verification.

📌 **Example**: An OSINT analyst investigating online extremism may subconsciously favor sources that confirm their pre-existing views while ignoring contradictory evidence.

3.5.2 Common Cognitive Biases in OSINT Investigations

1. Confirmation Bias – "Seeing What You Want to See"

🔍 **Definition**: The tendency to search for, interpret, and recall information that confirms existing beliefs while ignoring contradictory evidence.

📌 **Example**: An investigator tracking a cybercriminal assumes they are from a specific country and only focuses on evidence supporting this idea, ignoring alternative possibilities.

☐ **How to Mitigate:**

✔ Challenge assumptions by actively looking for contradictory evidence.

✔ Use structured analysis methods like the Analysis of Competing Hypotheses (ACH).

2. Anchoring Bias – "The First Piece of Information Sticks"

🔍 **Definition**: The tendency to rely too heavily on the first piece of information encountered (the "anchor"), even if later evidence contradicts it.

📌 **Example**: If an OSINT analyst's first search result labels someone a hacker, they may continue to view them as guilty, even when new evidence suggests otherwise.

☐ **How to Mitigate:**

✔ Delay conclusions until multiple independent sources are reviewed.

✔ Consider alternative explanations before finalizing an assessment.

3. Availability Heuristic – "If I Remember It, It Must Be True"

🔍 **Definition**: The tendency to judge the likelihood of an event based on how easily it comes to mind rather than actual probability.

📌 **Example**: After reading about a high-profile ransomware attack, an investigator overestimates the prevalence of similar incidents, leading to misguided risk assessments.

☐ **How to Mitigate:**

✅ Base conclusions on verifiable data and statistics, not just recent or memorable events.

✅ Use historical trends and threat intelligence rather than intuition.

4. Survivorship Bias – "Only Seeing the Successful Cases"

🔍 **Definition**: Focusing only on successful or known cases while ignoring failures or missing data, leading to distorted conclusions.

📌 **Example**: An OSINT analyst studying successful cybercrime arrests may conclude that law enforcement is highly effective, overlooking cases where criminals evaded capture.

☐ **How to Mitigate:**

✅ Look for "missing" data and question whether invisible cases exist.

✅ Analyze failures as well as successes for a complete picture.

5. Overconfidence Bias – "I Know More Than I Actually Do"

🔍 **Definition**: The tendency to overestimate one's knowledge, skills, or accuracy of predictions.

📌 **Example**: An investigator with years of experience assumes their judgment is always correct, leading them to dismiss dissenting opinions or warnings.

☐ **How to Mitigate:**

✅ Always seek peer reviews and second opinions.

✅ Approach investigations with humility and skepticism.

6. Hindsight Bias – "I Knew It All Along"

🔍 **Definition**: The tendency to believe, after an event has occurred, that it was predictable all along, leading to oversimplified conclusions.

📌 **Example**: After a major data breach, an analyst claims, "The signs were obvious," even though they weren't at the time.

◻ **How to Mitigate:**

✅ Document the decision-making process to track how conclusions were reached.

✅ Recognize that many outcomes are only clear in retrospect.

7. Groupthink – "Going with the Crowd"

🔍 **Definition**: The tendency to conform to group opinions instead of independent critical thinking, often leading to poor decision-making.

📌 **Example**: If a team of OSINT investigators all believe a hacker is from a certain country, individual members may avoid questioning this assumption to fit in.

◻ **How to Mitigate:**

✅ Encourage dissenting viewpoints and challenge consensus conclusions.

✅ Assign a "devil's advocate" to consider alternative perspectives.

3.5.3 How to Minimize Cognitive Bias in OSINT Investigations

🔎 **1. Use Structured Analytical Techniques (SATs)**

- **Analysis of Competing Hypotheses (ACH)** – Weighs multiple explanations against available evidence.
- **Red Teaming** – Forces analysts to adopt an opposing viewpoint to test conclusions.

- **Devil's Advocacy** – Assigning someone to challenge findings and uncover weaknesses.

📌 **Example**: Before finalizing an OSINT report, an analyst conducts a "devil's advocate" review, testing whether biases influenced their conclusions.

☐ 2. Keep a Bias Checklist

Before accepting any intelligence, ask:

✅ Am I favoring evidence that confirms my pre-existing beliefs?

✅ Have I considered contradictory data?

✅ Am I basing conclusions on emotions or intuition rather than facts?

📌 **Example**: A team of OSINT investigators uses a bias checklist before finalizing risk assessments.

🏛 3. Cross-Reference Multiple Sources

- Use at least three independent, credible sources before making conclusions.
- Compare differing viewpoints (e.g., international vs. local media coverage).

📌 **Example**: An analyst investigating online extremism checks reports from government sources, independent watchdogs, and news outlets before forming conclusions.

📝 4. Maintain a Decision Log

- Document key decisions and reasoning throughout an investigation.
- Review past decisions to identify patterns of bias.

📌 **Example**: An OSINT professional logs their research process, later discovering that they repeatedly favored Western news sources over regional ones.

Cognitive biases can significantly impact OSINT investigations, leading to misinterpretation, misinformation, and flawed decision-making. By recognizing and mitigating these biases, analysts can enhance the accuracy, objectivity, and reliability of their intelligence.

Using structured analysis techniques, diverse perspectives, and systematic verification methods, OSINT professionals can ensure their investigations are fact-driven, balanced, and free from unconscious distortions.

✓□ The best OSINT investigators are not just skilled at gathering data—they are also skilled at questioning their own assumptions.

3.6 How to Approach OSINT with a Threat Intelligence Perspective

Open-Source Intelligence (OSINT) plays a crucial role in threat intelligence (TI) by helping analysts identify, assess, and mitigate security risks. When OSINT is integrated with a threat intelligence mindset, it shifts from being a simple information-gathering process to a proactive strategy for detecting cyber threats, geopolitical risks, and criminal activities.

This chapter explores how to align OSINT with threat intelligence methodologies, the different types of threat intelligence, and best practices for using OSINT to anticipate and counter threats.

3.6.1 What is Threat Intelligence (TI)?

Threat intelligence involves the collection, analysis, and dissemination of information to understand and mitigate security threats. It helps organizations:

🔍 Identify emerging threats before they escalate.
□ Assess vulnerabilities and security gaps.
⚠ Detect malicious actors and their tactics.
🚀 Support decision-making in cybersecurity, law enforcement, and national security.

📌 **Example**: A company might use OSINT to monitor dark web forums for discussions about potential cyberattacks on their industry.

3.6.2 The Relationship Between OSINT and Threat Intelligence

While OSINT focuses on collecting publicly available data, threat intelligence applies analytical frameworks to transform that data into actionable security insights.

Aspect	OSINT	Threat Intelligence
Purpose	Gathering publicly available information	Analyzing data to predict and mitigate threats
Focus	Broad information collection	Security risks, cyber threats, and adversaries
Outcome	Raw data or reports	Actionable intelligence for decision-makers

📌 **Example**: OSINT can discover a leaked employee credential, but threat intelligence assesses how threat actors might use it and how to mitigate the risk.

3.6.3 Types of Threat Intelligence in OSINT

1. Strategic Threat Intelligence (High-Level, Long-Term)

◆ Focuses on global trends, geopolitical risks, and industry-wide threats.
◆ Used by executives, policymakers, and security leaders.
◆ **OSINT tools**: News aggregation, government reports, geopolitical analysis platforms.

📌 **Example**: Monitoring nation-state cyber activities to predict future threats to critical infrastructure.

2. Tactical Threat Intelligence (Attacker Methods & Techniques)

◆ Examines how adversaries operate, including their tools, techniques, and procedures (TTPs).
◆ Used by SOC teams, cybersecurity analysts, and red teams.
◆ **OSINT tools**: MITRE ATT&CK framework, malware analysis, social media monitoring.

📌 **Example**: Tracking ransomware groups to understand their attack patterns and target selection.

3. Operational Threat Intelligence (Real-Time Threat Monitoring)

◆ Provides actionable insights on ongoing or imminent attacks.
◆ Used by incident response teams and cybersecurity defenders.
◆ **OSINT tools**: Dark web monitoring, threat feeds, honeypots, and intrusion detection systems.

📌 **Example**: Identifying threat actor chatter about an upcoming phishing campaign targeting a company's employees.

4. Technical Threat Intelligence (Indicators of Compromise – IoCs)

◆ Focuses on technical data, such as IP addresses, malware signatures, and phishing URLs.
◆ Used by IT security teams and network administrators.
◆ **OSINT tools**: VirusTotal, Shodan, AlienVault OTX, Recorded Future.

📌 **Example**: Detecting a new malware strain by analyzing OSINT threat feeds and sandboxed samples.

3.6.4 The OSINT-Driven Threat Intelligence Workflow

Step 1: Define Intelligence Requirements

- What threats are we trying to detect?
- Who are the potential adversaries (hackers, nation-states, insiders)?
- What assets need protection?

📌 **Example**: A financial institution might focus on phishing campaigns targeting banking customers.

Step 2: OSINT Data Collection

- **Passive OSINT**: Gathering data without direct interaction (e.g., news, public records, leaked databases).
- **Active OSINT**: Engaging with sources (e.g., using fake social media accounts to monitor threat actors).

☐ **Key OSINT Sources:**

✅ **Dark web forums & marketplaces** – Monitoring cybercriminal activity.
✅ **Paste sites (e.g., Pastebin)** – Finding leaked credentials.
✅ **Threat intelligence feeds** – Real-time alerts on IoCs.
✅ **Social media monitoring** – Tracking disinformation and geopolitical threats.

📌 **Example**: Security teams monitor hacker forums for zero-day vulnerabilities affecting their software.

Step 3: Data Processing & Correlation

- Filtering useful intelligence from noisy data.
- Using AI and automation to process large datasets.
- Correlating OSINT findings with internal security logs.

☐ **Key Tools:**

✅ **Maltego** – Mapping threat actor networks.
✅ **MITRE ATT&CK** – Understanding adversary techniques.
✅ **Threat intelligence platforms (TIPs)** – Centralizing security data.

📌 **Example**: An analyst correlates a leaked employee password with recent phishing attempts targeting company emails.

Step 4: Threat Analysis & Attribution

- Identifying who is behind a threat (if possible).
- Assessing intent, capability, and likelihood of attack.
- Using adversary profiling based on OSINT intelligence.

📌 **Example**: Investigators attribute a cyberattack to a known ransomware group by analyzing TTPs and Bitcoin wallet transactions.

Step 5: Dissemination & Actionable Intelligence

- Reporting findings to decision-makers.
- Implementing mitigation strategies based on OSINT intelligence.
- Feeding new intelligence into security defenses (e.g., blocking malicious IPs, updating firewalls).

📌 **Example**: A threat intelligence team publishes an alert about an ongoing social engineering scam targeting executives.

3.6.5 OSINT Threat Intelligence Best Practices

✅ **Verify All Sources** – Cross-check intelligence to avoid misinformation.

✅ **Use Automation Wisely** – AI and machine learning can process OSINT faster, but human analysis is essential.

✅ **Stay Within Legal Boundaries** – OSINT should always adhere to data privacy laws (e.g., GDPR, CCPA).

✅ **Think Like an Attacker** – Adopt a Red Team approach to predict how adversaries might exploit vulnerabilities.

✅ **Collaborate with Intelligence Communities** – Share findings with trusted security networks (e.g., ISACs, threat sharing groups).

By approaching OSINT with a threat intelligence mindset, investigators can transform raw data into actionable security insights. This approach allows organizations to anticipate cyber threats, defend against attacks, and improve security postures.

◆ OSINT alone is powerful, but when combined with threat intelligence frameworks, it becomes a proactive tool for preventing cybercrime, espionage, and emerging threats.

4. Essential OSINT Tools & Resources

The power of OSINT lies not just in the information itself but in the tools used to collect, analyze, and verify data efficiently. From search engines and social media platforms to specialized databases and automation frameworks, a well-equipped OSINT practitioner leverages a diverse toolkit to uncover valuable intelligence. This chapter introduces essential OSINT tools, including web reconnaissance utilities, metadata extractors, geolocation services, and data visualization platforms. Whether you're a beginner or looking to expand your arsenal, understanding the strengths and limitations of these tools will help you conduct more effective and precise investigations.

4.1 Web-Based OSINT Tools: Free & Paid Solutions

Open-Source Intelligence (OSINT) relies on various web-based tools to gather, analyze, and verify publicly available information. These tools range from free open-source solutions to premium paid platforms that offer advanced analytics, automation, and integration with other intelligence systems.

This chapter explores key web-based OSINT tools, their functionalities, and how investigators, cybersecurity professionals, and businesses can leverage them for intelligence gathering.

4.1.1 Categories of OSINT Tools

OSINT tools are designed for different purposes, including:

1. Search & Discovery

◆ **Purpose**: Finding publicly available data across websites, databases, and search engines.

📌 **Example**: Investigating a person's digital footprint.

✅ **Google Dorking (Free)** – Advanced Google search operators for hidden data.
✅ **Shodan (Freemium)** – Search engine for internet-connected devices and vulnerabilities.
✅ **Censys (Freemium)** – Scans the internet for exposed assets and security risks.

2. Social Media Intelligence (SOCMINT)

◆ **Purpose**: Extracting and analyzing social media content, posts, and user activity.

📌 **Example**: Monitoring Twitter for political disinformation.

✅ **TweetDeck (Free)** – Real-time monitoring of Twitter activity.

✅ **SOCMINT (Paid)** – Advanced social media forensics for law enforcement.

✅ **Maltego (Freemium)** – Visual link analysis for mapping social networks.

3. Domain & IP Intelligence

◆ **Purpose**: Investigating domains, IP addresses, and network infrastructure.

📌 **Example**: Checking if a website is linked to cybercrime.

✅ **Whois Lookup (Free)** – Finds domain ownership and registration details.

✅ **VirusTotal (Freemium)** – Scans URLs, files, and IPs for malware.

✅ **RiskIQ PassiveTotal (Paid)** – Tracks historical DNS records and domain infrastructure.

4. Dark Web & Threat Intelligence

◆ **Purpose**: Monitoring hidden forums, marketplaces, and cybercriminal activity.

📌 **Example**: Detecting stolen credentials on the dark web.

✅ **DarkOwl (Paid)** – Deep web and dark web monitoring.

✅ **IntSights (Paid)** – Threat intelligence platform for cyber investigations.

✅ **Tor Browser (Free)** – Accesses onion sites on the dark web.

5. Image & Video Analysis

◆ **Purpose**: Extracting metadata, verifying authenticity, and geolocating media.

📌 **Example**: Confirming the origin of a viral video.

✅ **Google Reverse Image Search (Free)** – Finds similar images online.

✅ **ExifTool (Free)** – Extracts metadata from images and videos.

✅ **InVID (Freemium)** – Verifies and analyzes online videos.

6. Data Breach & Credential Monitoring

◆ **Purpose**: Checking if emails, passwords, or personal data have been leaked.

📌 **Example**: Investigating if an organization's credentials have been compromised.

✅ **Have I Been Pwned? (Free)** – Checks if an email is in a data breach.

✅ **DeHashed (Freemium)** – Searches leaked databases for user credentials.

✅ **SpyCloud (Paid)** – Enterprise-level breach monitoring and remediation.

7. Automated OSINT Platforms

◆ **Purpose**: Integrating multiple OSINT capabilities into a single platform.

📌 **Example**: Automating large-scale intelligence gathering for cyber defense.

✅ **SpiderFoot (Freemium)** – Automated reconnaissance for threat intelligence.

✅ **TheHarvester (Free)** – Gathers emails, subdomains, and IPs for cybersecurity.

✅ **Palantir Gotham (Paid)** – Enterprise-level intelligence platform for governments and corporations.

4.1.2 Choosing the Right OSINT Tool

◆ **For Beginners & Casual Users**: Google Dorking, Whois Lookup, Have I Been Pwned?

◆ **For Cybersecurity Professionals**: Shodan, VirusTotal, RiskIQ

◆ **For Law Enforcement & Investigators**: Maltego, SOCMINT, DarkOwl

◆ **For Business Intelligence**: IntSights, Palantir, SpyCloud

Web-based OSINT tools provide critical insights for cybersecurity, investigations, and business intelligence. Whether using free tools for basic searches or paid platforms for advanced threat detection, the right OSINT approach ensures accurate, ethical, and effective intelligence gathering.

4.2 OSINT Browser Extensions & Add-ons

Browser extensions and add-ons can significantly enhance OSINT investigations by providing quick access to data, automating searches, and improving security. These tools allow OSINT professionals to extract information, analyze metadata, investigate domains, and improve operational security (OPSEC) without leaving their web browsers.

This chapter explores some of the best browser extensions for OSINT, categorized by functionality.

4.2.1 Why Use Browser Extensions for OSINT?

◆ **Speed & Efficiency**: Automates repetitive tasks like reverse image searches and domain lookups.

◆ **Convenience**: Provides one-click access to OSINT tools directly from the browser.

◆ **Enhanced Analysis**: Extracts metadata, monitors website changes, and verifies online information.

◆ **Security & OPSEC**: Protects investigators from tracking, fingerprinting, and malicious websites.

4.2.2 OSINT Browser Extensions by Category

1. Search & Investigation Extensions

These extensions help investigators gather information from search engines, social media, and online databases.

☑ **Google Dorking Helper (Chrome, Firefox)** – Automates advanced Google search operators for hidden data.

☑ **Search by Image (Chrome, Firefox)** – Conducts reverse image searches across Google, Bing, Yandex, and TinEye.

☑ **Hunter.io (Chrome, Firefox)** – Finds email addresses associated with a website.

☑ **Intelligence X (Chrome, Firefox)** – Searches archived content, leaks, and darknet data.

📌 **Example**: An OSINT analyst uses Google Dorking Helper to find PDF files containing sensitive government documents.

2. Domain & IP Analysis Extensions

These tools help investigate domains, IP addresses, and website ownership.

✅ **Whois Lookup (Chrome, Firefox)** – Retrieves domain registration details and ownership history.

✅ **IPinfo.io (Chrome, Firefox)** – Provides geolocation and ASN information for IP addresses.

✅ **Shodan Plugin (Chrome, Firefox)** – Displays open ports, vulnerabilities, and exposed devices for any visited website.

✅ **Wappalyzer (Chrome, Firefox)** – Detects technologies used on a website (CMS, frameworks, hosting).

📌 **Example**: An OSINT investigator uses Shodan Plugin to check if a website is hosted on an exposed server with known vulnerabilities.

3. Social Media OSINT Extensions

These extensions streamline social media investigations by extracting user data and monitoring activity.

✅ **Social Analyzer (Chrome, Firefox)** – Searches for a person's username across multiple social media platforms.

✅ **OSINT Combine Twitter Tool (Chrome)** – Enhances Twitter investigations by collecting user metadata.

✅ **Facebook Pixel Helper (Chrome, Firefox)** – Identifies tracking pixels on Facebook-related sites, useful for ad intelligence.

✅ **LinkedIn Sales Navigator (Paid, Chrome)** – Extracts professional profiles and connections for business intelligence.

📌 **Example**: An investigator tracks a fake social media account using Social Analyzer to find linked profiles across different platforms.

4. Dark Web & Data Leak Detection

These tools assist in monitoring data breaches, darknet activity, and leaked credentials.

✅ **Have I Been Pwned? (HIBP) Checker (Chrome, Firefox)** – Checks if an email has been compromised in a data breach.

✅ **Dark Web Plugin (IntelTechniques) (Chrome)** – Searches for usernames, domains, and emails on dark web databases.

✅ **Pastebin Search (Firefox, Chrome)** – Monitors leaked credentials and pastebin dumps.

📌 **Example**: A cybersecurity team uses HIBP Checker to monitor employees' corporate emails for potential data breaches.

5. Image & Metadata Analysis Extensions

These extensions help extract metadata, verify images, and conduct reverse image searches.

✅ **Exif Viewer (Chrome, Firefox)** – Extracts metadata (EXIF) from images, including GPS location and device details.
✅ **InVID Verification Plugin (Chrome, Firefox)** – Assists in video forensics, deepfake detection, and media verification.
✅ **TinEye Reverse Image Search (Chrome, Firefox)** – Finds similar images and detects altered or manipulated content.

📌 **Example**: A journalist uses InVID to verify whether a viral video was manipulated or taken out of context.

6. Security & OPSEC Extensions

These extensions protect OSINT investigators from tracking, fingerprinting, and malicious content.

✅ **uBlock Origin (Chrome, Firefox)** – Blocks ads and tracking scripts to prevent fingerprinting.
✅ **Privacy Badger (Chrome, Firefox)** – Detects and blocks invisible trackers used by websites.
✅ **HTTPS Everywhere (Chrome, Firefox)** – Forces websites to use secure HTTPS connections.
✅ **NoScript (Firefox)** – Blocks JavaScript execution, reducing the risk of browser-based attacks.

📌 **Example**: An OSINT professional uses uBlock Origin and NoScript to investigate malicious websites without exposing their real identity.

4.2.3 Best Practices for Using OSINT Browser Extensions

✅ **Use Multiple Extensions** – Different extensions provide different insights. Combine Whois Lookup, Shodan, and Exif Viewer for a deeper analysis.

✅ **Protect Your Privacy** – Enable OPSEC extensions to prevent websites from tracking your OSINT activities.

✅ **Verify Findings** – Don't rely on a single tool—always cross-check information using multiple OSINT sources.

✅ **Be Aware of Legal & Ethical Boundaries** – Respect privacy laws (GDPR, CCPA) and avoid using OSINT tools for unauthorized access.

Browser extensions and add-ons significantly enhance OSINT capabilities by making investigations faster, more efficient, and more secure. From search automation and metadata extraction to social media tracking and cybersecurity analysis, these tools are invaluable for OSINT professionals, cybersecurity experts, journalists, and law enforcement.

◆ By leveraging the right mix of OSINT browser extensions, investigators can uncover critical intelligence while maintaining privacy and security.

4.3 Data Aggregators & People Search Engines

In Open-Source Intelligence (OSINT), data aggregators and people search engines play a critical role in collecting publicly available personal and business information. These tools gather data from multiple sources—such as public records, social media, and websites—allowing OSINT professionals to efficiently investigate individuals, organizations, and networks.

This chapter explores key data aggregators and people search engines, their use cases, ethical considerations, and best practices for effective OSINT investigations.

4.3.1 What Are Data Aggregators & People Search Engines?

◆ **Data Aggregators** – Large-scale platforms that collect, store, and organize public and commercial data from multiple sources.

◆ **People Search Engines** – Specialized tools that allow users to find personal information such as addresses, phone numbers, social media accounts, and court records.

📌 **Example**: A private investigator uses a people search engine to locate an individual's address, relatives, and phone number for a missing persons case.

4.3.2 Categories of Data Aggregators & People Search Engines

1. General People Search Engines

These tools collect publicly available data from various online sources to provide basic personal information.

✅ **Spokeo (Paid)** – Aggregates social media, phone numbers, addresses, and emails.
✅ **TruePeopleSearch (Free)** – Finds names, phone numbers, and relatives.
✅ **BeenVerified (Paid)** – Conducts background checks with public records.
✅ **PeekYou (Freemium)** – Searches for a person's online profiles.

📌 **Example**: A journalist uses PeekYou to find an individual's Twitter, LinkedIn, and Facebook accounts.

2. Public Records & Background Check Services

These platforms provide access to criminal records, property ownership, and legal filings.

✅ **Intelius (Paid)** – Background checks, criminal records, and financial history.
✅ **Instant Checkmate (Paid)** – Public records, court cases, and bankruptcies.
✅ **Whitepages (Freemium)** – Phone number lookup, addresses, and business records.
✅ **FastPeopleSearch (Free)** – Phone, email, and address searches.

📌 **Example**: A fraud investigator uses Instant Checkmate to check if an individual has prior fraud-related criminal records.

3. Social Media & Username Search Tools

These tools help identify social media accounts, usernames, and linked profiles across multiple platforms.

✅ **Pipl (Paid)** – Advanced identity verification using deep web searches.

☑ **UserSearch.org (Free)** – Searches usernames across forums, social media, and gaming platforms.

☑ **Social Searcher (Free)** – Finds mentions of a person on social media.

☑ **Namechk (Free)** – Checks username availability across 150+ sites.

📌 **Example**: A cybersecurity analyst uses Pipl to investigate a fake social media account linked to phishing scams.

4. Dark Web & Data Breach Search Engines

These platforms monitor leaked credentials, dark web forums, and cybercrime databases.

☑ **Have I Been Pwned? (Free)** – Checks if an email has been involved in a data breach.

☑ **DeHashed (Freemium)** – Searches leaked passwords, emails, and usernames.

☑ **IntSights (Paid)** – Monitors dark web forums for threat intelligence.

☑ **LeakCheck (Paid)** – Finds compromised accounts and stolen credentials.

📌 **Example**: A company's security team uses DeHashed to detect if employees' corporate credentials have been leaked.

5. Business & Corporate OSINT Tools

These tools help investigate companies, financial records, and business ownership structures.

☑ **OpenCorporates (Free)** – World's largest open database of companies.

☑ **Crunchbase (Freemium)** – Provides business insights, funding rounds, and key executives.

☑ **CorporationWiki (Free)** – Maps business relationships between executives.

☑ **SEC EDGAR (Free)** – Retrieves U.S. corporate filings, ownership, and financial reports.

📌 **Example**: A fraud analyst uses OpenCorporates to track shell companies linked to financial crimes.

4.3.3 Ethical & Legal Considerations

While data aggregators and people search engines provide valuable information, OSINT investigators must ensure ethical and legal compliance.

◆ Data Privacy & Regulations

✓ **GDPR (Europe):** Restricts how personal data is stored and shared.

✓ **CCPA (California):** Gives individuals rights over their personal information.

✓ **FCRA (U.S.):** Limits how consumer reports are used for employment and credit decisions.

➤ **Example**: Using BeenVerified for employment background checks without consent violates FCRA regulations.

◆ Best Practices for Ethical OSINT

✓ **Use Data Responsibly** – Avoid doxxing or unauthorized access to sensitive information.

✓ **Verify Information** – Cross-check data from multiple sources to prevent misinformation.

✓ **Follow Local Laws** – Be aware of jurisdictional restrictions on data collection and usage.

✓ **Use Tools Transparently** – Inform subjects if data is being collected for investigative or compliance purposes.

Data aggregators and people search engines streamline OSINT investigations by providing quick access to public records, online identities, and business intelligence. However, ethical and legal considerations must always be prioritized when conducting investigations.

◆ By combining multiple OSINT tools and verifying findings, investigators can ensure accurate, responsible, and compliant intelligence gathering.

4.4 Social Media Analysis Tools & Platforms

Social media is one of the richest sources of Open-Source Intelligence (OSINT), offering vast amounts of real-time data, user interactions, and behavioral insights. OSINT professionals, cybersecurity experts, law enforcement, and businesses rely on social media analysis tools to extract, analyze, and visualize data from platforms like Twitter, Facebook, Instagram, LinkedIn, and TikTok.

This chapter explores the best social media OSINT tools, their features, and ethical considerations when conducting investigations.

4.4.1 What Are Social Media Analysis Tools?

◆ **Definition**: Social media analysis tools help extract, monitor, and analyze publicly available data from platforms like Twitter, Facebook, Instagram, and LinkedIn.

◆ **Use Cases:**

✓ **Cybersecurity & Threat Intelligence** – Identifying fake accounts, scams, and disinformation campaigns.

✓ **Law Enforcement & Investigations** – Tracking criminal activity and missing persons.

✓ **Marketing & Business Intelligence** – Monitoring brand mentions and audience sentiment.

✓ **Journalism & Research** – Verifying viral content and tracking global events.

★ **Example**: An OSINT investigator monitors Twitter hashtags to track disinformation campaigns related to an election.

4.4.2 Top Social Media OSINT Tools

1. Cross-Platform Social Media Monitoring

These tools allow investigators to analyze multiple social media platforms at once.

✅ **SOCMINT (Paid)** – Advanced social media forensics for law enforcement.

✅ **Talkwalker (Paid)** – AI-powered social listening tool for brands and public sentiment analysis.

✅ **Social Searcher (Freemium)** – Real-time monitoring of keywords and hashtags across multiple platforms.

✅ **Hootsuite (Freemium)** – Tracks and manages multiple social media accounts in one dashboard.

📌 **Example**: A cybersecurity team uses Talkwalker to detect and analyze disinformation campaigns across Twitter and Facebook.

2. Twitter OSINT Tools

Twitter is one of the most open social media platforms for OSINT, making it a valuable source for real-time information.

☑ **TweetDeck (Free)** – Real-time Twitter monitoring, useful for tracking live events.
☑ **Twitonomy (Freemium)** – Provides in-depth analytics on Twitter accounts, mentions, and hashtags.
☑ **Followerwonk (Freemium)** – Analyzes Twitter followers, engagement, and influence.
☑ **Tweepy (Free, API-Based)** – Python library for advanced Twitter scraping.

📌 **Example**: A journalist uses Twitonomy to analyze influencers spreading misinformation about a crisis.

3. Facebook & Instagram OSINT Tools

Facebook and Instagram have strict API restrictions, but some tools can still extract valuable data.

☑ **Facebook Graph Search (Free, Limited)** – Advanced search queries for public posts, groups, and pages.
☑ **InSpy (Free)** – Extracts employee and company data from LinkedIn and Facebook.
☑ **Phantombuster (Paid)** – Scrapes social media profiles, comments, and user activity from Facebook and Instagram.
☑ **Pybliometrics (Python Library)** – Analyzes social network relationships and metadata.

📌 **Example**: A fraud investigator uses Phantombuster to track fake Instagram profiles running phishing scams.

4. LinkedIn & Professional Network Analysis

LinkedIn is a goldmine for corporate intelligence, allowing OSINT analysts to track professional connections, company hierarchies, and employment history.

☑ **Sales Navigator (Paid)** – Extracts business connections, employee roles, and industry trends.

☑ **Hunter.io (Freemium)** – Finds corporate email addresses associated with a LinkedIn profile.

☑ **LinkedIn Scraper (Python, Free)** – Extracts profile data, job postings, and company insights.

📌 **Example**: A business intelligence analyst uses Hunter.io to gather potential client email addresses from LinkedIn.

5. YouTube & Video OSINT Tools

These tools analyze YouTube videos, metadata, and engagement trends.

☑ **InVID (Free)** – Verifies videos, detects deepfakes, and extracts metadata.

☑ **YouTube Data API (Free, Advanced Users)** – Extracts video descriptions, comments, and engagement analytics.

☑ **CrowdTangle (Paid, Meta-Owned)** – Monitors viral content trends across Facebook, Instagram, and YouTube.

📌 **Example**: A researcher uses InVID to verify if a viral protest video is real or manipulated.

6. TikTok & Emerging Platforms OSINT Tools

TikTok's growing influence makes it an important platform for OSINT investigations.

☑ **TikTok API (Free, Advanced Users)** – Extracts video metadata, user interactions, and trends.

☑ **OSINTCombine TikTok Tool (Paid)** – Tracks TikTok account activity and location metadata.

☑ **Webmii (Free)** – Searches for people across multiple platforms, including TikTok.

📌 **Example**: An OSINT investigator uses OSINTCombine to track TikTok accounts spreading extremist content.

4.4.3 Ethical & Legal Considerations

While social media OSINT tools provide valuable insights, investigators must navigate privacy laws and ethical guidelines carefully.

◆ **Data Privacy & Platform Policies**

✓ **GDPR (Europe):** Limits how user data can be collected and stored.

✓ **CCPA (California):** Protects user privacy and personal data.

✓ **Twitter, Facebook, and LinkedIn Terms of Service**: Restrict unauthorized scraping and automated data collection.

➹ **Example**: Using unauthorized scrapers to collect private LinkedIn data violates terms of service and could lead to legal consequences.

◆ **Best Practices for Ethical Social Media OSINT**

✅ **Focus on Public Data** – Avoid collecting private or restricted information.
✅ **Cross-Verify Findings** – False information spreads easily on social media—always check multiple sources.
✅ **Be Transparent** – When possible, disclose investigations ethically (especially in journalism and law enforcement).
✅ **Use Tools Responsibly** – Follow social media platform policies to avoid bans or legal action.

Social media OSINT tools provide powerful capabilities for investigations, cybersecurity, business intelligence, and law enforcement. By leveraging AI-powered monitoring, data extraction, and real-time analysis, investigators can uncover hidden connections, detect misinformation, and track global trends.

◆ However, OSINT professionals must use these tools ethically, respecting privacy laws and platform policies to ensure responsible intelligence gathering.

4.5 Metadata & Image Analysis Tools

Images and metadata hold crucial information for OSINT investigations, helping analysts verify sources, track locations, and uncover hidden details. Metadata analysis tools extract details like timestamps, GPS coordinates, and camera models, while image analysis tools assist in reverse image searches, deepfake detection, and forensic analysis.

This chapter explores essential metadata and image analysis tools, their use cases, and best practices for ethical investigations.

4.5.1 What Are Metadata & Image Analysis Tools?

◆ **Metadata Analysis Tools** – Extract hidden information (EXIF data) from images, videos, and documents.

◆ **Image Analysis Tools** – Perform reverse image searches, detect manipulated media, and analyze visual content.

📌 **Example**: A journalist verifies whether an image of a war zone is authentic or digitally altered by analyzing metadata and running a reverse image search.

4.5.2 Metadata Extraction & Analysis Tools

1. EXIF & Metadata Extraction Tools

These tools retrieve embedded metadata from images, videos, and documents.

✅ **ExifTool (Free, Open-Source)** – Extracts and edits metadata from images, PDFs, and audio files.
✅ **Jeffrey's Image Metadata Viewer (Free, Online)** – Web-based EXIF data extraction.
✅ **FOCA (Free)** – Extracts metadata from PDFs, Word docs, and PowerPoint files.
✅ **EXIFPurge (Free)** – Removes metadata to enhance privacy.

📌 **Example**: A security analyst uses ExifTool to extract GPS coordinates from an image posted by a suspect to determine the photo's exact location.

2. Reverse Image Search Tools

These tools help track down original sources, find similar images, and detect manipulated content.

✅ **Google Reverse Image Search (Free)** – Finds similar images and web pages where the image appears.

✅ **Bing Visual Search (Free)** – Performs AI-powered visual searches.

✅ **Yandex Reverse Image Search (Free)** – More effective than Google for matching faces and objects.

✅ **TinEye (Freemium)** – Tracks an image's modifications and past appearances online.

📌 **Example**: A journalist uses Yandex Reverse Image Search to find the original source of a viral protest image, revealing it was taken years earlier in a different country.

3. Image Forensics & Deepfake Detection

These tools help analyze images for signs of tampering, Photoshop edits, and synthetic media (deepfakes).

✅ **InVID WeVerify (Free, Browser Plugin)** – Detects fake images, deepfakes, and manipulated media.

✅ **FotoForensics (Free)** – Performs error level analysis (ELA) to detect image tampering.

✅ **Forensically (Free, Online)** – Provides clone detection, noise analysis, and metadata extraction.

✅ **Deepware Scanner (Free, Online)** – Identifies deepfake images and videos.

📌 **Example**: A fact-checker uses InVID WeVerify to confirm whether a viral video of a political leader is AI-generated or authentic.

4. Facial Recognition & Object Detection

These tools analyze faces, objects, and patterns in images for OSINT investigations.

✅ **PimEyes (Paid)** – Facial recognition search engine to track faces across the internet.

✅ **Betaface (Paid)** – Extracts facial features and compares them to databases.

✅ **Google Cloud Vision (Freemium)** – Detects objects, logos, and text in images.

✅ **Amazon Rekognition (Paid)** – Identifies people, activities, and objects in photos/videos.

📌 **Example**: A missing persons investigator uses PimEyes to track a person's face appearing in different online photos.

5. Geolocation & Satellite Image Analysis

These tools identify locations, landmarks, and geographic features in images.

✅ **Google Earth Pro (Free)** – Examines historical satellite imagery for location verification.
✅ **GeoGuessr (Freemium)** – Helps OSINT analysts train their geolocation skills.
✅ **SunCalc (Free)** – Calculates shadows and sunlight angles to estimate time of day and location.
✅ **Mapillary (Free)** – Provides crowdsourced street-level imagery.

📌 **Example**: An OSINT investigator uses SunCalc to determine the exact time and location of a terrorist propaganda photo based on shadows and the sun's position.

4.5.3 Ethical & Legal Considerations

◆ **Privacy Laws & Image Metadata**

✔ **GDPR (Europe):** Prohibits storing personal metadata without consent.

✔ **CCPA (California):** Restricts unauthorized collection of facial recognition data.

✔ **Terms of Service**: Using facial recognition tools (like PimEyes) may violate website policies.

📌 **Example**: Publishing someone's GPS-tagged photos without consent can violate privacy laws and expose them to harm.

◆ **Best Practices for Ethical Image OSINT**

✅ **Use Open-Source Tools Ethically** – Avoid violating privacy laws and website policies.
✅ **Verify Image Origins** – Cross-check multiple sources before drawing conclusions.
✅ **Avoid Manipulation** – Do not alter images to create misleading narratives.
✅ **Anonymize Sensitive Data** – Blur faces and remove metadata when necessary.

Metadata and image analysis tools enhance OSINT investigations by revealing hidden details, verifying authenticity, and exposing digital forgeries. By leveraging reverse image searches, metadata extraction, and forensic analysis, OSINT professionals can track down sources, uncover fakes, and strengthen digital investigations.

◆ However, ethical and legal considerations must always be prioritized to ensure responsible use of image OSINT tools.

4.6 Bookmarking & Organizing OSINT Tools for Efficiency

Open-Source Intelligence (OSINT) investigations involve using multiple tools, databases, and resources across various platforms. To maintain efficiency and accuracy, OSINT professionals must organize, bookmark, and categorize their tools properly. Without a structured system, managing resources can become chaotic, leading to wasted time, redundant searches, and missed insights.

This chapter covers methods, tools, and best practices for bookmarking and organizing OSINT resources, ensuring smoother workflows and faster, more effective investigations.

4.6.1 Why Is Organization Essential in OSINT?

◆ **Saves Time** – Quickly access frequently used tools instead of repeatedly searching for them.
◆ **Enhances Accuracy** – Avoid using outdated or redundant tools by keeping an updated list.
◆ **Improves Collaboration** – Share categorized tools with teams for faster investigations.
◆ **Reduces Cognitive Load** – A structured system helps OSINT professionals stay focused.

📌 **Example**: A cybersecurity analyst investigating a phishing attack saves time by using a pre-organized set of tools for email analysis instead of searching manually.

4.6.2 Best Bookmarking & Organization Methods for OSINT

1. Browser-Based Bookmarking Systems

Modern browsers allow users to create folders and categorize tools for quick access.

✓ **Google Chrome & Firefox Bookmarks** – Organize OSINT tools into folders and subfolders.

☑ **Raindrop.io (Freemium)** – A cloud-based bookmarking manager with tagging and search functionality.

☑ **OneTab (Free, Chrome/Firefox)** – Saves and organizes multiple open tabs into a list format.

☑ **Start.me (Freemium)** – Creates a customized OSINT dashboard with categorized links.

📌 **Example**: An OSINT investigator creates separate bookmark folders for tools related to social media analysis, metadata extraction, and geolocation.

2. OSINT-Specific Toolkits & Repositories

Some platforms provide pre-organized collections of OSINT tools, reducing the need to manually bookmark everything.

☑ **OSINT Framework (Free, Online)** – A categorized directory of OSINT tools and techniques.

☑ **IntelTechniques Search Tool (Freemium)** – A structured search tool for finding people, websites, and metadata.

☑ **Awesome OSINT GitHub Repository (Free, Open-Source)** – A community-curated collection of OSINT resources.

📌 **Example**: A journalist uses OSINT Framework as a one-stop reference for searching social media, government databases, and news archives.

3. Note-Taking & Knowledge Management Tools

To enhance efficiency, OSINT professionals should use structured note-taking apps to store findings, workflows, and methodologies.

☑ **Obsidian (Free, Markdown-Based)** – Helps link related OSINT notes for an interconnected database.

☑ **Notion (Freemium)** – Organizes OSINT workflows, tools, and case studies in one platform.

☑ **Evernote (Freemium)** – Captures and categorizes OSINT findings with tags and notebooks.

☑ **Joplin (Free, Open-Source)** – A privacy-focused note-taking app that works offline.

📌 **Example**: A researcher investigating online scams logs their findings in Notion, linking each case to relevant OSINT tools and resources.

4. Mind Mapping & Visualization for OSINT Workflows

Mind mapping tools help visualize OSINT investigations, showing relationships between data sources, tools, and findings.

✅ **Maltego (Paid, Freemium for Community Edition)** – A powerful OSINT visualization tool for mapping connections.
✅ **MindMeister (Freemium)** – Creates interactive mind maps for OSINT workflows.
✅ **Obsidian Graph View (Free)** – Displays linked OSINT notes and data as a network graph.

📌 **Example**: A threat intelligence analyst uses Maltego to map social media connections between suspected cybercriminals.

5. Automation & Custom Dashboards

Automating OSINT tool management helps reduce manual effort and improve efficiency.

✅ **Harpoon (Paid)** – An OSINT automation tool that aggregates data from multiple sources.
✅ **TheHive (Free, Open-Source)** – Case management system for tracking OSINT investigations.
✅ **Hunchly (Paid)** – Automatically captures and organizes online investigations for documentation.

📌 **Example**: A private investigator uses Hunchly to automatically save and organize webpages during online research.

4.6.3 Best Practices for Organizing OSINT Tools Efficiently

✅ **Categorize by Investigation Type** – Create folders or dashboards for social media, geolocation, metadata, and people search tools.
✅ **Use Tags & Labels** – Assign keywords to bookmarks to quickly find relevant tools.
✅ **Keep Resources Updated** – Regularly remove outdated links and replace them with new, more effective tools.

✓ **Backup & Sync Data** – Use cloud-based platforms to ensure access across devices.

✓ **Test & Prioritize Tools** – Keep a shortlist of the most effective and reliable OSINT tools for quick access.

📌 **Example**: A cybersecurity investigator tags all social media OSINT tools with "Twitter," "Facebook," and "Instagram" labels for faster retrieval.

Bookmarking and organizing OSINT tools significantly enhances efficiency and effectiveness in investigations. By leveraging browser bookmarks, curated OSINT repositories, note-taking apps, and automation tools, professionals can streamline their workflow, save time, and stay focused on actionable intelligence.

◆ A well-organized OSINT toolkit ensures faster access to critical resources, leading to more accurate and efficient investigations.

5. Google Dorking & Search Techniques

Google is more than just a search engine—it's a powerful gateway to vast amounts of hidden information if you know how to search effectively. Google Dorking, or advanced search querying, allows OSINT practitioners to uncover publicly accessible but often overlooked data, from exposed documents and login portals to sensitive information unintentionally left online. This chapter explores essential search operators, advanced filtering techniques, and practical use cases for refining your queries. By mastering Google Dorking and other search strategies, you can transform basic searches into precise intelligence-gathering operations, maximizing the power of open-source information.

5.1 Understanding Google Search Operators

Google is one of the most powerful OSINT tools available, but most users don't leverage its full potential. Google search operators allow investigators to refine searches, extract specific data, and uncover hidden information that isn't immediately visible through standard searches.

This chapter explores Google search operators, advanced techniques, and best practices for OSINT investigations.

5.1.1 What Are Google Search Operators?

◆ **Definition**: Google search operators are special commands that help refine and filter search results.

◆ **Purpose**: They allow OSINT investigators to find hidden webpages, filter results, and search for specific file types or domains.

📌 **Example**: Searching for site:linkedin.com "cybersecurity analyst" will return only LinkedIn profiles containing "cybersecurity analyst" in the text.

5.1.2 Basic Google Search Operators

Operator	Function	Example	Use Case
"quotes"	Searches for an exact phrase	`"John Doe hacker"`	Find exact mentions of a name
site:	Searches within a specific website	`site:bbc.com "cyber attack"`	Find articles about cyber attacks only on BBC
filetype:	Finds a specific file type	`filetype:pdf "OSINT guide"`	Locate PDF reports on OSINT
intitle:	Searches for a keyword in page titles	`intitle:"data breach"`	Find webpages with "data breach" in the title
inurl:	Finds keywords in the URL	`inurl:login`	Locate login pages for websites
related:	Finds websites similar to a given URL	`related:forbes.com`	Discover sites similar to Forbes
cache:	Views Google's last cached version of a webpage	`cache:example.com`	See older versions of a webpage

📌 **Example**: A journalist searching for a leaked government report might use:

🔎 **filetype**:pdf site:gov "classified report"

5.1.3 Advanced Google Search Operators

Operator	Function	Example	Use Case
OR	Searches for one or the other keyword	`"cyber attack" OR "data breach"`	Find pages mentioning either term
AND	Requires both terms to be present	`"phishing attack" AND "credit card"`	Find cases where both terms appear
- (Minus Sign)*	Excludes a term from results	`"John Doe" -Facebook`	Remove Facebook results from searches
before:	Finds results published before a specific date	`"hacking tools" before:2022`	Find older resources
after:	Finds results published after a specific date	`"zero-day exploit" after:2023`	Find recent information

📌 **Example**: A hacker tracking dark web forums might use:

🔎 **inurl**:forum site:.onion "hacking tools"

5.1.4 Google Dorking for OSINT Investigations

What Is Google Dorking?

◆ Google Dorking (aka Google Hacking) uses advanced search queries to find exposed databases, login pages, and sensitive files.
◆ Used by OSINT analysts, cybersecurity professionals, and ethical hackers.

Common Google Dorks for OSINT

Dork Query	Function	Example
`intitle:"index of"`	Finds open directories with publicly accessible files	`intitle:"index of" passwords.txt`
`filetype:log`	Searches for log files	`filetype:log site:example.com`
`ext:sql OR ext:db`	Looks for exposed databases	`ext:sql site:.gov`
`intext:"username" AND intext:"password"`	Finds pages containing login credentials	`intext:"admin" AND intext:"12345"`
`inurl:/wp-admin/`	Searches for WordPress admin login pages	`inurl:/wp-admin/ site:.com`

📌 **Example**: A penetration tester looking for exposed passwords might use:
🔎 **filetype**:txt inurl:passwords site:.com

⚠ **Warning**: Google Dorking must be used ethically and legally. Accessing private information without permission is illegal under cybercrime laws.

5.1.5 Best Practices for OSINT Investigators

✅ **Use Multiple Operators Together** – Combine operators for highly targeted searches.
✅ **Monitor Real-Time Data** – Use after: and before: to filter recent leaks and reports.
✅ **Stay Ethical & Legal** – Google Dorking should only be used for legal investigations.
✅ **Automate Searches** – Tools like Google Alerts can notify you of new search results.

📌 **Example**: A corporate investigator searching for recent PDF reports on cybersecurity threats could use:

🔍 **filetype**:pdf "cyber threat report" after:2023

Google search operators are powerful tools for OSINT professionals, allowing them to find hidden information, uncover leaked documents, and verify sources efficiently. By mastering advanced queries and Google Dorking, investigators can enhance their intelligence-gathering process while staying within legal and ethical boundaries.

◆ Using search operators strategically helps uncover deep, valuable insights that standard searches miss.

5.2 Advanced Google Dorking Techniques

Google Dorking, also known as Google hacking, is an advanced OSINT technique that leverages Google's powerful search engine to find hidden information, exposed databases, sensitive files, and misconfigured web servers. While Google Dorking can uncover valuable intelligence, it must be used ethically and legally to avoid unauthorized access to sensitive data.

In this section, we will explore advanced Google Dorking techniques, use cases, and best practices for OSINT investigations.

5.2.1 What Is Google Dorking?

◆ **Definition**: Google Dorking involves using advanced search queries (dorks) to uncover hidden, exposed, or forgotten information on the web.
◆ **Purpose**: It helps OSINT analysts, penetration testers, and cybersecurity professionals locate sensitive data, misconfigured servers, and exposed credentials.

📌 **Example**: A Google search for filetype:sql site:gov may reveal publicly accessible government SQL databases that were never intended to be exposed.

⚠ **Warning**: Accessing sensitive data without authorization may violate laws such as the Computer Fraud and Abuse Act (CFAA) and GDPR.

5.2.2 Common Google Dorking Use Cases

◆ **Finding Exposed Login Pages** – Identifying admin panels and login portals.

◆ **Locating Open Directories** – Discovering publicly accessible file repositories.

◆ **Extracting Metadata & Credentials** – Uncovering sensitive documents with usernames and passwords.

◆ **Discovering Vulnerable Websites** – Finding outdated software, misconfigured servers, and exploitable pages.

◆ **Tracking Leaked Information** – Searching for leaked reports, credentials, and classified data.

📌 **Example**: A journalist searching for a leaked report might use:

🔍 **filetype**:pdf "confidential" site:.gov

5.2.3 Advanced Google Dorking Operators

Here are some of the most powerful Google Dorking operators and their applications:

Dork Query	Function	Example	Use Case
`intitle:"index of"`	Finds open directories with accessible files	`intitle:"index of" "passwords.txt"`	Locate publicly exposed files
`filetype:sql OR filetype:db`	Searches for exposed databases	`filetype:sql "customer data"`	Find unprotected databases
`inurl:/wp-admin/ OR inurl:/admin/login`	Finds admin login panels	`inurl:/wp-admin/ site:.com`	Locate WordPress admin panels
`ext:log OR ext:cfg OR ext:ini`	Searches for configuration or log files	`ext:cfg "ftp password"`	Uncover server credentials
`site:pastebin.com OR site:github.com`	Finds leaked credentials on paste sites	`site:pastebin.com "email password"`	Identify data breaches
`intext:"username" AND intext:"password"`	Searches for hardcoded login credentials	`intext:"admin" AND intext:"12345"`	Find exposed credentials in text files
`site:.onion`	Searches for hidden Tor (.onion) websites	`site:.onion "hacker forum"`	Discover dark web resources

📌 **Example**: An investigator looking for leaked passwords might use:

🔍 **intext**:"password" filetype:txt site:.com

5.2.4 Advanced Google Dorking for Specific OSINT Use Cases

1. Finding Exposed Databases & Sensitive Documents

Many organizations accidentally expose databases, spreadsheets, and sensitive PDFs.

🔎 filetype:xls OR filetype:csv site:.gov "password"
🔎 filetype:pdf "confidential" site:example.com

📌 **Example**: A researcher looking for publicly available government reports might use:

🔎 filetype:pdf site:.gov "classified"

2. Identifying Vulnerable Websites

Older websites often contain outdated plugins, which attackers exploit.

🔎 inurl:"phpinfo.php" OR inurl:"phpmyadmin"
🔎 intitle:"Apache Status" site:.edu

📌 **Example**: A penetration tester searching for outdated server configurations might use:

🔎 intitle:"Apache Server Status" site:.com

3. Tracking Leaked Credentials & Data Breaches

Hackers often post stolen credentials on Pastebin, GitHub, or other leak sites.

🔎 site:pastebin.com "email password"
🔎 site:github.com "AWS_SECRET_KEY"

📌 Example: A security analyst checking for exposed company credentials might use:

🔎 site:pastebin.com "companyname.com password"

4. Discovering Open Directories & Publicly Shared Files

Open directories contain folders of images, videos, and PDFs that anyone can access.

🔎 intitle:"index of" "mp4"
🔎 intitle:"index of" "financial report"

📌 **Example**: A financial investigator looking for publicly available reports might use:

🔎 intitle:"index of" "annual report"

5.2.5 Automating Google Dorking for OSINT

◆ **Google Alerts** – Automates searches for new data leaks or sensitive info.
◆ **GHDB (Google Hacking Database)** – A curated list of known dorks used in OSINT and cybersecurity.
◆ **Python Scripts (e.g., Googlesearch-Py)** – Automates bulk Google Dorking queries.

📌 **Example**: A cybersecurity researcher sets a Google Alert for:

🔎 filetype:sql "password" site:.com

5.2.6 Ethical & Legal Considerations

◆ **Legality**: Accessing unauthorized information using Google Dorking may violate cybercrime laws (CFAA, GDPR, CCPA).
◆ **Ethics**: Never exploit found data—instead, follow responsible disclosure if sensitive data is discovered.
◆ **Terms of Service:** Using automated tools to scrape Google results may violate Google's policies.

📌 **Example**: If an investigator finds an exposed database, the ethical step is to report it to the company's security team, not exploit it.

Google Dorking is a powerful OSINT technique that uncovers hidden data, exposed credentials, and vulnerable websites. By mastering advanced search operators, investigators can discover valuable intelligence quickly. However, ethics and legality must always be a top priority—responsible use is key.

◆ When used correctly, Google Dorking is one of the most effective tools in an OSINT investigator's arsenal.

5.3 Searching for Hidden or Deleted Webpages

The internet is constantly evolving, with websites being updated, moved, or deleted. However, deleted or hidden webpages often leave behind digital traces that can still be accessed, recovered, or analyzed using specialized OSINT techniques.

In this section, we explore how OSINT investigators can use cached pages, web archives, and forensic techniques to uncover hidden or deleted web content.

5.3.1 Why Search for Hidden or Deleted Webpages?

♦ **Investigating Misinformation** – Find evidence of edited, deleted, or retracted content.
♦ **Tracking Online Footprints** – Discover hidden user activity on websites.
♦ **Recovering Lost Information** – Access deleted news articles, reports, or forum posts.
♦ **Digital Forensics & Cybercrime Investigations** – Identify altered webpages in fraud cases.

📌 **Example**: A journalist researching corporate corruption might look for an old version of a company's website that was deleted after a scandal.

5.3.2 Methods for Finding Deleted or Hidden Pages

1. Using Google's Cached Pages

♦ Google stores cached versions of websites that may no longer be accessible.

🔎 How to Access a Cached Page?

- Search for a website on Google.
- Click the three dots (⋮) next to a result.
- Click "Cached" to view Google's stored version.

✅ Google Cache Direct URL:

📌 cache:example.com/page

📌 **Example:**

🔎 cache:bbc.com/news/cyberattack – Shows an older version of a BBC news article.

⚠ **Limitations**: Google does not cache all pages, and caches expire quickly.

2. Searching the Internet Archive (Wayback Machine)

◆ Wayback Machine (archive.org) is one of the best tools for accessing historical versions of websites.

🔎 **How to Use It?**

- Go to https://web.archive.org/
- Enter the URL of the website.
- Select a date to view past versions.

✓ **Direct Wayback Machine Search:**

📌 https://web.archive.org/web/*/example.com

📌 **Example**: A researcher looking for a deleted government press release might check:

🔎 https://web.archive.org/web/*/whitehouse.gov/news/

⚠ **Limitations**: Not all websites allow Wayback Machine to archive them.

3. Checking Google Search Snapshots (Google Dorking)

◆ If a webpage has been deleted recently, Google may still have a search result snippet with relevant information.

🔎 **Google Dork for Deleted Pages:**

📌 "Keyword from deleted page" site:example.com

📌 **Example**: A cybersecurity analyst tracking a removed blog post about a data breach might use:

🔍 "customer data leaked" site:example.com

⚠ **Limitations**: Snippets disappear once Google updates its index.

4. Using Other Web Archiving Services

Several alternatives to Wayback Machine exist:

✅ **Archive.is** – Manually saves pages (better for blocked or restricted sites).
✅ **CachedView.com** – Aggregates Google Cache, Bing Cache, and Web Archive.
✅ **Memento Project** – Searches across multiple web archives at once.
✅ **Resurrect Pages (Browser Extension)** – Finds archived versions of dead links.

📌 **Example**: An OSINT investigator trying to access a deleted social media profile might check:

🔍 https://archive.is/twitter.com/user123

5. Recovering Deleted Content via RSS Feeds

◆ Some websites publish RSS feeds that retain deleted content.

🔍 **How to Check RSS for Deleted Content?**

- Use an RSS reader like Feedly or Inoreader.
- Check if old posts are still visible in the feed.
- Search for archived RSS snapshots in Wayback Machine.

📌 **Example**: A researcher tracking deleted blog posts might use:

🔍 site:example.com "RSS" – Finds feed URLs.

⚠ **Limitations**: RSS feeds don't always store full posts, just summaries.

6. Using Search Engine Caches (Bing, Yandex, Baidu, DuckDuckGo)

◆ Other search engines (besides Google) may still have cached versions of deleted pages.

✅ **Bing Cache:**

📌 https://www.bing.com/search?q=cache:example.com

✅ **Yandex Cache:**

📌 https://yandex.com/search/?text=cache:example.com

📌 **Example**: If Google Cache is missing a deleted article, an investigator might check:

🔍 cache:example.com site:bing.com

⚠ **Limitations**: Some search engines update caches frequently, deleting old versions.

7. Finding Deleted Social Media Posts

◆ Social media posts are often deleted, but traces can remain.

✅ **Facebook & Twitter Cached Searches:**

📌 "deleted post keyword" site:facebook.com
📌 "deleted tweet keyword" site:twitter.com

✅ **OSINT Tools for Social Media Archiving:**

- Wayback Machine (for public social media pages).
- PolitiTweet (for archived political tweets).
- UnTweetable (for tracking deleted tweets).

📌 **Example**: An OSINT analyst tracking a politician's deleted tweets might use:
🔍 "statement about cyber law" site:twitter.com

⚠ **Limitations**: Private accounts, closed groups, and deleted media may be difficult to recover.

5.3.3 Best Practices for OSINT Investigators

✅ **Act Fast** – Web pages disappear quickly after deletion, so check caches and archives ASAP.

✅ **Use Multiple Sources** – Combine Google Cache, Wayback Machine, and Bing/Yandex archives.

✅ **Document Findings** – Screenshots and archived links preserve evidence before it disappears.

✅ **Stay Ethical** – Only investigate publicly accessible information; avoid illegal data scraping.

📌 **Example**: A journalist documenting corporate website changes might create a timeline of archived snapshots to show when specific claims were removed.

Finding hidden or deleted webpages is a crucial OSINT skill that allows investigators to recover lost data, track website changes, and investigate digital footprints. By using Google Cache, Wayback Machine, search engine caches, and social media archives, OSINT professionals can uncover valuable intelligence that might otherwise be lost.

♦ In the digital world, nothing truly disappears—traces always remain for those who know where to look.

5.4 Using Filetype & Metadata Searches for Intelligence

OSINT investigations often rely on extracting intelligence from files such as PDFs, Word documents, Excel spreadsheets, images, and other publicly available documents. By using filetype-specific searches and metadata analysis, investigators can uncover sensitive information, document authors, hidden data, and security vulnerabilities.

This section will cover how OSINT professionals can use Google Dorking, metadata extraction tools, and filetype searches to gather intelligence effectively.

5.4.1 Why Use Filetype & Metadata Searches in OSINT?

♦ **Finding Leaked or Exposed Documents** – Locate publicly accessible PDFs, spreadsheets, or PowerPoint presentations.

♦ **Extracting Hidden Metadata** – Discover document authors, timestamps, software versions, and revision history.

◆ **Uncovering Security Vulnerabilities** – Identify sensitive data leaks in government or corporate documents.
◆ **Tracking Digital Footprints** – Connect individuals to files through metadata traces.
◆ **Investigating Cybercrime** – Find malicious file signatures, embedded links, or manipulated documents.

📌 **Example**: A researcher investigating corporate leaks might look for internal documents by searching for:

🔍 filetype:pdf "confidential" site:example.com

5.4.2 Using Google Dorking for Filetype Searches

Google Dorking allows investigators to search for specific file types on websites, potentially revealing misconfigured servers or publicly accessible documents.

Search Query	Use Case	Example
`filetype:pdf`	Finds PDF reports, manuals, and research papers	`filetype:pdf "internal report" site:example.com`
`filetype:xls OR filetype:csv`	Locates spreadsheets with financial or personal data	`filetype:xls "employee salaries" site:.gov`
`filetype:doc OR filetype:docx`	Finds Word documents that may contain internal memos	`filetype:doc "confidential" site:example.com`
`filetype:ppt`	Searches for PowerPoint presentations with business or academic content	`filetype:ppt "strategy meeting" site:.org`
`filetype:log OR filetype:cfg`	Finds configuration or log files that may contain credentials	`filetype:log "password" site:example.com`

📌 **Example**: An OSINT analyst searching for government memos might use:

🔍 filetype:doc "internal use only" site:.gov

⚠ **Limitations**: Accessing sensitive files without permission may violate privacy laws.

5.4.3 Extracting Metadata from Documents

Metadata is hidden information stored within a file, including:

✅ **Author Name** – Reveals who created the document.

✅ **Creation & Modification Dates** – Shows when and how the file was edited.

✅ **Software Used** – Identifies software versions (useful for finding vulnerabilities).

✅ **Hidden Comments & Edits** – May contain sensitive information.

✅ **Geolocation Data (EXIF)** – Found in images and media files.

Tools for Metadata Extraction

Tool	Function	URL
ExifTool	Extracts metadata from images, PDFs, and documents	https://exiftool.org/
FOCA	Finds metadata in public documents	https://elevenpaths.com/labstools/foca
PDF Examiner	Extracts metadata from PDFs	https://www.pdfexaminer.com/
Metagoofil	Scrapes metadata from online documents	https://github.com/laramies/metagoofil

📌 **Example**: A security analyst investigating leaked government reports might analyze a PDF with:

🔍 exiftool report.pdf

5.4.4 Searching for Exposed Metadata in Public Files

1. Finding Author Information

🔍 Google Dork:

📌 filetype:pdf "Author: John Doe"

📌 **Example**: A journalist researching corporate whistleblowers might check:

🔍 filetype:docx "Author: Anonymous"

2. Identifying Hidden Comments in Documents

🔍 Google Dork:

📌 filetype:xls "hidden comments"

📌 **Example**: A cybersecurity analyst looking for unredacted financial data might check:

🔎 filetype:xls "notes" site:.gov

3. Tracking Geolocation Data in Images (EXIF Metadata)

Many images contain EXIF metadata, which can reveal:

✅ **GPS Coordinates** – Exact location where the photo was taken.
✅ **Camera Model** – Identifies the device used.
✅ **Timestamps** – Shows when the photo was captured.

📌 **Example**: A journalist tracking military activities might extract EXIF data from leaked photos using:

🔎 exiftool image.jpg

⚠ **Limitations**: Some social media platforms strip EXIF data before uploading.

5.4.5 Investigating Leaked or Misconfigured File Repositories

Many organizations accidentally expose sensitive files on cloud storage or FTP servers.

1. Searching Open Directories

🔎 Google Dork:

📌 intitle:"index of" "confidential"

📌 **Example**: A researcher looking for publicly available financial reports might check:

🔎 intitle:"index of" "financial report" site:.com

2. Finding Unsecured Cloud Storage (Google Drive, Dropbox, AWS S3)

🔎 Google Dork for Google Drive:

📌 site:drive.google.com "confidential"

🔎 Google Dork for AWS Buckets:

📌 site:s3.amazonaws.com "database backup"

📌 **Example**: A cybersecurity analyst checking for exposed customer data might search:

🔎 site:s3.amazonaws.com "passwords.csv"

⚠ **Legal Note**: Accessing private cloud storage without permission is illegal.

5.4.6 Best Practices & Ethical Considerations

✅ **Act Responsibly** – Avoid accessing private or confidential information.
✅ **Verify Metadata Sources** – Some metadata may be altered or misleading.
✅ **Use Metadata to Corroborate Evidence** – Always cross-check metadata with other sources.
✅ **Report Data Leaks Ethically** – Follow responsible disclosure if sensitive files are exposed.

📌 **Example**: If an investigator finds a leaked government report, the ethical step is to inform the responsible agency, not exploit the data.

Filetype searches and metadata analysis are essential OSINT techniques for finding hidden, leaked, or misconfigured files. By using Google Dorking, metadata extraction tools, and open-source file repositories, investigators can uncover critical intelligence while maintaining legal and ethical standards.

◆ Every file tells a story—learning how to read metadata can unlock powerful insights.

5.5 Finding Exposed Databases & Open Directories

In OSINT investigations, exposed databases and open directories can provide valuable intelligence, revealing sensitive information, leaked credentials, financial data, and more.

Organizations sometimes misconfigure servers, leaving databases, backups, and file repositories publicly accessible.

This section explores how OSINT analysts can use Google Dorking, specialized tools, and ethical best practices to identify open databases and unsecured file directories while staying within legal and ethical boundaries.

5.5.1 Why Search for Exposed Databases & Open Directories?

◆ **Discovering Leaked Credentials** – Exposed databases may contain usernames, passwords, and personal data.
◆ **Investigating Data Breaches** – Open directories may store confidential documents, backups, or logs.
◆ **Tracking Misconfigured Cloud Storage** – Organizations sometimes leave Amazon S3 buckets, Google Drive folders, and FTP servers unprotected.
◆ **Uncovering Security Vulnerabilities** – Finding open databases allows organizations to fix security issues before attackers exploit them.

📌 **Example**: A cybersecurity researcher investigating a leaked customer database might search for open MongoDB or Elasticsearch instances.

⚠ **Warning**: Accessing private or sensitive data without authorization may be illegal. Always adhere to ethical guidelines.

5.5.2 Using Google Dorking to Find Open Directories

Google Dorking can help locate publicly accessible directories and files that were not intended for public access.

1. Searching for Open Index Pages

🔎 Google Dork:

📌 intitle:"index of" "parent directory"

✓ Variations:

- intitle:"index of" "database backup"
- intitle:"index of" "passwords"

- intitle:"index of" "confidential"

📌 **Example**: Searching for open FTP servers containing financial reports:

🔎 intitle:"index of" "financial report" site:.gov

2. Finding Exposed Files in Open Directories

🔎 Google Dork:

📌 intitle:"index of" filetype:sql (Finds exposed SQL databases)
📌 intitle:"index of" filetype:csv (Finds spreadsheets with possible personal data)
📌 intitle:"index of" "backup.zip" (Finds compressed backup files)

📌 **Example**: An OSINT analyst looking for exposed credentials might search for:

🔎 intitle:"index of" "passwords.txt"

⚠ **Risk**: If a file is found, do not download or access private information without permission.

3. Searching for Openly Accessible Database Dumps

🔎 Google Dork:

📌 filetype:sql "INSERT INTO" site:.com

✅ Variations:

- filetype:sql "mysql dump" – Finds database exports.
- filetype:json "user_password" – Searches for JSON files with stored credentials.
- filetype:csv "email,password" – Finds CSV files containing login credentials.

📌 **Example**: Searching for publicly exposed SQL database dumps:

🔎 filetype:sql "customer data" site:.org

5.5.3 Finding Exposed Databases (MongoDB, Elasticsearch, etc.)

Many NoSQL and relational databases are accidentally left exposed due to misconfigured security settings. These include:

✅ **MongoDB** – Often exposed on port 27017.
✅ **Elasticsearch** – Usually found on port 9200.
✅ **PostgreSQL & MySQL** – Commonly left open without passwords.
✅ **Redis** – Frequently misconfigured and publicly accessible.

1. Using Shodan & Censys to Find Open Databases

◆ Shodan and Censys are search engines that scan the internet for publicly accessible databases and devices.

🔎 Shodan Query for Open MongoDB:

📌 port:27017 product:MongoDB

🔎 Censys Query for Open Elasticsearch:

📌 services.service_name: "Elasticsearch" AND services.tls.status: "NO_TLS"

📌 **Example**: A cybersecurity researcher checking for open Elasticsearch instances might search:

🔎 **port**:9200 product:Elasticsearch on Shodan.

⚠ **Risk**: Accessing exposed databases without authorization is illegal.

5.5.4 Investigating Misconfigured Cloud Storage (S3, Google Drive, FTP, etc.)

Many organizations accidentally expose cloud storage due to poor configurations.

1. Finding Public Amazon S3 Buckets

🔎 Google Dork for AWS S3:

📌 site:s3.amazonaws.com "confidential"

✅ **Common Searches:**

- site:s3.amazonaws.com filetype:csv – Searches for CSV files in AWS buckets.
- site:s3.amazonaws.com "database backup" – Looks for exposed database backups.
- site:s3.amazonaws.com "AWS_ACCESS_KEY" – Finds exposed AWS credentials.

📌 **Example**: A security analyst checking for misconfigured S3 buckets might search:

🔍 site:s3.amazonaws.com "customer data"

2. Searching for Public Google Drive & Dropbox Links

🔍 Google Drive Dork:

📌 site:drive.google.com "private"

🔍 Dropbox Dork:

📌 site:dropbox.com "passwords"

📌 **Example**: Searching for exposed Google Drive spreadsheets:

🔍 site:drive.google.com "employee salaries"

3. Identifying Open FTP Servers

🔍 Google Dork for FTP:

📌 intitle:"index of" "ftp"

✅ **Common FTP Dorks:**

- intitle:"index of" "ftp" site:.gov – Searches for government FTP servers.
- intitle:"index of" "ftp" filetype:zip – Looks for compressed backups.

📌 **Example**: Searching for publicly accessible FTP servers with medical data:

🔎 intitle:"index of" "ftp" "medical records"

⚠ **Legal Note**: Accessing unauthorized FTP servers is illegal.

5.5.5 Best Practices for OSINT Investigators

✅ **Act Ethically** – Avoid accessing private or sensitive information.
✅ **Verify Public Access** – If an organization has inadvertently exposed data, consider reporting it responsibly.
✅ **Use Only Legal Tools** – Shodan, Censys, and Google Dorking are legal tools, but accessing restricted databases is illegal.
✅ **Document Findings** – Maintain detailed logs and screenshots when performing security research.

📌 **Example**: A cybersecurity analyst finding an exposed corporate database should report it responsibly rather than exploit the data.

Exposed databases and open directories are common sources of OSINT intelligence, but they also pose serious security risks when misconfigured. Using Google Dorking, Shodan, and OSINT tools, investigators can identify leaked data, security vulnerabilities, and digital footprints—but ethical and legal considerations must always come first.

◆ In OSINT, finding information is easy—acting responsibly is what matters most.

5.6 Practical Google Hacking for OSINT Investigations

Google is one of the most powerful OSINT tools available, and Google Hacking (also known as Google Dorking) is a technique used to uncover sensitive information, exposed files, misconfigured databases, and hidden web pages. By using advanced search operators, OSINT investigators can filter results and discover intelligence that might not be easily visible through a normal search.

This section will cover:

◆ How Google Hacking works for OSINT

- Practical Google Dorking techniques
- Finding hidden files, login pages, and unsecured databases
- Ethical and legal considerations

5.6.1 What is Google Hacking?

Google Hacking involves using special search queries, called "dorks," to find specific types of information on public websites. These queries help uncover:

✓ Exposed login pages

✓ Publicly accessible directories & databases

✓ Leaked credentials & sensitive documents

✓ Misconfigured security settings

✓ Hidden website vulnerabilities

⚠ Warning: Accessing sensitive or private data without permission is illegal. OSINT should always follow ethical guidelines.

5.6.2 Common Google Dorking Techniques

Google Dorking uses advanced search operators to refine search results. Below are some of the most useful operators for OSINT investigations:

1. Finding Exposed Login Pages

Many web applications have login portals that are publicly accessible but not meant to be found via search engines.

🔎 Google Dork:

📌 inurl:login OR inurl:signin

✓ Variations:

- inurl:admin login – Searches for admin login panels.
- inurl:signin site:example.com – Finds the sign-in page for a specific domain.

- inurl:wp-login.php – Locates WordPress login pages.

📌 **Example**: Searching for login pages on government websites:

🔎 inurl:login site:.gov

2. Finding Publicly Accessible Directories

Web directories sometimes contain open file listings due to misconfigured server settings.

🔎 **Google Dork:**

📌 intitle:"index of" "parent directory"

✅ **Variations:**

- intitle:"index of" "passwords" – Searches for open directories containing password files.
- intitle:"index of" "financial report" – Looks for financial documents.
- intitle:"index of" site:example.com – Finds open directories on a specific site.

📌 **Example**: Searching for open file directories on university websites:

🔎 intitle:"index of" site:.edu

3. Searching for Exposed Documents & Databases

Sometimes, sensitive documents are accidentally indexed by Google, making them publicly accessible.

🔎 **Google Dork:**

📌 filetype:pdf "confidential"

✅ **Variations:**

- filetype:xls "password" – Searches for Excel spreadsheets containing credentials.
- filetype:sql "insert into" – Finds SQL database dumps.

- filetype:doc "internal use only" – Looks for Word documents labeled as internal.

📌 **Example**: Searching for leaked corporate financial reports:

🔎 filetype:xls "budget report" site:.com

4. Discovering Exposed Email Lists & Credentials

Organizations sometimes accidentally expose email lists and login credentials in online documents.

🔎 **Google Dork:**

📌 "username" "password" filetype:txt

✅ **Variations:**

- "email" "password" filetype:csv – Looks for email-password combinations.
- "admin" "login" filetype:log – Searches for log files containing login attempts.

📌 **Example**: Searching for exposed user credentials in CSV format:

🔎 "user,password" filetype:csv

⚠ **Warning**: Accessing sensitive login credentials without authorization is illegal.

5. Finding Vulnerable Websites (SQL Injection, XSS, etc.)

Google can be used to identify web vulnerabilities, helping organizations secure their systems.

🔎 **Google Dork:**

📌 inurl:php?id=1

✅ **Variations:**

- inurl:".php?id=" – Searches for potentially vulnerable PHP pages.

- intext:"Warning: mysql_fetch_array()" – Finds web pages with SQL errors.
- inurl:"view.php?id=" – Looks for pages that might be vulnerable to SQL injection.

📌 **Example**: Searching for web pages with SQL errors:

🔎 intext:"Warning: mysql_fetch_array()"

⚠ **Warning**: Exploiting vulnerabilities is illegal unless you have explicit permission from the website owner.

5.6.3 Using Google Dorking to Investigate a Target

Case Study: Investigating an Organization

Scenario:

A journalist is investigating Company X and wants to find internal documents, login portals, and exposed databases.

✅ **Step 1: Find Company X's Login Portals**

🔎 inurl:login site:companyx.com

✅ **Step 2: Search for Internal Documents**

🔎 filetype:pdf "internal use only" site:companyx.com

✅ **Step 3: Locate Open Directories**

🔎 intitle:"index of" site:companyx.com

✅ **Step 4: Check for Exposed Emails**

🔎 "@companyx.com" filetype:xls

◆ **Findings**: The search reveals an exposed directory containing old employee salary spreadsheets. The journalist reports this responsibly to the company.

5.6.4 Ethical & Legal Considerations

✅ DO:

- Use Google Dorking responsibly for OSINT and cybersecurity research.
- Report security vulnerabilities through responsible disclosure.
- Stay within the law—searching is legal, but accessing private data is not.

🚫 **DON'T:**

- Access private databases, credentials, or login portals without authorization.
- Exploit vulnerabilities or use found data for malicious purposes.
- Download or share confidential or sensitive information.

Google Dorking is a powerful OSINT technique that can uncover exposed data, misconfigured security settings, and leaked credentials. By mastering advanced search operators, OSINT investigators can efficiently filter search results and find hidden information—while ensuring that their work remains ethical and legal.

◆ Google doesn't just find what's on the surface—it reveals what others didn't mean to expose. Use it wisely.

6. Social Media Basics for OSINT

Social media platforms are treasure troves of real-time information, making them essential resources for OSINT investigations. From user profiles and location check-ins to hidden metadata and network connections, social media can reveal valuable insights when analyzed strategically. This chapter introduces the fundamentals of social media intelligence (SOCMINT), covering platform-specific search techniques, profile analysis, and content verification. Whether tracking digital footprints, verifying identities, or mapping social networks, mastering the basics of social media OSINT will equip you with the skills to extract actionable intelligence from the world's most dynamic information sources.

6.1 Social Media as an OSINT Goldmine

Social media is one of the richest sources of Open-Source Intelligence (OSINT). Billions of users share personal, professional, and location-based information across platforms like Facebook, Twitter (X), Instagram, LinkedIn, TikTok, and Reddit. This data can be leveraged for investigations, cybersecurity, law enforcement, competitive intelligence, and more.

This section explores:

- The value of social media for OSINT
- Types of intelligence that can be gathered
- Methods and tools for collecting and analyzing data
- Ethical and legal considerations

6.1.1 Why Social Media is a Powerful OSINT Source

Unlike traditional intelligence sources, social media provides:

✅ **Real-time updates** – Users constantly post about events, locations, and opinions.

✅ **Publicly accessible data** – Many profiles and posts are openly available without restrictions.

✅ **Rich multimedia content** – Photos, videos, and live streams can reveal locations, activities, and associations.

✅ **Network insights** – Friends, followers, and interactions can map out connections between individuals or organizations.

✅ **Searchability** – Most platforms allow searching by keywords, hashtags, geolocation, and usernames.

📌 **Example**: Law enforcement tracking a fugitive might use social media posts to determine their current location or connections to accomplices.

6.1.2 What Can Be Collected from Social Media?

1. User Profiles & Biographical Data

- Name, username, aliases
- Profile pictures
- Location (self-reported or inferred)
- Employment history (LinkedIn, Facebook)
- Hobbies, interests, political views

📌 **Example**: An investigator looking into a cybersecurity threat actor might check their LinkedIn to see past employers, technical skills, and connections.

2. Geolocation & Travel Patterns

- Check-ins & location tags
- Photos & videos with identifiable landmarks
- GPS metadata in uploaded content
- Posts about recent or future travel

📌 **Example**: A journalist investigating a war zone can analyze social media posts from civilians for on-the-ground intelligence.

3. Connections & Social Networks

- Friends, followers, group memberships
- Mentions & tagged posts
- Mutual connections
- Engagement with other users (likes, shares, comments)

📌 **Example**: A corporate investigator may examine an executive's LinkedIn connections to identify business relationships and potential conflicts of interest.

4. Multimedia Analysis (Photos, Videos, Metadata)

- ◆ Reverse image searches for tracking individuals
- ◆ Identifying objects, tattoos, or surroundings in photos
- ◆ Extracting EXIF metadata (if available)

📌 **Example**: A human rights group analyzing video footage might determine where and when a conflict occurred by identifying landmarks, weather conditions, and shadows.

5. Hashtags & Keyword Monitoring

- ◆ Tracking trending topics and conversations
- ◆ Identifying movements, protests, or criminal activities
- ◆ Monitoring misinformation or fake news campaigns

📌 **Example**: A cybersecurity analyst monitoring #DataBreach can track companies that have suffered leaks in real time.

6.1.3 OSINT Collection Methods for Social Media

1. Manual Searching

Most social media platforms have built-in search functions that allow keyword, hashtag, and location-based searches.

🔍 **Examples:**

- **Twitter (X):** from:username (to find posts from a specific user)
- **Instagram**: #hashtag (to track discussions)
- **Facebook**: Searching for public posts & group discussions

📌 **Tip**: Advanced searches like "site:twitter.com keyword" on Google can find specific posts.

2. Automated OSINT Tools for Social Media

Various OSINT tools automate social media data collection:

- ♠ **Sherlock** – Finds usernames across multiple social media platforms.
- ♠ **Twint** – Scrapes Twitter (X) data without an API.

- ◆ **SOCMINT Tools (Social Media Intelligence):**

  - **Maltego** – Maps social connections.
  - **Geofeedia** – Monitors geotagged posts.

IntelTechniques OSINT Toolset – Provides deep searches into social media platforms.

📌 **Example**: A fraud investigator might use Maltego to map out relationships between suspicious accounts.

3. Geolocation & Image Analysis

- ♠ **Google Reverse Image Search** – Finds where a profile picture was previously used.
- ♠ **Yandex Reverse Image Search** – More accurate for finding faces and objects.
- ♠ **EXIF Metadata Extractors** – Tools like ExifTool analyze image metadata for location, camera type, and timestamp.
- ♠ **SunCalc.net** – Estimates time of day based on shadows in an image.

📌 **Example**: A journalist verifying a protest photo can check SunCalc.net to confirm whether the shadows match the reported time of day.

4. Hashtag & Sentiment Analysis

- ♠ **Trendsmap** – Tracks trending Twitter (X) hashtags worldwide.
- ♠ **Social Bearing** – Analyzes Twitter (X) user engagement and sentiment.
- ♠ **CrowdTangle (Meta tool)** – Monitors Facebook, Instagram, and Reddit trends.

📌 **Example**: Law enforcement tracking a protest movement might monitor hashtags like #ProtestCityName to predict escalation points.

6.1.4 Ethical & Legal Considerations

✔ DO:

✓ Collect only publicly available data.

✓ Follow the terms of service of each platform.

✓ Respect user privacy and avoid harassment.

✓ Use findings for ethical investigations (law enforcement, security, journalism, etc.).

⊘ DON'T:

✗ Access private accounts without permission.

✗ Use fake accounts (some platforms ban sockpuppet accounts).

✗ Download or share private information without consent.

✗ Engage in social engineering or phishing to gain access.

📌 **Example**: A security researcher reporting an exposed database is ethical, but using OSINT for doxxing or harassment is illegal.

6.1.5 Case Study: Tracking a Missing Person Using OSINT

Scenario:

A missing college student was last seen posting on Instagram from a bar.

OSINT Investigation Steps:

✅ Step 1: Analyze the Student's Social Media

- **Instagram**: Last post shows a bar's neon sign in the background.
- **Facebook**: Parents reported the disappearance in a local group.
- **Twitter (X):** Friends tweeted about her last known outfit & location.

✅ Step 2: Reverse Search the Image

- A Google Reverse Image Search reveals the bar's location.

✅ Step 3: Check Nearby Geotagged Posts

- Searching Instagram's location tags for the bar shows another patron's video from the same night.

✅ **Step 4: Confirm Sightings & Timeline**

- The video confirms the missing person left with an unknown individual.
- Authorities use this data to locate security footage and track the suspect's vehicle.

📌 **Outcome**: The student is found safe, thanks to OSINT and geolocation analysis.

Social media is an OSINT goldmine that provides real-time, public intelligence for investigators, journalists, law enforcement, and security professionals. By leveraging manual searches, automation tools, and geolocation techniques, analysts can uncover key insights while ensuring that privacy laws and ethical standards are respected.

◆ In OSINT, information is everywhere—you just need to know where (and how) to look.

6.2 Facebook OSINT: Public Profiles & Hidden Data

Facebook remains one of the largest social media platforms, with nearly 3 billion active users worldwide. Because users often share personal details, Facebook is a goldmine for OSINT investigations. Whether you're a journalist, investigator, or cybersecurity professional, Facebook OSINT can help uncover key information about individuals, organizations, and events.

This section covers:

◆ How to collect intelligence from public Facebook profiles
◆ Techniques for finding hidden data
◆ Facebook Graph Search alternatives
◆ Ethical & legal considerations

6.2.1 What Makes Facebook a Valuable OSINT Source?

Facebook is one of the most data-rich platforms available for OSINT. Some key types of intelligence that can be gathered include:

☑ **User Information** – Names, aliases, profile pictures, education, employment, and location.

☑ **Friends & Social Connections** – Friend lists, mutual friends, group memberships, and tagged posts.

☑ **Photos & Videos** – Self-uploaded images, tagged photos, and shared content.

☑ **Location Data** – Check-ins, geo-tagged posts, and past locations.

☑ **Events & Groups** – Participation in events and private/public groups.

☑ **Interactions & Likes** – Posts, comments, reactions, and shared content.

📌 **Example**: An investigator looking into a fraud case might analyze a suspect's Facebook posts to find their connections, past employers, or locations.

6.2.2 Collecting OSINT from Public Facebook Profiles

Even if a user limits their privacy settings, some data remains publicly accessible. Here's what you can check:

1. Profile & Cover Photos

- Public profile pictures and cover photos remain visible even if the account is private.
- Reverse image searching can help track a person's online presence.

📌 **Tool**: Google Reverse Image Search

📌 **Alternative**: Yandex Image Search (Better for facial recognition)

2. About Section & Workplace History

- Current & past jobs (useful for corporate investigations)
- Education history (helps track former classmates or locations)
- Relationship status & family members

📌 **Tip**: If an account is private, check comments on public posts from friends or family— they may reveal hidden connections.

3. Posts & Comments

◆ Even if a profile is private, public posts & comments can reveal:

✅ Political views

✅ Personal opinions

✅ Shared locations or events

📌 **Tip**: Searching for a user's name on Facebook's search bar can show public posts and comments they've interacted with.

4. Friends List & Mutual Connections

◆ Even if friend lists are private, checking mutual friends can help map relationships.
◆ Some people leave their friends list open—this is useful for network mapping.

📌 **Tool**: Maltego – Helps visualize social networks.

5. Facebook Groups & Events

◆ Many groups are public, and their posts/members can be analyzed.
◆ Events show who is attending, helping track movement & activity patterns.

📌 **Example**: A journalist investigating a protest can check who organized it, attendees, and discussions in public groups.

6.2.3 Finding Hidden Facebook Data

Even if a user locks down their profile, some hidden data can still be accessed using advanced OSINT techniques.

1. Facebook Search Operators (Manual Dorking)

Using Google Dorking, you can find Facebook posts, profiles, and comments indexed by Google.

🔍 **Find public Facebook posts with a specific keyword:**

📌 site:facebook.com "keyword"

🔍 **Find posts by a specific person (if public):**

📌 site:facebook.com "John Doe" "keyword"

🔍 **Find images from a specific user:**

📌 site:facebook.com "John Doe" filetype:jpg

📌 **Example**: Searching for leaked job complaints about a company:

🔍 site:facebook.com "Company Name" "toxic workplace"

2. Tracking Deleted or Hidden Posts

Even if a user deletes or hides a post, it might still be:

✅ Cached by Google

✅ Archived by Wayback Machine

✅ Screenshotted or shared elsewhere

📌 **Tools to check:**

◆ **Google Cache** – Shows saved versions of pages.
◆ **Wayback Machine** – Archives old Facebook pages.

3. Using Facebook's Internal ID System

Every Facebook profile, post, and image has a unique numerical ID. Even if a username changes, this ID stays the same.

How to Find Facebook Profile ID:

1️⃣ Right-click on a profile picture → Copy Image Address
2️⃣ Look for the numeric ID in the URL (e.g., fbid=1234567890).

📌 **Use Case**: If a user changes their username, the old ID can still be used to track their history.

6.2.4 Advanced OSINT Tools for Facebook Investigations

Several tools help automate Facebook OSINT investigations:

◆ **OSINT Combine Facebook Tool** – Extracts data from Facebook profiles & groups.
◆ **IntelTechniques Facebook Search Tool** – Deep searches within Facebook's ecosystem.
◆ **Maltego** – Graph-based analysis of Facebook connections.

📌 **Example**: A cybercrime investigator might use Maltego to map connections between scam accounts.

6.2.5 Ethical & Legal Considerations

✅ **DO:**

✔ Only collect publicly available data.

✔ Follow Facebook's Terms of Service.

✔ Use findings for ethical investigations (journalism, law enforcement, cybersecurity).

🚫 **DON'T:**

✘ Hack, scrape, or bypass Facebook's security measures.

✘ Access private accounts without permission.

✘ Use OSINT for stalking, harassment, or doxxing.

📌 **Example**: Investigating a scammer using OSINT is ethical, but using Facebook OSINT for personal revenge is unethical and illegal.

6.2.6 Case Study: Tracking a Fake Profile

Scenario:

A company is investigating a fake profile impersonating its CEO to scam customers.

OSINT Investigation Steps:

✅ **Step 1: Reverse Image Search** – The scammer's profile picture is found on multiple fake accounts.

✅ **Step 2: Google Dorking** – site:facebook.com "CEO Name" scam reveals past complaints.

✅ **Step 3: Checking Mutual Friends** – Some mutual connections expose other fake accounts linked to the scam.

✅ **Step 4: Reporting to Facebook** – The company submits findings to Facebook's security team, leading to profile takedown.

📌 **Outcome**: The scam is disrupted, and the company prevents customer fraud.

Facebook remains one of the most valuable OSINT sources, offering personal, business, and geolocation intelligence. By using manual searches, advanced tools, and ethical OSINT techniques, investigators can extract hidden data while respecting privacy laws.

◆ "The key to Facebook OSINT is knowing where (and how) to look!"

6.3 Twitter OSINT: Hashtags, Lists & Historical Tweets

Twitter (now known as X) is one of the most valuable platforms for Open-Source Intelligence (OSINT). Unlike Facebook, which emphasizes private networks, Twitter is designed for public conversations, news updates, and real-time event tracking.

This chapter explores how OSINT investigators can use hashtags, Twitter Lists, and historical tweets to gather intelligence effectively.

6.3.1 Why Twitter (X) is an OSINT Goldmine

Twitter is a real-time information hub where users share:

✅ Breaking news before mainstream media

✅ Geotagged tweets revealing locations

✅ Conversations & discussions around events and movements

✅ Political opinions, protests, and cyber threats

✅ Company & industry trends

📌 **Example**: During global crises (e.g., natural disasters, conflicts), OSINT investigators can track eyewitness tweets and geolocated images for real-time intelligence.

6.3.2 Using Hashtags for OSINT Investigations

Hashtags help categorize tweets, making them searchable and useful for monitoring trends, events, or movements.

1. Searching for Hashtags Manually

Use Twitter's search bar or Google Dorking to find relevant hashtags.

🔎 **Basic Twitter Search:**

📌 **#ProtestCityName** – Find tweets related to a specific protest.
📌 **#DataBreach** – Track cybersecurity incidents.
📌 **#MissingPerson** – Monitor missing persons reports.

🔎 **Google Dorking to Search Twitter Hashtags:**

📌 site:twitter.com "#Keyword" – Finds tweets containing the keyword.

2. Tracking Hashtags in Real-Time

Some tools allow live monitoring of hashtags:

◆ **Trendsmap** – Shows trending hashtags by location.
◆ **TweetDeck** – Customizable dashboard for tracking multiple hashtags at once.
◆ **Twitonomy** – Analyzes hashtag usage, engagement, and mentions.

📌 **Example**: A security analyst monitoring a cyberattack can track hashtags like #Ransomware, #DataLeak, or #DDoSAttack in real time.

6.3.3 Twitter Lists: Mapping Networks & Influence

Twitter Lists are collections of accounts that users create to follow specific groups of people. Investigators can:

✅ Find curated lists of experts, journalists, or threat actors.

✅ Analyze who follows whom in niche industries or extremist groups.

✅ Identify bot networks by comparing list memberships.

1. Finding Public Twitter Lists

📌 site:twitter.com/*/lists "keyword" – Finds public lists related to a topic.

📌 **Example**: Searching site:twitter.com/*/lists "cybersecurity" finds lists containing cybersecurity professionals.

2. Monitoring Lists for Investigations

◆ List members reveal connections between individuals or groups.
◆ Lists followed by a person indicate their interests or affiliations.
◆ Bot accounts often appear in multiple suspicious lists.

📌 **Example**: A journalist investigating disinformation campaigns can analyze lists followed by known fake news accounts.

6.3.4 Extracting & Analyzing Historical Tweets

1. Searching for Old Tweets (Manual & Google Dorking)

Twitter's Advanced Search allows filtering by:

✅ Date range

✅ Username

✅ Hashtags or keywords

📌 **Google Dorking to Find Historical Tweets:**

🔎 site:twitter.com inurl:status "keyword" before:YYYY-MM-DD after:YYYY-MM-DD

📌 **Example:**

◈ Find tweets about a hacking group before 2022:

site:twitter.com inurl:status "hacker group" before:2022-01-01

2. Automating Historical Tweet Extraction

Some tools allow bulk extraction of old tweets:

◈ **Twint** – Scrapes historical tweets without API limitations.
◈ **Wayback Machine** – Checks archived Twitter pages.
◈ **TweetBeaver** – Exports old tweets for analysis.

📌 **Example**: A fraud investigator looking into a scammer's deleted tweets might use Wayback Machine to retrieve snapshots.

6.3.5 Twitter Geolocation OSINT

Many tweets contain location metadata, either manually tagged by users or inferred from content.

1. Finding Geotagged Tweets Manually

📌 geocode:LATITUDE,LONGITUDE,RADIUS – Searches tweets from a specific area.

📌 **Example**: Find tweets from New York City (within 10km):

🔎 geocode:40.7128,-74.0060,10km

2. Automated Geolocation OSINT Tools

◈ **GeoSocial Footprint** – Extracts geotagged tweets.
◈ **Echosec** – Visualizes tweets on a map interface.
◈ **OSINT Combine Geolocation Tool** – Finds geolocation clues in tweets.

📌 **Example**: During a riot, law enforcement can use Echosec to track tweets from eyewitnesses and geolocate hotspots.

6.3.6 Case Study: Identifying a Cyber Threat Actor on Twitter

Scenario:

A company suspects that a Twitter account is linked to a hacker group leaking sensitive data.

OSINT Investigation Steps:

☑ **Step 1: Analyze Hashtags & Mentions**

- Search for #DataLeak #DarkWeb to find related tweets.
- Identify accounts frequently mentioning hacking forums.

☑ **Step 2: Check Twitter Lists**

- Look at lists they belong to (e.g., hacker forums, cybersecurity threats).
- Identify other accounts in the same lists.

☑ **Step 3: Extract Historical Tweets**

- Use Google Dorking to find old tweets linking the account to hacking groups.

☑ **Step 4: Reverse Image Search**

- If the hacker has a profile picture, check if it was stolen or linked to other accounts.

📌 **Outcome**: The company connects the suspect's Twitter account to a known hacker forum, confirming their involvement in leaked data sales.

6.3.7 Ethical & Legal Considerations for Twitter OSINT

☑ **DO:**

✔ Collect only publicly available tweets.

✔ Follow Twitter's Terms of Service.

✔ Report threat actors or criminal activity responsibly.

⊘ DON'T:

✘ Hack, scrape, or access private Twitter accounts.

✘ Engage in harassment, impersonation, or doxxing.

✘ Violate data protection laws (GDPR, CCPA).

📌 **Example**: A journalist analyzing Twitter disinformation campaigns is ethical, but tracking individuals' private tweets without consent is illegal.

Twitter (X) is a real-time intelligence goldmine, offering insights into breaking events, networks, geolocation data, and historical trends. By leveraging hashtags, lists, and tweet history, OSINT investigators can uncover hidden connections while staying within legal and ethical boundaries.

◆ "Every tweet leaves a footprint—if you know where to look."

6.4 Instagram OSINT: Reverse Image & Story Analysis

Instagram is one of the most visual-driven social media platforms, with millions of users sharing photos, videos, and stories daily. While it may seem harder to extract intelligence compared to text-heavy platforms like Twitter (X), Instagram OSINT can uncover valuable insights—from geolocated images to hidden social connections.

This chapter explores how to:

◆ Use reverse image search to track people and photos
◆ Analyze Instagram Stories for real-time intelligence
◆ Extract metadata & hidden details from images
◆ Navigate privacy settings & OSINT limitations

6.4.1 Why Instagram is a Valuable OSINT Source

Unlike Twitter, which focuses on text-based content, Instagram revolves around images, videos, and stories. Despite privacy restrictions, investigators can still gather key intelligence, including:

✅ **Profile Information** – Usernames, bio, website links, and mutual followers
✅ **Geotagged Posts** – Locations where photos were taken or tagged
✅ **Connections & Followers** – Public interactions, mutual followers, and tagged users
✅ **Instagram Stories** – Time-sensitive posts with location, music, and hashtags
✅ **Metadata in Photos** – Hidden details like timestamps and camera models

📌 **Example**: A missing persons investigator can use Instagram OSINT to find recent photos, tagged locations, and mutual followers to trace the individual's movements.

6.4.2 Reverse Image Search on Instagram

Since Instagram is primarily image-based, reverse image search is one of the most effective OSINT techniques to:

✔ Track fake profiles & catfish accounts

✔ Find other social media accounts using the same profile picture

✔ Detect image theft & fake product scams

1. How to Perform a Reverse Image Search

◆ **Google Reverse Image Search** – Upload an image to find similar versions across the web.
◆ **Yandex Image Search** – More effective for finding faces across different sites.
◆ **TinEye** – Tracks where an image has appeared online.

📌 **Steps:**

1️⃣ Save the Instagram photo (screenshot if necessary).

2️⃣ Upload it to Google Images, Yandex, or TinEye.

3️⃣ Check if the image appears on other profiles, websites, or forums.

📌 **Example**: An investigator tracking an online scammer finds that their Instagram profile photo is actually stolen from a random model's LinkedIn account using reverse image search.

6.4.3 Extracting Metadata & Hidden Information from Instagram Photos

1. Checking for Metadata (EXIF Data)

When users upload images to Instagram, most EXIF metadata (geolocation, camera details) is stripped. However, if you can obtain the original file from other sources (like a message or a linked site), you can use:

◆ **ExifTool** – Extracts timestamps, camera models, and geolocation from original images.

◆ **Jeffrey's Image Metadata Viewer** – Online EXIF viewer for quick analysis.

📌 **Example**: A fraud investigator analyzing a leaked Instagram photo might find GPS coordinates hidden in the original file, revealing the suspect's real location.

2. Extracting Image Clues Without Metadata

Even without metadata, you can still analyze:

✓ **Reflections & Backgrounds** – Objects or landmarks in the image may indicate a location.

✓ **Time & Weather Conditions** – Shadows and lighting can help estimate when the photo was taken.

✓ **Objects & Branding** – Store names, license plates, or street signs may reveal real-world details.

📌 **Example**: An OSINT analyst tracking a cybercriminal's Instagram post notices a reflection of a street sign in sunglasses, helping pinpoint their location.

6.4.4 Analyzing Instagram Stories for OSINT

Instagram Stories are temporary posts that disappear after 24 hours but can provide:

✅ Real-time activity tracking

✅ Geotags & location data

✅ Mentions & tagged users

1. Finding Public Instagram Stories

◆ **Instagram Web Version** – Open https://www.instagram.com/USERNAME/ to check public stories.

◆ **Third-party Story Viewers** – Sites like InstaStories allow anonymous viewing.

◆ **Google Dorking** – Find cached Instagram Stories with:

📌 site:instagram.com "story" "username"

2. Archiving Instagram Stories for OSINT

Since stories disappear after 24 hours, archiving is crucial. Some tools include:

◆ **StorySaver** – Downloads Instagram Stories.

◆ **Wayback Machine** – May have cached versions of Instagram profiles.

◆ **Screenshot & Screen Recording** – A simple but effective method.

📌 **Example**: A law enforcement officer monitoring a gang's Instagram Stories finds a gun sale advertisement, but before it disappears, they record it as evidence.

6.4.5 Finding Hidden Social Connections on Instagram

1. Checking Tagged Users & Mentions

Even if an Instagram account is private, you can:

✔ Search for their username in other people's posts.

✔ Look at who they tag in public comments or stories.

✔ Check their mutual followers for connections.

📌 **Example**: A journalist investigating a politician's hidden connections finds that they are tagged in vacation photos by an undisclosed business partner.

2. Tracking Comment Interactions

Even if a profile is locked, comments on public posts remain visible.

✓ Check what public posts they've commented on.

✓ Find accounts they frequently interact with.

📌 **Example**: A cybersecurity team tracking a hacker's Instagram finds they frequently comment on cryptocurrency scam pages, linking them to fraudulent activities.

6.4.6 Case Study: Tracking a Missing Person via Instagram OSINT

Scenario:

A 19-year-old student is reported missing, and the last known contact was via Instagram Stories. Investigators use OSINT to track them.

OSINT Investigation Steps:

✅ Step 1: Reverse Image Search

Investigators check Instagram profile photos and find the student's other social media accounts.

✅ Step 2: Analyzing Instagram Stories

Last story posted 24 hours ago shows the student in a car with a visible road sign.

Investigators geolocate the road sign to identify the potential travel route.

✅ Step 3: Checking Tagged Users & Comments

Friends tagged in their last Instagram posts are contacted for information.

A tagged user confirms they were last seen at a specific location.

📌 **Outcome**: The student is found safe after OSINT methods helped pinpoint their last known location.

6.4.7 Ethical & Legal Considerations in Instagram OSINT

✅ **DO:**

✓ Use only publicly available data.

✓ Follow Instagram's Terms of Service.

✓ Report findings ethically (e.g., missing persons, fraud investigations).

🚫 **DON'T:**

✗ Hack, scrape, or access private accounts without permission.

✗ Use OSINT for harassment, stalking, or doxxing.

✗ Violate privacy laws (e.g., GDPR, CCPA).

📌 **Example**: Investigating scams or criminal activities on Instagram is legal, but using OSINT for personal revenge is unethical and illegal.

Instagram OSINT is powerful for tracking individuals, identifying social connections, and analyzing real-time events through reverse image searches and story analysis. By using ethical intelligence-gathering techniques, investigators can extract valuable insights while respecting privacy laws.

◆ "Every Instagram post tells a story—if you know how to read between the lines."

6.5 LinkedIn OSINT: Corporate & Employment Investigations

LinkedIn is the world's largest professional networking platform, making it a goldmine for OSINT (Open-Source Intelligence) investigations related to businesses, employees, and industry trends. Unlike other social media platforms, LinkedIn is specifically designed for corporate networking, job listings, and professional interactions, allowing investigators to extract valuable intelligence on companies, executives, hiring trends, and connections.

In this chapter, we'll explore:

✅ How to extract intelligence from public LinkedIn profiles

✅ Investigating companies, employees, and hiring trends

✅ Using LinkedIn search operators & Google Dorking

✅ Identifying corporate vulnerabilities & social engineering risks

✅ Ethical considerations in LinkedIn OSINT

6.5.1 Why LinkedIn is a Valuable OSINT Source

LinkedIn provides structured and self-reported data from professionals, making it highly reliable for OSINT. Key data points include:

✅ **Full names & aliases** – Often includes real names, unlike pseudonyms on other social platforms.

✅ **Employment history** – Previous jobs, promotions, and career shifts.

✅ **Company affiliations** – Insights into corporate structures and partnerships.

✅ **Skills & certifications** – Verifies expertise in specific fields.

✅ **Connections & networks** – Shows mutual connections, employees, and industry influencers.

✅ **Public posts & articles** – Corporate announcements, opinions, and personal insights.

📌 **Example**: A cybersecurity firm investigating a data breach may use LinkedIn OSINT to find employees who recently posted about internal company changes, potentially revealing security weaknesses.

6.5.2 Investigating Companies on LinkedIn

1. Extracting Key Company Information

To investigate a company, start by analyzing its LinkedIn company page, which typically reveals:

✔ Headquarters location

✔ Number of employees

✓ Recent job postings

✓ Industry & sector

✓ Notable executives & founders

📌 **Example**: A competitor investigating a startup's hiring trends may notice multiple job listings for cybersecurity professionals, suggesting the company is building a security team—possibly due to a recent data breach.

2. Finding Employees & Corporate Networks

✅ Search for employees using Google Dorking:

🔍 site:linkedin.com/in "company name" – Lists all LinkedIn profiles mentioning the company.

✅ Find key personnel & decision-makers:

🔍 site:linkedin.com/in "CTO" OR "Chief Technology Officer" "company name" – Identifies top executives.

✅ Analyze employment trends:

- Mass exits or layoffs suggest internal instability.
- Rapid hiring in cybersecurity suggests a recent security incident.
- Executives leaving before a scandal may indicate a cover-up.

📌 **Example**: An investigator researching fraud in a financial firm finds that several senior employees left the company just before an SEC investigation—suggesting internal knowledge of misconduct.

6.5.3 Extracting Intelligence from Public LinkedIn Profiles

Even without being connected, public LinkedIn profiles reveal a lot of information:

✓ **Work history & promotions** – Tracks career growth and industry experience.

✓ **Endorsements & recommendations** – Identifies key skills & credibility.

✓ **Mutual connections** – Maps out networks & affiliations.

✓ **Published articles & posts** – Corporate opinions & insider knowledge.

1. Using LinkedIn Search Operators

🔎 site:linkedin.com/in "John Doe" "Company Name" – Finds a specific employee's profile.

🔎 site:linkedin.com/in "cybersecurity analyst" "Google" – Finds cybersecurity analysts at Google.

🔎 site:linkedin.com/in "ex-CompanyName" OR "formerly at CompanyName" – Finds ex-employees who may reveal insider info.

📌 **Example**: A journalist investigating a government contractor finds an ex-employee's LinkedIn post criticizing the company's security practices, revealing potential vulnerabilities.

2. Identifying Fake LinkedIn Profiles

Fake LinkedIn profiles are used for social engineering, corporate espionage, and phishing attacks. Red flags include:

⚑ Few connections (under 100)
⚑ Profile photo from a stock image site
⚑ Unrealistic job history (e.g., CEO at 20 years old)
⚑ Lack of posts or engagement
⚑ Generic or poorly written profile summaries

📌 **Example**: A security team finds a suspicious LinkedIn account posing as a recruiter, attempting to connect with employees in high-security roles—likely a phishing attempt.

6.5.4 Social Engineering Risks & LinkedIn OSINT

Hackers and threat actors use LinkedIn for social engineering attacks, gathering intelligence to target individuals and companies.

1. How Attackers Use LinkedIn for OSINT

✓ **Spear-phishing** – Using job roles to craft realistic phishing emails.

✓ **CEO fraud** – Impersonating executives to manipulate employees.

✓ **Credential harvesting** – Scanning job listings for software/tools used by a company.

✓ **Pretexting & impersonation** – Creating fake recruiter profiles to lure victims.

📌 **Example**: A hacker finds a LinkedIn post by a junior employee mentioning their company uses "Okta for authentication". The hacker then sends a phishing email disguised as an Okta update to steal login credentials.

2. Protecting Against LinkedIn-Based Threats

✅ **Limit profile visibility** – Restrict public access to sensitive details.
✅ **Educate employees** – Train staff on social engineering tactics.
✅ **Be cautious with connection requests** – Avoid accepting unknown people.
✅ **Monitor executive profiles** – Detect fake impersonation accounts.

📌 **Example**: A corporate security team monitors LinkedIn for fake accounts impersonating executives to prevent CEO fraud scams.

6.5.5 Case Study: Uncovering Corporate Fraud via LinkedIn OSINT

Scenario:

A financial analyst suspects a startup is exaggerating its valuation to attract investors.

OSINT Investigation Steps:

✅ Step 1: Analyze employee count & hiring trends

Despite claiming rapid growth, the company has only 5 employees listed on LinkedIn.

✅ Step 2: Investigate executives' backgrounds

The CEO's past job history appears inconsistent, with overlapping job roles at different companies.

✅ Step 3: Identify ex-employees & whistleblowers

A former employee's LinkedIn post criticizes the company's financial mismanagement.

📌 **Outcome**: The analyst uncovers inconsistencies in the company's claims, warning investors before a potential fraud scandal erupts.

6.5.6 Ethical & Legal Considerations in LinkedIn OSINT

✅ DO:

✔ Investigate only publicly available information.

✔ Follow LinkedIn's Terms of Service.

✔ Use OSINT for ethical purposes (e.g., cybersecurity, fraud prevention).

🚫 DON'T:

✘ Use fake profiles to deceive or impersonate others.

✘ Scrape LinkedIn data with automated bots (violates LinkedIn's policies).

✘ Harass or target individuals for personal revenge.

📌 **Example**: Conducting corporate due diligence using LinkedIn OSINT is legal, but using OSINT for identity theft or blackmail is illegal.

LinkedIn is a powerful OSINT tool for investigating companies, employees, and hiring trends. By using search operators, analyzing profiles, and mapping corporate networks, investigators can uncover hidden business insights, security vulnerabilities, and fraud risks while maintaining ethical boundaries.

◆ "A company's LinkedIn presence reveals more than just job listings—it exposes corporate intelligence waiting to be uncovered."

6.6 Social Media Archiving & Monitoring Techniques

Social media platforms generate vast amounts of data in real time, making them valuable for OSINT (Open-Source Intelligence) investigations. However, posts, comments, and stories can disappear quickly due to deletion, privacy changes, or platform policies, making it crucial to archive and monitor social media activity effectively.

This chapter explores:

✅ Why social media archiving is essential

✅ Tools & methods for real-time monitoring

✅ How to capture deleted or disappearing content

✅ Legal & ethical considerations in social media archiving

6.6.1 Why Social Media Archiving Matters

Since social media content is dynamic and temporary, archiving ensures that:

✔ **Critical evidence is preserved** – Posts, tweets, and comments can be deleted.

✔ Trends and sentiment analysis can be tracked over time.

✔ Fake news, scams, and misinformation are documented.

✔ Legal & regulatory compliance is maintained (e.g., corporate investigations).

📌 **Example**: A journalist tracking disinformation campaigns archives tweets from bots spreading propaganda before Twitter (X) removes them.

6.6.2 Real-Time Social Media Monitoring Techniques

Real-time monitoring helps investigators track:

✔ Trending hashtags & keywords

✔ Public posts & user activity

✔ Emerging threats & cyberattacks

✔ Geolocated social media activity

1. Keyword & Hashtag Monitoring

Tools:

- ◆ **TweetDeck** (for Twitter monitoring)
- ◆ **Talkwalker** (social media alerts)
- ◆ **Brandwatch** (AI-powered sentiment analysis)

📌 **Example**: A cybersecurity team monitors hashtags related to a data breach (#leak, #breach, #hacked) to detect early signs of leaked corporate data.

2. Location-Based Monitoring (Geo-OSINT)

Tools:

- ◆ **Echosec** – Tracks geotagged posts across platforms.
- ◆ **GeoSocial Footprint** – Analyzes location-based social media activity.
- ◆ **Google Earth & Maps** – Cross-references geotagged images.

📌 **Example**: Law enforcement tracks Instagram posts near a crime scene to identify potential witnesses.

6.6.3 How to Capture & Archive Social Media Content

Since platforms like Twitter, Facebook, and Instagram frequently remove posts, archiving ensures evidence is not lost.

1. Manual Archiving Methods

✓ **Screenshots** – Simple but can be altered (use timestamping tools).

✓ **PDF or HTML Save** – Right-click and save web pages for documentation.

✓ **Video Recording** – Tools like OBS Studio capture live streams.

📌 **Example**: A journalist investigating political corruption takes screenshots of deleted tweets by government officials for evidence.

2. Automated Archiving Tools

◆ **Wayback Machine (Archive.org)** – Saves past versions of web pages.

◆ **Hunchly** – Automatically captures & saves web pages for OSINT investigations.

◆ **Snagit** – Screenshots and records scrolling web pages.

📌 **Example**: An OSINT analyst investigating a cybercriminal's dark web activities uses Hunchly to save their Twitter posts before they disappear.

3. Social Media API Scraping

Some platforms provide APIs (Application Programming Interfaces) that allow structured data collection.

✓ **Twitter API** – Extracts tweets based on keywords, users, and locations.

✓ **Facebook Graph API** – Collects public posts & interactions (with restrictions).

✓ **YouTube API** – Gathers video metadata and comments.

📌 **Example**: A researcher studying misinformation campaigns uses the Twitter API to collect thousands of tweets promoting fake news articles.

⚖ **Warning**: Web scraping social media without permission may violate Terms of Service—always check platform policies.

6.6.4 Capturing Deleted & Disappearing Content

Many social media posts are deleted, hidden, or altered after being posted. However, OSINT techniques can still recover them.

1. Using Cached & Archived Versions

◆ **Google Cache** – Find old versions of deleted posts.

◆ **Bing Cache** – Similar to Google's cache for web pages.

◆ **Wayback Machine** – Retrieves deleted pages.

📌 **Example**: An investigator looking for a suspect's deleted Facebook post finds it in Google's cache before it disappears.

2. Finding Deleted Tweets & Posts

- ◆ **Politwoops** – Archives deleted tweets from politicians.
- ◆ **Resavr** – Saves long Reddit comments before deletion.
- ◆ **Unddit** – Recovers deleted Reddit comments.

📌 **Example**: A journalist uses Politwoops to retrieve a deleted tweet from a senator admitting to financial misconduct.

3. Tracking Changes in Edited Content

- ◆ **Facebook's Edit History** – View changes made to posts.
- ◆ **Wikipedia Revision History** – Track article edits.
- ◆ **Wayback Machine Diff Tool** – Compare old vs. new web pages.

📌 **Example**: A misinformation researcher monitors Facebook post edits, noticing how a political group changes misleading claims after backlash.

6.6.5 Case Study: Investigating a Cyber Threat via Social Media OSINT

Scenario:

A cybersecurity team detects a potential data breach at a major company.

OSINT Investigation Steps:

✅ **Step 1: Monitor real-time Twitter & Telegram discussions**

Team sets up keyword alerts for "leaked database," "company breach," and "password dump."

✅ **Step 2: Archive suspicious posts before deletion**

Using Hunchly, they save Telegram messages where hackers discuss selling stolen data.

✅ **Step 3: Cross-check deleted posts via cache & archive tools**

Investigators find a deleted forum post where a hacker originally leaked a sample of compromised credentials.

📌 **Outcome**: The company issues a security alert and forces a password reset before the breach worsens.

6.6.6 Ethical & Legal Considerations in Social Media Archiving

✅ **DO:**

✓ Archive only publicly available content.

✓ Follow platform Terms of Service.

✓ Obtain proper legal authorization when required.

🚫 **DON'T:**

✗ Use hacking or unauthorized scraping.

✗ Archive private content without consent.

✗ Use OSINT for malicious purposes (e.g., harassment, stalking).

📌 **Example**: A journalist tracking fake news networks can ethically archive public Facebook posts, but scraping private messages without consent violates privacy laws.

Social media OSINT requires efficient archiving & monitoring techniques to capture and analyze disappearing content. By using real-time monitoring tools, archiving services, and ethical methods, investigators can preserve critical evidence, track online threats, and uncover misinformation campaigns.

◆ "Social media never forgets—if you know where to look and how to archive it."

7. Website & Domain Investigations for Beginners

Every website leaves behind a digital footprint, and OSINT practitioners can leverage domain investigations to uncover valuable intelligence about organizations, individuals, and hidden infrastructures. By analyzing domain registrations, server details, website metadata, and historical records, investigators can trace ownership, detect potential security vulnerabilities, and reveal connections between seemingly unrelated entities. This chapter introduces fundamental techniques for conducting website and domain research using WHOIS lookups, DNS analysis, historical archives, and other essential tools. Whether you're verifying a source, uncovering hidden assets, or tracking online activities, mastering website investigations is a crucial step in your OSINT journey.

7.1 Finding Information About a Website's Owner

When conducting OSINT (Open-Source Intelligence) investigations, identifying the owner of a website can reveal valuable insights about individuals, businesses, or cybercriminal operations. Whether you're researching a scam website, tracking a competitor, or investigating cyber threats, knowing who owns a website helps in attribution, risk assessment, and legal actions.

This chapter explores:

✓ How to identify a website's owner

✓ WHOIS lookups and domain registration data

✓ Technical footprints (IP addresses, hosting, DNS records)

✓ Tracking website history & ownership changes

✓ Legal & ethical considerations

7.1.1 Why Website Ownership Matters in OSINT

Understanding who owns a website can help:

✓ **Identify scams & fraud** – Track down fraudulent e-commerce or phishing sites.

✓ **Investigate cyber threats** – Discover who is behind malicious domains.

✓ **Verify credibility** – Assess the legitimacy of news sites and businesses.

✓ **Support legal actions** – Assist in lawsuits or regulatory enforcement.

📌 **Example**: A cybersecurity analyst investigates a website impersonating a bank's login page. By tracing the domain owner, they uncover a network of phishing sites run by the same actor.

7.1.2 Using WHOIS Lookups to Identify Domain Owners

WHOIS is a global database that stores domain registration details, including:

✓ Registrant Name & Organization

✓ Email Address & Phone Number

✓ Domain Registration & Expiry Dates

✓ Registrar (e.g., GoDaddy, Namecheap)

✓ Hosting & Name Server Information

1. WHOIS Lookup Tools

◆ **Whois.domaintools.com** – Detailed domain records.
◆ **ICANN WHOIS** – Official WHOIS lookup.
◆ **WhoisXML API** – Bulk domain lookups.

📌 **Example**: A journalist investigating a fake news website finds that multiple domains spreading misinformation are registered using the same email and company name.

2. What If WHOIS Data Is Hidden?

Many website owners use privacy protection services to hide their WHOIS details (e.g., "PrivacyGuard" or "DomainsByProxy").

✓ Look for historical WHOIS records (sometimes past ownership data is visible).

✓ Check for related domains using the same registrar details.

✓ Investigate technical data (IP addresses, hosting, and SSL certificates).

📌 **Example**: A fraud investigator finds that a scam website's WHOIS data is private, but historical WHOIS records reveal a registrant email used in previous scams.

7.1.3 Analyzing a Website's IP Address & Hosting Provider

Even if WHOIS data is hidden, you can still trace a website's hosting and IP address to gather intelligence.

1. Find the IP Address of a Website

◆ **Ping Command**: Run ping example.com in Command Prompt (Windows) or Terminal (Mac/Linux).
◆ **Online IP Lookup**: Use IPinfo.io or ViewDNS.info to check hosting locations.
◆ **nslookup Command**: Run nslookup example.com to find the authoritative name server.

📌 **Example**: A cybercrime analyst discovers that multiple scam sites share the same IP address, indicating they belong to the same network.

2. Checking Hosting Providers

◆ **Hosting Checker** – Identifies the hosting provider.
◆ **IPinfo.io** – Reveals IP ownership details.
◆ **HackerTarget** – Finds hosting details.

📌 **Example**: A researcher finds that a fake e-commerce site is hosted on a known bulletproof hosting provider, commonly used by cybercriminals.

7.1.4 Tracking Website History & Ownership Changes

Websites often change ownership, design, and purpose over time. Tracking past versions can uncover hidden connections and previously exposed data.

1. Using the Wayback Machine to View Past Versions

◆ **Wayback Machine (Archive.org)** – View archived snapshots of websites.

📌 **Example**: A journalist investigating a rebranded disinformation site uses the Wayback Machine to reveal its past as a known propaganda blog.

2. Checking Historical WHOIS Data

◆ **WhoisXML API** – Retrieves old WHOIS records.
◆ **ViewDNS.info** – Shows domain ownership history.

📌 **Example**: A fraud investigator finds that a newly registered "legitimate" website was previously flagged as a phishing site under the same owner.

7.1.5 Identifying Linked Domains & Hidden Connections

Sometimes, an individual or company owns multiple related domains. Finding these connections helps uncover networks of scam sites, propaganda networks, or cybercriminal operations.

1. Reverse WHOIS Lookups

◆ **WhoisXML API** – Finds domains registered with the same email.
◆ **DomainBigData** – Searches domains by registrant details.

📌 **Example**: A cybersecurity researcher finds that a phishing website is linked to dozens of similar domains, all registered with the same email and phone number.

2. Reverse IP Lookups

◆ **ViewDNS Reverse IP Lookup** – Finds all domains hosted on the same IP.

📌 **Example**: A fraud investigator discovers that multiple fake shopping sites are hosted on the same server, linking them to a larger scam operation.

7.1.6 Case Study: Exposing a Fraudulent Website's Owner

Scenario:

A group of victims report losing money on a fake cryptocurrency investment site.

OSINT Investigation Steps:

✅ Step 1: Perform WHOIS Lookup

The domain's WHOIS record is hidden with privacy protection, but historical records show a registrant email linked to past scams.

✅ Step 2: Check IP Address & Hosting

The website's IP is traced to a data center known for hosting fraudulent websites.

✅ Step 3: Investigate Related Domains

A reverse WHOIS search reveals the scammer also owns several other fraudulent investment sites.

📌 **Outcome**: The scam network is exposed, and authorities take down multiple fraudulent domains.

7.1.7 Ethical & Legal Considerations in Website OSINT

✅ DO:

✓ Use only publicly available data.

✓ Follow terms of service for WHOIS lookups and website analysis tools.

✓ Report fraudulent sites to authorities when necessary.

🚫 DON'T:

✗ Hack or gain unauthorized access to domain data.

✗ Use OSINT for malicious purposes (e.g., stalking, harassment).

✗ Violate privacy laws (e.g., GDPR or CCPA) when handling sensitive registrant data.

📌 **Example**: A security researcher can legally investigate scam websites, but illegally accessing private databases would be a crime.

Investigating a website's owner is a critical OSINT skill for uncovering cyber threats, fraud, and misinformation networks. By using WHOIS lookups, IP analysis, historical records, and linked domain searches, investigators can trace hidden connections and expose online deception.

◆ "A website's domain history tells a story—if you know how to read it."

7.2 Using WHOIS & Domain History Lookups

When conducting OSINT (Open-Source Intelligence) investigations, uncovering a website's ownership details, history, and technical information is crucial for identifying scam websites, cyber threats, fraudulent businesses, and misinformation networks. WHOIS lookups and domain history analysis help investigators track who registered a domain, past ownership changes, and linked websites.

This chapter explores:

✅ What WHOIS is and how it works

✅ How to perform a WHOIS lookup

✅ Investigating domain history to track past ownership

✅ Finding connected domains for deeper investigations

✅ Legal and ethical considerations

7.2.1 What is WHOIS?

WHOIS is a publicly accessible database that stores domain registration details, including:

✔ Registrant Name & Organization

✔ Email Address & Phone Number (if public)

✔ Registration & Expiry Dates

✔ Registrar (e.g., GoDaddy, Namecheap)

✓ Hosting Provider & Name Servers

WHOIS data is useful for:

🔍 Identifying who owns a domain
🔍 Detecting connections between websites
🔍 Investigating scam & phishing sites
🔍 Tracking cybercriminal activity

📌 **Example**: A cybersecurity analyst investigates a phishing website impersonating PayPal. A WHOIS lookup reveals that the domain was registered using an email associated with multiple other scam sites.

7.2.2 Performing a WHOIS Lookup

1. Free WHOIS Lookup Tools

◆ **ICANN WHOIS Lookup** – Official WHOIS database.
◆ **Whois.domaintools.com** – Provides detailed records.
◆ **WhoisXML API** – Bulk and historical WHOIS lookups.
◆ **ViewDNS.info WHOIS Lookup** – Shows registrant details.

📌 **Example**: An investigator researching a fake online store performs a WHOIS lookup and finds the registrant's name, email, and country of registration, which links to previous fraud reports.

7.2.3 Understanding WHOIS Lookup Results

A WHOIS lookup provides structured information:

🔎 Example WHOIS Data for "example.com"

Domain Name: EXAMPLE.COM
Registrar: GoDaddy.com, LLC
Registrant Name: John Doe
Registrant Email: johndoe@examplemail.com
Registrant Country: US
Creation Date: 2020-06-15

Expiration Date: 2025-06-15
Name Servers: NS1.EXAMPLESERVER.COM, NS2.EXAMPLESERVER.COM

Key Fields to Analyze

✓ **Registrant Name & Email** – May reveal the domain owner's identity.

✓ **Registrar & Hosting Provider** – Useful for tracking where the domain is hosted.

✓ **Registration & Expiry Dates** – Newly registered domains may indicate scams.

✓ **Name Servers** – Shows where the domain is hosted.

📌 **Example**: A cybersecurity team investigating a malware site finds that its domain was recently registered (less than a month old)—a red flag for potential fraud.

7.2.4 Investigating Domains with Privacy Protection

Many domain owners hide their WHOIS details using privacy protection services like:

◆ Domains By Proxy (GoDaddy)
◆ WhoisGuard (Namecheap)
◆ Contact Privacy (Google Domains)

How to Bypass WHOIS Privacy

✓ Look for historical WHOIS records (section 7.2.5).

✓ Check related domains using reverse WHOIS (section 7.2.6).

✓ Investigate website metadata (SSL certificates, hosting data).

📌 **Example**: A journalist tracking a disinformation website finds that WHOIS data is hidden but discovers an old WHOIS record listing the registrant's real email.

7.2.5 Tracking Domain History with WHOIS Archives

Many websites change ownership over time, making historical WHOIS data valuable.

Tools for Checking Domain History

- **WhoisXML API** – Shows previous owners.
- **ViewDNS.info Historical WHOIS** – Past registrant data.
- **Wayback Machine (Archive.org)** – Snapshots of old website versions.

📌 **Example**: A fraud investigator finds that a new cryptocurrency website was previously flagged as a scam under a different name. The historical WHOIS record confirms the same registrant email used for both sites.

7.2.6 Identifying Linked Domains & Hidden Connections

Cybercriminals and fraudsters often own multiple related websites. Tracking these connections can reveal fraud networks, phishing campaigns, or misinformation sources.

1. Reverse WHOIS Lookup (Find all domains registered with the same email or phone number)

- **WhoisXML API** – Finds domains by registrant details.
- **DomainBigData** – Tracks linked domains.

📌 **Example**: A researcher finds that a fake government website is linked to 20 other fraudulent sites, all registered with the same contact email.

2. Reverse IP Lookup (Find all domains hosted on the same server)

- **ViewDNS.info Reverse IP** – Finds all domains sharing the same IP.
- **SecurityTrails** – Reveals hosted domains.

📌 **Example**: A cybersecurity analyst discovers that several phishing websites are hosted on the same server, confirming a coordinated scam operation.

7.2.7 Case Study: Investigating a Fake Charity Website

Scenario:

A suspicious charity website claims to raise money for disaster relief but is suspected of fraud.

OSINT Investigation Steps:

✅ **Step 1: Perform a WHOIS Lookup**

WHOIS data is hidden with privacy protection.

✅ **Step 2: Check Historical WHOIS Records**

An old WHOIS record reveals the domain was previously owned by an individual linked to past scams.

✅ **Step 3: Investigate Linked Domains**

A reverse WHOIS search finds the same registrant email associated with multiple fake donation websites.

📌 **Outcome**: The scam network is reported, and authorities shut down the fraudulent websites.

7.2.8 Ethical & Legal Considerations

✅ **DO:**

✔ Use only publicly available WHOIS data.

✔ Follow domain registrars' terms of service.

✔ Report fraudulent websites to authorities.

🚫 **DON'T:**

✖ Hack or gain unauthorized access to registrant data.

✖ Use OSINT for malicious purposes (e.g., harassment, stalking).

✖ Violate privacy laws (e.g., GDPR, CCPA).

📌 **Example**: A researcher can legally investigate public WHOIS data, but using hacking tools to access private records would be illegal.

Using WHOIS lookups and domain history tools, OSINT investigators can uncover website owners, track fraud networks, and investigate cyber threats. Even if WHOIS data is hidden, historical records, linked domains, and hosting data can provide critical intelligence.

◆ "A domain's history never truly disappears—it just takes the right tools to uncover it."

7.3 Investigating Website Hosting & IP Addresses

When conducting OSINT (Open-Source Intelligence) investigations, identifying a website's hosting provider, IP address, and server details can reveal who controls the site, its location, and potential links to other domains. Cybercriminals often use bulletproof hosting, shared servers, or cloud services to hide their identities, making IP and hosting analysis a crucial step in tracking scams, phishing sites, or malicious networks.

This chapter covers:

✓ How to find a website's IP address

✓ Identifying a website's hosting provider

✓ Tracking shared hosting & related domains

✓ Investigating server locations & geolocation

✓ Using reverse IP lookup to find linked websites

✓ Legal & ethical considerations

7.3.1 Why Website Hosting & IP Analysis Matters

Understanding where a website is hosted helps in:

✓ Attributing a website to an individual or group

✓ Detecting scam websites that use the same server

✓ Finding connections between multiple domains

✓ Identifying malicious hosting providers

✓ Reporting abuse to hosting companies

📌 **Example**: A fraud investigator finds that a fake online bank is hosted on a server known for hosting phishing websites, strengthening the case against it.

7.3.2 Finding a Website's IP Address

Every website has an IP address, which can be traced to a server, data center, or cloud provider.

1. Using the Command Line

You can use basic network commands to find a website's IP.

Windows (Command Prompt)

Run the following command:

ping example.com

✓ This will return the website's IP address.

Mac/Linux (Terminal)

Run:

nslookup example.com

or

dig example.com +short

✓ This will reveal the website's server IP.

📌 **Example**: An investigator finds that a phishing site uses the same IP address as multiple other scam sites, suggesting they are run by the same actor.

7.3.3 Identifying a Website's Hosting Provider

Once you have an IP address, you can use online tools to trace the hosting provider.

Online Tools for Hosting Lookup

- **IPinfo.io** – Provides hosting provider & IP details.
- **Hosting Checker** – Finds hosting company.
- **Whois.domaintools.com** – Shows hosting provider.
- **HackerTarget** – IP & DNS analysis.

📌 **Example**: A journalist investigating a fake news website discovers it is hosted on a Russian data center known for disinformation campaigns.

7.3.4 Tracking Shared Hosting & Linked Websites

Many websites share the same hosting server, especially on cheap or free hosting providers. This can expose networks of related websites operated by scammers, cybercriminals, or political propaganda groups.

1. Reverse IP Lookup (Finding Other Sites on the Same Server)

- **ViewDNS.info Reverse** IP – Lists domains sharing the same IP.
- **SecurityTrails** – Tracks server activity & related domains.
- **Shodan.io** – Advanced server fingerprinting.

📌 **Example**: A fraud investigator finds that a fake shopping website shares a server with 20 other fraudulent stores, revealing a large-scale scam network.

7.3.5 Investigating Server Locations & Geolocation

Tracking a website's physical hosting location can help attribute ownership or detect foreign influence campaigns.

1. IP Geolocation Tools

- **IPinfo.io** – Shows country, city, and ISP of an IP.
- **MaxMind GeoIP** – Advanced geolocation.
- **IPLocation.net** – Multiple geolocation sources.

📌 **Example**: A government cybersecurity team finds that a suspicious political website is hosted in a foreign country, suggesting foreign interference.

2. Checking If a Website Uses a CDN (Content Delivery Network)

CDNs (like Cloudflare, Akamai, or Fastly) mask the true server location, making direct tracking difficult.

- ◆ Use CrimeFlare to bypass Cloudflare and find real IPs.
- ◆ Perform DNS lookups to detect hidden servers.

📌 **Example**: A hacker hides a phishing site behind Cloudflare, but an investigator uses CrimeFlare to find the real hosting provider.

7.3.6 Using DNS Analysis to Gather More Intel

DNS records reveal who controls a website's domain and email services.

1. Tools for DNS Analysis

- ◆ **MXToolbox** – Checks mail servers & DNS settings.
- ◆ **ViewDNS.info DNS Records** – Shows A, MX, and NS records.
- ◆ **HackerTarget DNS Lookup** – Advanced DNS tracking.

📌 **Example**: An OSINT investigator finds that a suspicious website uses the same mail server as other scam sites, confirming a linked fraud operation.

7.3.7 Case Study: Exposing a Cybercrime Network

Scenario:

A cybersecurity team is investigating a network of phishing sites impersonating banks.

OSINT Investigation Steps:

✅ **Step 1: Find the Website's IP Address**

A ping command reveals the phishing site's IP address.

✅ Step 2: Check the Hosting Provider

The site is hosted on a bulletproof hosting provider in Russia, commonly used by cybercriminals.

✅ Step 3: Perform a Reverse IP Lookup

20+ other phishing sites are hosted on the same server.

✅ Step 4: Investigate Server Geolocation

The IP traces back to a known cybercrime hub.

📌 **Outcome**: The findings are reported, leading to takedowns of multiple phishing sites.

7.3.8 Ethical & Legal Considerations

✅ DO:

✔ Use only publicly available data.

✔ Follow the terms of service for OSINT tools.

✔ Report malicious websites to authorities.

🚫 DON'T:

✖ Hack into servers or gain unauthorized access.

✖ Use OSINT tools for illegal activities.

✖ Violate privacy laws (e.g., GDPR, CCPA).

📌 **Example**: A researcher can legally investigate a website's public IP and hosting data but cannot perform unauthorized penetration testing without permission.

Investigating website hosting and IP addresses is a critical OSINT skill for tracking scam networks, cybercriminals, and foreign influence campaigns. Even if a website hides behind a CDN or WHOIS privacy, using reverse IP lookups, DNS records, and geolocation tools can uncover its real infrastructure and linked domains.

◆ "A website's true identity is often hidden, but its technical footprint never lies."

7.4 Analyzing Website Metadata & Tracking Codes

When conducting OSINT (Open-Source Intelligence) investigations, analyzing a website's metadata and tracking codes can reveal crucial insights about its ownership, network connections, and hidden affiliations. Websites often leave behind fingerprints in the form of metadata, analytics IDs, and embedded scripts, which can be used to link multiple sites, track their history, or uncover hidden identities.

This chapter covers:

✅ What website metadata is and why it matters

✅ How to extract metadata from a webpage

✅ Tracking Google Analytics & other unique IDs

✅ Investigating website technologies & scripts

✅ Case study: Uncovering hidden connections between websites

✅ Legal & ethical considerations

7.4.1 What is Website Metadata?

Metadata refers to hidden information within a webpage's source code that describes its structure, authorship, technologies, and tracking mechanisms.

Key Types of Website Metadata:

✓ **Meta Tags** – Descriptions, keywords, author names

✓ **HTML Comments** – Hidden notes from developers

✓ **Embedded Scripts** – JavaScript, analytics trackers

✓ **Content Management System (CMS) Data** – WordPress, Joomla, Drupal

✓ **Tracking Codes & Analytics IDs** – Google Analytics, Facebook Pixels

✓ **Server Headers** – Server type, security configurations

📌 **Example**: A journalist investigating a misinformation website finds that its Google Analytics ID is also used on several other fake news sites, linking them to the same operator.

7.4.2 Extracting Website Metadata

There are several ways to view a website's metadata for investigation.

1. Inspecting the Page Source (Manual Method)

1️ Right-click on a webpage and select "View Page Source" (Chrome/Firefox)

2️ Press Ctrl + F (Windows) / Cmd + F (Mac)

3️ Search for keywords like:

```
<meta name="author" content="John Doe">
<meta name="description" content="Fake Bank Inc.">
<!-- Developer notes: Testing new tracking script →
```

📌 **Example**: An investigator finds a comment in the page source that contains a developer's email address, linking the site to an offshore scam network.

2. Using Online Metadata Extraction Tools

◈ **BuiltWith** – Identifies website technologies
◈ **Netcraft Site Report** – Server & hosting details
◈ **URLScan.io** – Scans a website for security risks
◈ **Wappalyzer** – Detects CMS, analytics, and frameworks

📌 **Example**: A cybersecurity analyst uses BuiltWith to find that a fraudulent investment website uses the same backend technology as several known Ponzi schemes.

7.4.3 Tracking Google Analytics & Unique IDs

Many websites use Google Analytics, Facebook Pixels, and other tracking tools to monitor visitors. These trackers have unique IDs that can link multiple websites to the same owner or organization.

1. Identifying Google Analytics IDs

Google Analytics IDs follow the format:

UA-12345678-1 (Old format)
G-ABC123XYZ (New Google Analytics 4 format)

How to Find Google Analytics IDs:

1️⃣ View Page Source (Ctrl + U on Chrome)

2️⃣ Search for "UA-" or "G-"

3️⃣ Copy the Analytics ID and search for it online

2. Tracking Websites with the Same Google Analytics ID

◆ **SpyOnWeb** – Finds all websites using the same tracker
◆ **BuiltWith** – Detects analytics & tracking codes
◆ **DNSlytics** – Reverse searches tracking IDs

📌 **Example**: An OSINT investigator finds that a fake government grant website shares its Google Analytics ID with multiple phishing sites, confirming a fraud network.

7.4.4 Investigating Website Technologies & Embedded Scripts

Analyzing what technologies a website uses can provide clues about its ownership, security, and hidden affiliations.

1. Detecting CMS, Hosting, & Plugins

◆ **WhatCMS** – Detects if a site runs WordPress, Joomla, etc.
◆ **Wappalyzer** – Identifies web frameworks & CMS.

📌 **Example**: A fraud investigator finds that a fake PayPal login page is built using a common phishing kit that has been used in other scams.

2. Analyzing JavaScript & External Scripts

Websites often embed JavaScript from third-party services (e.g., tracking, chatbots, payment processing).

How to Find JavaScript Trackers

1□ Open Developer Tools (F12 in Chrome/Firefox)

2□ Go to Network → JS to see external scripts

3□ Look for hidden tracking services or suspicious domains

📌 **Example**: A cybersecurity analyst finds that a news website spreading propaganda is loading a JavaScript file from a foreign intelligence service's server.

7.4.5 Case Study: Uncovering a Network of Fake E-commerce Websites

Scenario:

A group of fraudulent e-commerce stores is scamming users with fake products.

OSINT Investigation Steps:

✅ **Step 1: Extract Metadata & Analytics IDs**

The websites all use the same Google Analytics ID (UA-87654321-1).

✅ **Step 2: Perform a Reverse Google Analytics Search**

SpyOnWeb reveals that 15 other scam sites use the same ID.

✅ **Step 3: Analyze Website Technologies**

All websites use the same WordPress theme and Shopify payment gateway.

✅ **Step 4: Investigate Embedded Scripts**

The checkout pages load a malicious JavaScript file that steals credit card info.

📌 **Outcome**: The findings are reported to authorities, leading to domain takedowns and fraud warnings.

7.4.6 Ethical & Legal Considerations

✅ **DO:**

✓ Use only publicly available metadata.

✓ Follow the terms of service for OSINT tools.

✓ Report fraudulent sites to authorities or hosting providers.

🚫 **DON'T:**

✗ Hack or modify website source code.

✗ Use OSINT for illegal activities (e.g., doxxing, harassment).

✗ Violate privacy laws (e.g., GDPR, CCPA).

📌 **Example**: An OSINT investigator can legally extract metadata from a website's public source code, but cannot hack into its admin panel.

Analyzing website metadata, tracking codes, and embedded scripts is a powerful OSINT technique for linking multiple websites, exposing fraud networks, and identifying hidden operators. Even if a site hides its WHOIS details, tracking its Google Analytics ID, CMS, or JavaScript scripts can reveal connections to other domains.

◆ "A website may lie about who owns it, but its metadata always tells the truth."

7.5 Extracting Data from Websites with OSINT Tools

Extracting data from websites is a core skill in Open-Source Intelligence (OSINT) investigations. Whether you're analyzing a suspect domain, gathering social media data, or tracking hidden connections, using the right OSINT tools can automate data collection and improve efficiency.

This chapter covers:

✅ Why web data extraction is essential for OSINT

✅ Legal & ethical considerations

✅ Techniques for extracting website data

✅ Best OSINT tools for scraping & automation

✅ Case study: Investigating a fraudulent website

7.5.1 Why Website Data Extraction Matters in OSINT

Websites contain vast amounts of publicly available data that can reveal:

✔ **Hidden ownership details** (e.g., WHOIS, metadata)

✔ **Connections between websites** (e.g., shared IPs, Google Analytics IDs)

✔ **Exposed sensitive information** (e.g., misconfigured databases)

✔ **Patterns of online activity** (e.g., archived pages, social media links)

📌 **Example**: An OSINT investigator extracts customer reviews and transaction logs from a scam e-commerce website, linking it to multiple fraudulent stores.

7.5.2 Legal & Ethical Considerations

Before extracting data, it's crucial to stay within legal boundaries.

✅ **Permitted OSINT Methods:**

✔ Viewing publicly accessible website data

✔ Using legal OSINT tools (e.g., web scrapers, browser plugins)

✔ Extracting non-sensitive metadata

⊘ Illegal or Unethical Methods:

✗ Hacking or bypassing authentication

✗ Accessing private databases without permission

✗ Violating terms of service (ToS) of a website

📌 **Example**: A journalist can scrape public news articles, but cannot extract data from a private members-only forum without consent.

7.5.3 Techniques for Extracting Website Data

There are multiple OSINT techniques to collect structured and unstructured data from websites.

1. Manual Data Collection (For Small-Scale Investigations)

- Use browser developer tools (F12 → Inspect Element → Network)
- Copy and paste structured data (e.g., lists, tables)
- Take screenshots for documentation

📌 **Best for**: Small investigations, legal compliance

2. Automated Web Scraping

Web scrapers extract large amounts of data quickly.

Common Web Scraping Tools:

- ◆ **Scrapy** – Python-based advanced web scraper
- ◆ **ParseHub** – No-code scraping solution
- ◆ **Octoparse** – User-friendly visual web scraper
- ◆ **BeautifulSoup** – Python library for parsing HTML

📌 **Best for**: Large-scale data extraction (e.g., tracking scam websites)

3. Using Web APIs to Extract Data

Many websites provide public APIs that allow structured data extraction.

Example API Sources:

- **Twitter API** – Extracts tweets, hashtags, mentions
- **Facebook Graph API** – Collects public Facebook posts
- **Wayback Machine API** – Retrieves archived webpages
- **Shodan API** – Finds exposed devices & databases

📌 **Best for**: Social media monitoring, archived website analysis

4. Google Dorking for Hidden Data

Google search operators can reveal exposed directories & sensitive data.

Useful Google Dorks:

site:example.com filetype:pdf

(Finds PDF files on a website)

intitle:"index of" site:example.com

(Finds open directories on a website)

📌 **Best for**: Finding leaked documents, misconfigured servers

7.5.4 Best OSINT Tools for Web Data Extraction

1. Online Web Scraping Tools

✓ **Web Scraper Chrome Extension** – Extracts structured data
✓ **DataMiner** – Browser-based web scraper

📌 **Use Case**: Extracting company employee lists from LinkedIn

2. Social Media Scrapers

✓ **Twint** – Scrapes Twitter without an API

✅ **Socid-extractor** – Collects social media profiles

📌 **Use Case**: Investigating bot networks on Twitter

3. Metadata & Exif Data Extraction

✅ **ExifTool** – Extracts metadata from images & PDFs
✅ **FOCA** – Extracts metadata from documents

📌 **Use Case**: Finding hidden author names in leaked PDFs

4. Website Structure & Tracking Analysis

✅ **BuiltWith** – Identifies website tech & tracking scripts
✅ **Wappalyzer** – Detects CMS, analytics, and frameworks

📌 **Use Case**: Linking multiple fake e-commerce sites based on their tracking IDs

7.5.5 Case Study: Investigating a Fraudulent Website

Scenario:

An OSINT investigator is tracking a fraudulent investment website that is scamming victims with fake promises.

Investigation Steps:

✅ **Step 1: Extract Website Metadata**

Using Wappalyzer, the investigator finds that the site is built on WordPress.

✅ **Step 2: Find Related Websites via Google Analytics ID**

Using BuiltWith, the site is linked to five other fraudulent domains.

✅ **Step 3: Scrape Public User Reviews**

Using ParseHub, all customer complaints are extracted from forums & review sites.

✅ Step 4: Investigate with Google Dorking

Searching site:scaminvestment.com filetype:pdf reveals a hidden investor report.

📌 **Outcome**: The extracted data is reported to authorities, leading to a domain takedown & warnings to potential victims.

7.5.6 Ethical & Legal Considerations in Web Data Extraction

✅ DO:

✔ Extract only publicly available data

✔ Follow terms of service (ToS) for websites

✔ Cite sources when publishing findings

🚫 DON'T:

✖ Use hacking techniques to bypass login pages

✖ Extract private or sensitive user data

✖ Violate GDPR, CCPA, or other privacy laws

📌 **Example**: Scraping public LinkedIn job postings is legal, but scraping private profiles without permission is a violation of LinkedIn's ToS.

Extracting data from websites is a crucial OSINT skill, but must be done legally and ethically. By using the right scraping tools, APIs, and Google Dorking techniques, investigators can collect valuable intelligence while staying within legal boundaries.

◆ "The internet is full of hidden clues – you just need the right tools to extract them."

7.6 Identifying Fake or Malicious Websites

The internet is full of fake and malicious websites designed to deceive users, spread misinformation, or conduct cybercrime. OSINT (Open-Source Intelligence) investigators, cybersecurity analysts, and law enforcement officials often need to determine whether a website is legitimate or fraudulent.

This chapter covers:

✅ Common types of fake & malicious websites

✅ Key red flags to spot fraudulent sites

✅ Technical analysis methods (WHOIS, IP lookup, metadata)

✅ OSINT tools for investigating website legitimacy

✅ Case study: Exposing a scam website

7.6.1 Common Types of Fake & Malicious Websites

Fraudulent websites can be used for scamming, phishing, spreading malware, or misinformation. Some common types include:

1. Phishing Websites

✔ Designed to steal login credentials or payment info

✔ Often mimic legitimate sites (e.g., fake bank login pages)

📌 **Example**: paypa1.com (instead of paypal.com) tricks users into entering their PayPal login.

2. Scam E-Commerce Stores

✔ Fake online shops that never deliver products

✔ Often have cheap prices, stolen images, & no contact details

📌 **Example**: A site selling PlayStation 5 consoles at 70% off, but never shipping orders.

3. Fake News & Misinformation Websites

✓ Publish false or misleading news stories

✓ Often use clickbait headlines & manipulated images

📌 **Example**: A site claiming a celebrity has died to generate traffic and ad revenue.

4. Malware-Hosting Websites

✓ Distribute viruses, spyware, or ransomware

✓ Often disguised as software downloads or video streaming

📌 **Example**: A website offering "free" cracked software but actually installing malware.

5. Investment & Crypto Scams

✓ Promise high returns with low risk

✓ Often use fake testimonials & aggressive marketing

📌 **Example**: A site claiming "Invest $100 today and make $10,000 in a week!"

7.6.2 Red Flags of Fake or Malicious Websites

🚩 **1. Suspicious Domain Name**

- Look for misspellings or extra characters (e.g., amaz0n.com instead of amazon.com).
- Be wary of recently registered domains (often used for scams).

🚩 **2. No HTTPS / Unsecure Connection**

- Fake sites often lack SSL certificates (http:// instead of https://).
- Some scams use free SSL, so HTTPS alone isn't proof of legitimacy.

🚩 **3. Poor Website Design & Grammar Mistakes**

- Many scams copy-paste content from real sites but have broken links, missing images, or errors.

⚑ 4. Fake Contact Information

- No real address, phone number, or support email.
- If contact info exists, it may be fake or unverified.

⚑ 5. Too-Good-To-Be-True Offers

- Extremely low prices, fake discounts, or guaranteed high investment returns.

⚑ 6. No Social Media Presence or Fake Reviews

- Scam sites often have no verifiable social media pages.
- Some use fake reviews or testimonials (e.g., AI-generated profile pictures).

⚑ 7. Website Blocks or Warnings

- Browsers like Chrome or Firefox may warn "This site may be unsafe".
- Antivirus software may flag the website.

📌 **Example**: A website offering "free Netflix accounts" is flagged as dangerous when accessed.

7.6.3 Technical Analysis of a Website

1. Checking WHOIS & Domain Registration

The WHOIS database reveals who registered the domain, when it was created, and its expiration date.

Tools for WHOIS Lookups:

- ◆ **Whois Lookup** – Checks domain registration details
- ◆ **ICANN WHOIS** – Official domain lookup
- ◆ **DomainBigData** – Finds related domains

📌 Red Flags:

⚑ Recently registered domain (scam sites rarely last long)

⚑ Private or hidden WHOIS details (often used by fraudsters)

⚑ Frequent ownership changes

📌 **Example**: A crypto investment website is found to have been registered only 3 weeks ago, raising suspicions.

2. Checking a Website's IP Address & Hosting Details

Sometimes, multiple scam websites share the same hosting server or IP address.

Tools for IP & Hosting Checks:

◆ **IPinfo.io** – Checks website IP address

◆ **VirusTotal** – Scans a website for malware

◆ **Netcraft Site Report** – Reveals hosting details

📌 **Red Flags:**

⚑ IP address linked to multiple scam sites

⚑ Server located in a high-risk country

⚑ Blacklisted by security databases

📌 **Example**: A scam e-commerce store is hosted on the same server as 20 other fraudulent sites.

3. Investigating Website Metadata & Tracking Codes

Websites often use Google Analytics, Facebook Pixels, or similar tracking IDs. If multiple suspicious sites share the same tracking ID, they may be connected.

Tools for Tracking Analysis:

◆ **BuiltWith** – Checks website technologies & analytics IDs

◆ **Wappalyzer** – Identifies tracking scripts

📌 **Example**: A phishing website is linked to five other scam sites using the same Google Analytics ID.

4. Analyzing Website Content & Images

Fake sites often steal images and text from legitimate websites.

How to Detect Stolen Content:

- **Google Reverse Image Search** – Checks if images exist elsewhere
- **Tineye.com** – Finds image duplicates & sources
- **Copyscape.com** – Detects plagiarized text

📌 **Example**: An e-commerce scam store uses product photos stolen from Amazon.

7.6.4 OSINT Tools for Investigating Website Legitimacy

- ✓ **Whois Lookup** – Checks domain details
- ✓ **IPinfo.io** – Finds website IP & hosting details
- ✓ **VirusTotal** – Scans websites for malware
- ✓ **BuiltWith** – Identifies website tracking codes
- ✓ **Wayback Machine** – Views archived website versions
- ✓ **Google Reverse Image Search** – Finds stolen images

📌 **Use Case**: Confirming if an investment website is real or a scam.

7.6.5 Case Study: Exposing a Fake Cryptocurrency Exchange

Scenario:

An investigator is analyzing "CryptoWealthPro.com", a website promising guaranteed profits from Bitcoin investments.

Investigation Steps:

✓ **Step 1: WHOIS Lookup**

- Domain was registered just 1 month ago ▶
- WHOIS details are hidden ▶

✅ Step 2: IP Address & Hosting Check

- Hosted in a high-risk country known for scams ▶
- Shares IP with 5 other scam sites ▶

✅ Step 3: Reverse Image Search

- The CEO's profile picture is a stock photo ▶

✅ Step 4: Google Dorking

- Searching site:cryptowealthpro.com scam reveals many complaints ▶

📌 **Outcome**: The website is reported and blacklisted, preventing further victims.

Identifying fake or malicious websites is a critical OSINT skill. By checking domain registration, IP addresses, metadata, and content, investigators can expose fraud, phishing scams, and misinformation sites before they cause harm.

◆ "A fake website may look real, but OSINT always reveals the truth."

8. Image & Video Verification Fundamentals

In the era of deepfakes, misinformation, and digitally altered media, verifying the authenticity of images and videos is a critical OSINT skill. A single manipulated image or misattributed video can spread false narratives, making fact-checking essential for analysts and investigators. This chapter covers the core techniques of media verification, including reverse image searches, metadata extraction, geolocation analysis, and error level analysis. By mastering these methods, you'll be able to assess the credibility of visual content, detect manipulation, and ensure that your intelligence is based on accurate and verifiable evidence.

8.1 Introduction to Image & Video OSINT

Image and video analysis is a critical aspect of Open-Source Intelligence (OSINT). With the rise of social media, news, and user-generated content, visual data has become one of the most powerful sources of intelligence. Analysts use images and videos to verify events, track locations, identify individuals, and detect misinformation.

This chapter covers:

✓ Why image & video OSINT is important

✓ Basic principles of visual intelligence analysis

✓ Types of intelligence that can be extracted

✓ Common challenges & ethical considerations

8.1.1 Why Image & Video OSINT Matters

Images and videos can provide critical evidence in investigations across various fields:

🔍 1. Cybersecurity & Threat Intelligence

✓ Identifying fake social media accounts using stolen images

✓ Analyzing threat actor videos for location clues

📌 **Example**: A cybersecurity team analyzes leaked hacker group videos to track their origins.

☐ 2. Law Enforcement & Criminal Investigations

✓ Facial recognition for identifying suspects

✓ Analyzing security footage for movement patterns

📌 **Example**: Investigators extract vehicle license plates from a blurry CCTV recording.

☐ 3. Geolocation & Verification

✓ Confirming where an image or video was taken

✓ Matching landmarks & weather conditions to timestamps

📌 **Example**: OSINT analysts geolocate a viral warzone video using satellite imagery.

🖼 4. Fact-Checking & Misinformation Detection

✓ Detecting AI-generated deepfake videos

✓ Verifying authenticity of protest footage

📌 **Example**: Journalists debunk a faked political rally video by analyzing metadata.

☐☐ 5. Corporate & Business Intelligence

✓ Identifying competitor supply chains from leaked factory images

✓ Monitoring unauthorized brand usage in social media posts

📌 **Example**: A company uses image OSINT to track counterfeit products online.

8.1.2 Basic Principles of Image & Video Analysis

🔎 1. Metadata Extraction

Every digital image and video contains hidden metadata, which can reveal:

✓ Date & time it was captured

✓ Device used (e.g., iPhone, DSLR camera)

✓ GPS coordinates (if location tagging was enabled)

□ **Tools for Metadata Analysis:**

✓ **ExifTool** – Extracts metadata from images & videos
✓ **FOCA** – Finds hidden metadata in documents
✓ **Jeffrey's Image Metadata Viewer** – Online Exif data viewer

📌 **Example**: Analyzing a leaked military image shows it was taken at a classified location.

□ **2. Geolocation & Reverse Image Search**

By analyzing landmarks, signs, shadows, and weather conditions, analysts can determine where and when an image or video was taken.

□ **Tools for Geolocation & Image Search:**

✓ **Google Reverse Image Search** – Finds similar images online
✓ **Tineye** – Identifies altered or duplicated images
✓ **Yandex Reverse Image Search** – Often finds uncropped originals
✓ **Google Earth & Street View** – Matches real-world locations

📌 **Example**: OSINT investigators geolocate a terrorist training camp using satellite images.

🎭 **3. Deepfake & AI-Generated Image Detection**

With the rise of deepfake technology, spotting synthetic images and videos has become crucial.

□ **Tools for Deepfake Detection:**

✓ **Deepware Scanner** – Identifies AI-generated faces

✅ **InVID & WeVerify** – Verifies video authenticity

✅ **Forensically** – Analyzes image manipulation

📌 **Example**: Investigators expose a fake political speech video as AI-generated.

☐ 4. Object & Facial Recognition

By using AI-powered recognition tools, OSINT analysts can:

✔ Identify individuals in images (facial recognition)

✔ Detect objects like weapons, logos, or vehicles

☐ Facial Recognition & Object Detection Tools:

✅ **PimEyes** – Finds faces across the internet

✅ **Clearview AI** – Law enforcement facial recognition (restricted use)

✅ **Google Vision AI** – Identifies objects & text in images

📌 **Example**: Analysts confirm a terrorist's identity from a leaked photo using PimEyes.

☐☐ 5. Video Analysis & Frame Extraction

Videos can be analyzed frame by frame to detect:

✔ Hidden objects in specific frames

✔ Inconsistencies (e.g., poor deepfake rendering)

✔ Changes in lighting, reflections, or timestamps

☐ Tools for Video Analysis:

✅ **ffmpeg** – Extracts frames from videos

✅ **InVID & WeVerify** – Video verification & forensic analysis

✅ **Forensic Video Analysis (FVA)** – Detects video tampering

📌 **Example**: Investigators extract license plate details from a blurry video.

8.1.3 Challenges & Limitations of Image & Video OSINT

✗ **Metadata can be removed** – Many social media platforms strip metadata from uploaded photos.

✗ **Deepfakes & AI manipulation** – Fake videos and AI-generated faces make verification harder.

✗ **Legal & ethical concerns** – Facial recognition can raise privacy violations.

✗ **Image alterations** – Images can be photoshopped or misrepresented.

📌 **Example**: A viral protest image is proven fake when metadata shows it was taken 10 years earlier.

8.1.4 Ethical & Legal Considerations

🔎 **Legal Boundaries:**

✓ Ensure public interest & investigative legitimacy

✓ Avoid violating privacy laws (GDPR, CCPA, etc.)

✓ Never use OSINT for malicious purposes

📌 **Example**: Journalists use OSINT responsibly to fact-check government claims.

Image & video OSINT is a powerful intelligence tool, but it requires careful analysis, verification, and ethical considerations. By using metadata extraction, reverse image search, geolocation, and AI detection, analysts can uncover hidden truths in visual data.

♦ "A picture is worth a thousand words – but only if it's real."

8.2 Reverse Image Searching: Google, Yandex & Bing

Reverse image searching is a powerful OSINT (Open-Source Intelligence) technique used to find the origins of an image, detect edited versions, identify people or objects, and uncover related information online. Instead of searching with keywords, users upload an image, and search engines return visually similar or related results from across the web.

This chapter covers:

✓ How reverse image search works

✓ When & why to use reverse image search

✓ How to conduct searches on Google, Yandex & Bing

✓ OSINT tools & techniques for better results

✓ Case study: Tracking down a fake social media profile

8.2.1 Why Use Reverse Image Search in OSINT?

Reverse image search is useful in a variety of investigations, including:

□□ 1. Verifying Fake Social Media Profiles

✓ Identify if a profile picture is stolen from someone else.

✓ Detect catfishing & impersonation scams.

📌 **Example**: A suspicious Facebook profile uses an image that actually belongs to a professional model in Russia.

□ 2. Geolocating Images

✓ Find the real location of an image by comparing it to online photos.

✓ Match landmarks, buildings, or natural features.

📌 **Example**: An investigator finds that a warzone photo was actually taken in another country years earlier.

🖼 3. Detecting Fake News & Misinformation

✓ Check if an image was reused from an older event.

✓ Identify photoshopped or AI-generated content.

📌 **Example**: A viral protest photo is found to be from 2014, not from a recent event.

🎭 4. Identifying AI-Generated or Altered Images

✔ Detect deepfake profile pictures.

✔ Find original, unedited images.

📌 **Example**: A dating scammer's profile picture is actually an AI-generated fake (detected using Yandex).

☐ 5. Law Enforcement & Cybercrime Investigations

✔ Track leaked sensitive photos.

✔ Identify hidden connections between websites using similar images.

📌 **Example**: A scammer is found using the same profile picture across multiple fake websites.

8.2.2 How Reverse Image Search Works

Reverse image search engines use computer vision and pattern recognition to compare the uploaded image with billions of indexed images on the web. They analyze:

- ◆ Colors, shapes & textures
- ◆ Facial & object recognition
- ◆ Text & logos within the image

Each search engine (Google, Yandex, Bing) has different strengths, making it important to use multiple tools for best results.

8.2.3 Reverse Image Search Using Google, Yandex & Bing

🔎 1. Google Reverse Image Search

✅ **Best for**: Finding duplicate images on news sites, blogs, and social media.
✖ **Weaknesses**: Doesn't always return faces & cropped images effectively.

How to Use Google Reverse Image Search:

1️⃣ Go to Google Images.

2️⃣ Click the camera icon 📷 in the search bar.

3️⃣ Upload an image or paste an image URL.

4️⃣ Google will show matching and similar images from indexed websites.

📌 **Example**: A fake Twitter account uses a celebrity's stolen image, which is found via Google.

◆ Google Lens (on mobile) can also analyze images directly from the phone's gallery.

🔲 2. Yandex Reverse Image Search

✅ **Best for**: Finding faces, Russian & Eastern European content, cropped images.

✖ **Weaknesses**: Less effective for English-language websites.

How to Use Yandex Reverse Image Search:

1️⃣ Go to Yandex Images.

2️⃣ Click on the camera icon 📷.

3️⃣ Upload an image or paste an image URL.

4️⃣ Yandex returns highly accurate face matches & visually similar images.

📌 **Example**: A LinkedIn scammer's profile picture is found to belong to a real businessman in Ukraine.

◆ **Pro Tip**: Yandex is particularly good at finding uncropped original versions of images.

🔍 3. Bing Reverse Image Search

✅ **Best for**: Identifying images in Microsoft-related platforms, shopping, and social media.

✖ **Weaknesses**: Smaller image index compared to Google & Yandex.

How to Use Bing Reverse Image Search:

1️⃣ Go to Bing Visual Search.

2️⃣ Click Upload Image or Paste Image URL.

3️⃣ Bing will return matches, similar images, and website links.

📌 **Example**: A researcher finds that an e-commerce scam site is using product images from Amazon.

◆ Bing's AI integration sometimes suggests context about the image, making it useful for basic investigations.

8.2.4 OSINT Techniques for Better Reverse Image Search Results

✅ 1. Crop & Rotate for Better Matches

◆ Sometimes, search engines fail to detect an image if it has extra text or logos.

◆ Try cropping out watermarks or irrelevant areas before searching.

📌 **Example**: A cropped version of an image finds the original unedited version.

✅ 2. Use Multiple Search Engines

◆ Google is best for general searches.

◆ Yandex is best for faces & uncropped images.

◆ Bing is useful for social media & e-commerce images.

📌 **Example**: A suspect's photo appears on Yandex but not Google, revealing a Russian connection.

✅ 3. Use Reverse Image Search Extensions & Tools

☐ **Browser Extensions for Quick Searches:**

◆ **RevEye Reverse Image Search** – Searches Google, Bing, Yandex & TinEye at once.

◆ **Search by Image** – Firefox extension for multi-engine searches.

✦ **Example**: A journalist quickly checks an image's origin across multiple platforms with one click.

✅ 4. Use OSINT-Specific Reverse Image Tools

- ◆ **TinEye** – Finds older versions of images.
- ◆ **PimEyes** – Advanced facial recognition search (paid).
- ◆ **ExifTool** – Extracts hidden metadata from images.

✦ **Example**: PimEyes reveals that a scammer's face appears in 10 different fake profiles.

8.2.5 Case Study: Catching a Fake Social Media Profile

Scenario:

A cybersecurity analyst is investigating a suspicious LinkedIn profile named "John Miller" with a profile picture that seems too professional.

Investigation Steps:

✅ Step 1: Google Reverse Image Search

No results. The image might be cropped or AI-generated.

✅ Step 2: Yandex Reverse Image Search

The image matches a Russian businessman's personal website.

✅ Step 3: Metadata Extraction with ExifTool

The image was originally taken with a Canon DSLR in Moscow.

✦ **Outcome**: The LinkedIn profile is confirmed as fake, and the scam attempt is reported.

Reverse image search is a critical OSINT skill that can expose fake identities, misinformation, and scams. By using Google, Yandex, and Bing together, along with metadata tools, investigators can uncover the hidden history of an image.

◆ "Every image has a story—it's your job to find it."

8.3 Extracting Metadata from Photos & Videos

Every digital photo or video contains hidden metadata—invisible data stored within the file that provides details about its origin, editing history, and technical specifications. Extracting metadata is a key OSINT (Open-Source Intelligence) technique used for:

✅ Verifying the authenticity of images & videos

✅ Determining when and where a file was created

✅ Tracking modifications & detecting forgeries

✅ Connecting files to specific devices or software

This chapter covers:

- What metadata is & why it matters
- How to extract metadata from images & videos
- OSINT tools for metadata analysis
- Real-world applications in cybersecurity, law enforcement, and journalism
- Challenges & limitations of metadata extraction

8.3.1 What is Metadata?

Metadata is data about data—it describes the properties of a file and can include:

📷 **Common Metadata in Photos**

EXIF Data (Exchangeable Image File Format)

📍 GPS coordinates (if location services were enabled)
🗓 Date & time the photo was taken
📷 Camera model, lens type, and exposure settings
▢▢ Software used for editing
👤 Photographer name (if embedded)

🎥 Common Metadata in Videos

- File format & codec information
- Frame rate, resolution, and bit rate
- Audio track details
- Editing software used (e.g., Adobe Premiere, Final Cut Pro)
- Timestamps & geolocation (if available)

📌 **Example**: A leaked video's metadata reveals it was edited with Adobe Premiere Pro, suggesting possible manipulation.

8.3.2 How to Extract Metadata from Photos & Videos

☐ Tools for Extracting Metadata

Tool	Best For	Platform
ExifTool	Comprehensive EXIF data extraction	Windows, macOS, Linux
Jeffrey's Image Metadata Viewer	Online metadata viewer	Web-based
FotoForensics	Metadata & image forensics	Web-based
InVID & WeVerify	Video metadata & verification	Web-based, Chrome Extension
FFmpeg	Extracting video metadata	Windows, macOS, Linux

🔍 Extracting Metadata from Photos

Using ExifTool (Command Line – Advanced Users)

1☐ Download and install ExifTool from here.

2☐ Open a command prompt or terminal.

3☐ Type:

exiftool image.jpg

4☐ The tool will display detailed metadata, including timestamp, camera model, and GPS data (if available).

📌 **Example**: An OSINT analyst extracts metadata from a suspicious protest photo and discovers it was actually taken years earlier in a different country.

Using Jeffrey's Image Metadata Viewer (Online – Easy Method)

1️⃣ Go to Jeffrey's Image Metadata Viewer.

2️⃣ Upload the image or paste its URL.

3️⃣ Click "View Image Data."

4️⃣ The metadata will display date, camera settings, and location (if available).

📌 **Example**: A journalist debunks a fake war photo by showing its timestamp doesn't match the claimed event date.

🎥 **Extracting Metadata from Videos**

Using InVID & WeVerify (Best for Journalists & Fact-Checkers)

1️⃣ Install InVID & WeVerify (Chrome extension).

2️⃣ Upload or paste the video link (e.g., YouTube, Twitter).

3️⃣ Click "Analyze" to extract:

- Video timestamps
- Thumbnails for reverse image search
- Metadata like resolution & encoding

📌 **Example**: A deepfake political speech video is exposed because its metadata shows it was created with AI software.

Using FFmpeg (Command Line – Advanced Users)

1️⃣ Download FFmpeg.

2️⃣ Open a terminal or command prompt.

3️⃣ Run:

ffmpeg -i video.mp4 -f ffmetadata metadata.txt

4️⃣ The extracted metadata will include frame rate, encoding details, and timestamps.

📌 **Example**: Investigators use FFmpeg to confirm a terrorist propaganda video was edited and re-uploaded from an older source.

8.3.3 Case Studies: Real-World OSINT Investigations Using Metadata

Case Study 1: Verifying a Leaked Government Photo

A controversial "secret military operation" photo is circulating online. OSINT analysts extract its EXIF metadata and discover:

📅 **Timestamp**: 2012 (not 2024 as claimed).
📍 **GPS Location**: A training site in California, not the Middle East.
🖥 **Editing software**: Photoshop CS6.

⚖ **Conclusion**: The image was reused & manipulated to spread false information.

Case Study 2: Tracking a Cybercriminal via Video Metadata

A hacker group posts a ransomware threat video. Investigators extract metadata using InVID and find:

📍 **Time Zone**: UTC+3 (suggesting Eastern Europe).
🖥 **Editing software**: Sony Vegas Pro.
📅 **Timestamp mismatch**: The video was recorded before the claimed cyberattack.

⚖ **Conclusion**: Authorities trace the hacker's origins based on metadata clues.

8.3.4 Challenges & Limitations of Metadata Extraction

✖ **Metadata Can Be Stripped** – Many social media platforms remove EXIF data from uploaded images/videos.
✔ **Solution**: Look for original uploads or archived versions.

✖ **Geolocation Data Isn't Always Available** – GPS data is only stored if the device had location services enabled.
✔ **Solution**: Use visual clues (buildings, weather, street signs) for geolocation.

✗ Metadata Can Be Faked – Hackers can edit EXIF data to mislead investigators.

✓ Solution: Cross-check with other OSINT techniques, like reverse image search & video analysis.

✦ Example: A deepfake video's metadata falsely claims it was filmed in Paris, but analysis shows landmarks from Moscow.

Metadata extraction is an essential OSINT technique for verifying digital evidence, uncovering hidden details, and exposing disinformation. While metadata can be stripped or manipulated, combining it with reverse image search, geolocation, and forensic analysis strengthens investigations.

◆ "Metadata never lies—unless someone edits it."

8.4 Using Shadows & Landmarks for Geolocation OSINT

Geolocation is a critical OSINT (Open-Source Intelligence) technique that helps analysts determine the exact location of an image or video by analyzing visual clues such as landmarks, shadows, terrain, signs, and architectural styles.

This method is widely used in:

✅ Fact-checking viral images and videos

✅ Tracking criminal or terrorist activities

✅ Identifying unknown locations in social media posts

✅ Locating missing persons or fugitives

In this chapter, we will cover:

- How shadows help determine time & location
- Identifying landmarks & unique terrain features
- OSINT tools for geolocation
- Real-world case studies

8.4.1 How Shadows Help in Geolocation

Shadows provide valuable information about time, date, and geographic location. By analyzing the length and angle of shadows in an image, you can estimate:

✓ The time of day when the image was taken

✓ The direction the camera was facing

✓ The approximate latitude of the location

☐ The Science Behind Shadows

The position of the sun changes throughout the day depending on:

- Latitude & longitude
- Season (summer vs. winter)
- Time of day

By measuring the shadow's angle, you can estimate the sun's position and narrow down a possible location.

☐ Tools for Shadow Analysis

Tool	Purpose	Link
SunCalc	Estimates sun position & shadow length at specific times	suncalc.org
Shadow Calculator	Calculates shadow length based on objects & time	shadowcalculator.com
Google Earth Pro	Historical satellite imagery & sun position overlay	earth.google.com

🔍 How to Use Shadows for Geolocation

1☐ Measure the Shadow Length

1☐ Identify an object in the image with a known height (e.g., a streetlight).

2☐ Measure the shadow's length in the image.

3☐ Use a shadow calculator to estimate the time of day.

📌 **Example**: A terrorist propaganda video shows a mosque with long morning shadows. OSINT analysts estimate the time of filming and compare it to satellite imagery.

2⃣ Determine Cardinal Directions

- Shadows in the Northern Hemisphere point northward at noon.
- Shadows in the Southern Hemisphere point southward at noon.

📌 **Example**: A viral protest photo claims to be from New York, but shadows indicate a south-facing sun, proving it was taken in the Southern Hemisphere.

8.4.2 Using Landmarks for Geolocation

Landmarks are one of the most powerful geolocation clues. These include:

✅ **Famous buildings & monuments** (Eiffel Tower, Burj Khalifa)
✅ **Unique architecture** (churches, temples, minarets)
✅ **Street signs & billboards** (language & writing style)
✅ Mountain ranges, coastlines, & vegetation

🗺 Tools for Landmark Identification

Tool	Best For	Link
Google Earth Pro	Finding real-world locations using satellite imagery	earth.google.com
Mapillary	Crowdsourced street-level imagery	mapillary.com
Yandex Maps	Street view in Russia & Eastern Europe	yandex.com/maps
PeakFinder	Identifying mountains & skyline features	peakfinder.org

🔍 How to Use Landmarks for Geolocation

1⃣ Identifying Buildings & Unique Structures

- Look for distinctive architecture that is common in specific regions (e.g., pagodas in East Asia, minarets in the Middle East).
- Use Google Lens to find visually similar buildings.
- Compare with Google Earth Pro to find a satellite view of the area.

📌 **Example**: A hostage video contains a minaret with a unique dome design. Analysts match it with a mosque in Syria using Google Earth.

2️⃣ Analyzing Street Signs & Billboards

- Language clues: Arabic script suggests the Middle East; Cyrillic suggests Russia/Eastern Europe.
- Phone numbers: Country codes can reveal location (e.g., +44 = UK, +91 = India).
- Company names: Search business names in Google Maps to pinpoint location.

📌 **Example**: A scammer's Facebook profile shows a restaurant sign with Thai script. A quick search reveals the business is located in Bangkok, Thailand.

3️⃣ Recognizing Terrain & Vegetation

- Mountain shapes can be matched using PeakFinder.
- Deserts, forests, or coastline help narrow down regions.
- Cloud patterns & climate can also provide location hints.

📌 **Example**: A fake warzone photo claimed to be from Ukraine, but the presence of palm trees and desert terrain proved it was actually from Libya.

8.4.3 Real-World Case Studies

Case Study 1: Locating an ISIS Training Camp

🔍 **Scenario**: A propaganda video shows men training near a mountain range with shadows visible.

✅ **Step 1: Shadow Analysis** – Shadows suggest a southern-facing sun, meaning the video was filmed north of the equator.
✅ **Step 2: Landmark Matching** – The mountain range matches satellite imagery in Syria.
✅ **Step 3: Cross-checking with OSINT Tools** – Terrain matches historical images from Google Earth Pro.

📟 **Outcome**: Intelligence agencies confirm the exact location of the training camp.

Case Study 2: Debunking a Fake News Image

🔍 **Scenario**: A viral Twitter post claims to show riots in Paris, but analysts suspect it's fake.

✅ **Step 1: Street Sign Analysis** – The signs contain Portuguese text, not French.
✅ **Step 2: Google Street View Comparison** – Matches a street in São Paulo, Brazil.
✅ **Step 3: Shadow Analysis** – Shadows confirm the image was taken in the Southern Hemisphere.

🚨 **Outcome**: The image is exposed as misinformation.

8.4.4 Challenges & Limitations of Geolocation OSINT

✗ **Image Manipulation** – Photos can be edited or cropped to remove location clues.
✓ **Solution**: Use reverse image search to find uncropped versions.

✗ **Lack of Unique Features** – Some areas look similar worldwide (e.g., generic urban streets).
✓ **Solution**: Look for smaller clues (e.g., license plates, traffic lights, street markings).

✗ **Time & Weather Variability** – Cloud cover or seasonal changes can affect landmarks.
✓ **Solution**: Use historical satellite imagery on Google Earth Pro.

📌 **Example**: A missing person's last-known photo shows trees with autumn leaves, indicating it was taken between September and November.

Shadows, landmarks, and terrain analysis are powerful OSINT tools for geolocation. Whether you're verifying viral images, tracking criminals, or identifying unknown locations, these techniques can provide crucial insights. By combining shadow analysis, street signs, and Google Earth, you can accurately determine where an image or video was taken.

◆ "Every image tells a story—it's your job to find out where it happened."

8.5 Identifying Deepfakes & Manipulated Media

In today's digital world, manipulated media—including deepfakes, doctored images, and AI-generated content—pose significant challenges to trust, security, and intelligence gathering. Open-Source Intelligence (OSINT) analysts must develop skills to detect and analyze fake media used for misinformation, fraud, and cybercrime.

This chapter will cover:

- What deepfakes and manipulated media are
- Common signs of fake videos & images
- OSINT tools for detecting manipulated content
- Real-world case studies of deepfake deception
- Limitations and future challenges

8.5.1 What Are Deepfakes & Manipulated Media?

𝓞 Deepfakes

Deepfakes are AI-generated videos or images that use machine learning (ML) & artificial intelligence (AI) to manipulate a person's face, voice, or body in a way that looks real.

Common uses of deepfakes:

✓ Fake political speeches (disinformation campaigns)

✓ AI-generated celebrity videos (scams & defamation)

✓ Fraudulent identity theft (fake interviews, scams)

✓ Fake adult content (blackmail & revenge attacks)

📌 **Example**: A deepfake video showed Ukrainian President Volodymyr Zelensky "surrendering" to Russia, but analysts exposed it as AI-generated.

🎭 Manipulated Images

Beyond deepfakes, images can also be edited, cropped, or distorted using software like Photoshop or AI generators.

Common manipulation tactics:

✓ **Photoshop edits** – Adding or removing objects/people

✅ **Face-swapping** – Replacing a person's face in a real image

✅ **Cropping & context manipulation** – Misleading narratives by removing key details

✅ **AI-generated images** – Entirely synthetic, with no real-world source

📌 **Example**: A viral image claimed to show mass protests in Paris, but the original was actually a 2019 protest in Chile.

8.5.2 Common Signs of Deepfakes & Fake Media

🔍 **How to Spot Deepfake Videos**

🏳 **Unnatural Blinking & Facial Movements** – AI struggles with natural eye movements.

🏳 **Blurred or Flickering Facial Features** – Look for distortions around the mouth, ears, or hairline.

🏳 **Asynchronous Speech & Lip Movements** – If the lips don't match the speech, it's likely fake.

🏳 **Weird Lighting & Shadows** – AI struggles to maintain realistic light reflections.

🏳 **Hands & Fingers Look Odd** – AI-generated hands often appear melted or misshapen.

📌 **Example**: A fake Tom Cruise deepfake fooled millions on TikTok, but closer analysis revealed blurry transitions around his jawline.

☐ **How to Detect Manipulated Images**

🏳 **Strange Pixel Patterns** – Zoom in to check for pixelation or mismatched details.

🏳 **Reflections & Shadows Don't Match** – Fake objects often don't cast proper shadows.

🏳 **Oddly Smooth Skin or Over-Sharpened Features** – AI-generated faces often lack natural imperfections.

🏳 **Mismatched Background Details** – Watch for repeating patterns or warped text.

🏳 **Metadata Anomalies** – File properties may reveal an image was edited.

📌 **Example**: A fake "UFO landing" image had inconsistent shadows and was later confirmed as AI-generated content.

8.5.3 OSINT Tools for Deepfake & Fake Media Detection

Tool	Best For	Link
InVID & WeVerify	Deepfake detection & video forensics	invid-project.eu
Forensically	Error level analysis (ELA) & metadata	29a.ch/forensically
Deepware Scanner	Detecting deepfake videos	deepware.ai
PimEyes	Reverse face search for AI-generated images	pimeyes.com
FotoForensics	Analyzing digital image manipulation	fotoforensics.com

☐ How to Analyze a Suspected Fake Video or Image

1☐ Reverse Image Search (Verify the Source)

- Upload the image to Google Reverse Image Search, Yandex, or TinEye.
- If multiple versions exist, compare them for edits or manipulations.
- Check date stamps—if an image existed years before an event, it's fake.

📌 **Example**: A "breaking news" image claimed to show flooding in New York, but a reverse search revealed it was from Bangladesh in 2017.

2☐ Use InVID & WeVerify for Video Analysis

1☐ Install the InVID plugin on Chrome.

2☐ Extract keyframes from the video.

3☐ Run a reverse image search on keyframes.

4☐ Check for inconsistencies in face movements, lip-syncing, and lighting.

📌 **Example**: A video showing a fake Joe Biden speech was flagged by InVID for frame inconsistencies and AI blur artifacts.

3☐ Perform Error Level Analysis (ELA) with FotoForensics

1☐ Upload the suspect image to FotoForensics.

2☐ Look for color anomalies—fake areas will show different pixel compression.

3☐ Cross-check with metadata for signs of Photoshop manipulation.

📌 **Example**: A fake news photo of a missile strike was debunked when ELA showed digital alterations around the explosion area.

8.5.4 Real-World Case Studies

Case Study 1: Fake Zelensky Surrender Video

- A deepfake video of Ukraine's President Volodymyr Zelensky appeared online, showing him announcing surrender to Russia.
- OSINT analysts detected weird facial distortions & mismatched voice syncing.
- Reverse searches found no original source, proving it was AI-generated.
- Official sources debunked the video within hours.

🏛 **Outcome**: The deepfake was quickly removed, preventing widespread disinformation.

Case Study 2: Fake Celebrity Scam Using AI Face Swaps

- Scammers used deepfake technology to create a fake Elon Musk video promoting cryptocurrency scams.
- Analysts noted unnatural blinking, robotic speech, and inconsistent lighting.
- Deepware Scanner flagged the video as AI-generated.
- The scam was reported to authorities, and the fraudulent ads were removed.

🏛 **Outcome**: Millions in potential fraud were prevented through early deepfake detection.

8.5.5 Challenges & Future of Deepfake Detection

✗ **AI Continues to Improve** – Deepfakes are becoming more realistic and harder to detect.

✓ **Solution**: OSINT tools must evolve with better forensic detection & AI countermeasures.

✗ **Metadata Can Be Stripped** – Many platforms remove file metadata, making verification harder.

✓ **Solution**: Use reverse searches & forensic analysis to cross-check details.

✗ **Public Misinformation Is Growing** – Deepfakes spread faster than fact-checking can catch up.

✓ **Solution**: Public awareness campaigns & AI detection tools are critical.

📌 **Future**: Blockchain & cryptographic watermarks may help secure authentic videos/images.

The rise of deepfakes and manipulated media presents serious risks to OSINT investigations, journalism, and cybersecurity. Detecting fakes requires a combination of technical tools, forensic analysis, and critical thinking. By using reverse image searches, metadata extraction, and deepfake detection AI, analysts can expose fake media before it spreads misinformation.

◆ "Trust nothing at face value—analyze, verify, and expose the truth."

8.6 OSINT Case Study: Fact-Checking Viral Content

In the age of social media, viral content spreads rapidly, often without verification. Misinformation and disinformation campaigns use manipulated images, deepfake videos, and misleading narratives to influence public opinion, create panic, or push an agenda. OSINT (Open-Source Intelligence) techniques allow analysts, journalists, and researchers to verify the authenticity of viral content before it spreads further.

This case study will cover:

- How viral misinformation spreads
- OSINT techniques for verifying viral images, videos, and news
- Real-world case study of a viral hoax
- Challenges and limitations in fact-checking viral content

8.6.1 How Viral Misinformation Spreads

Viral misinformation spreads quickly due to:

✅ **Emotional appeal** – People react strongly to shocking, emotional, or controversial content.
✅ **Echo chambers** – Social media algorithms amplify content within like-minded groups.
✅ **Lack of verification** – Most users share content without checking its authenticity.
✅ **Bots & fake accounts** – Automated accounts artificially boost fake news.

☑️ **Manipulated media** – Deepfakes and altered images make false claims look real.

📌 **Example**: A photoshopped image of Notre Dame Cathedral "fully intact" after the 2019 fire went viral, misleading people into believing the fire had been staged.

8.6.2 OSINT Techniques for Fact-Checking Viral Content

🔍 **1️⃣ Reverse Image Search**

📌 **Purpose**: Determine if an image is old, modified, or taken out of context.

🔧 **Tools:**

- **Google Reverse Image Search** → images.google.com
- **TinEye** → tineye.com
- **Yandex Reverse Search** → yandex.com/images

📌 **Example**: A viral image claimed to show a flood in New York in 2023, but a reverse search showed it was from Hurricane Sandy in 2012.

🎥 **2️⃣ Verifying Videos with InVID & WeVerify**

📌 **Purpose**: Extract video frames and compare them to known footage.

🔧 **Tools:**

- InVID WeVerify Plugin → invid-project.eu
- FFmpeg (for extracting frames manually)

📌 **Example**: A deepfake of Ukrainian President Zelensky "surrendering" was debunked using frame analysis, showing unnatural facial distortions.

📍 **3️⃣ Geolocation & Landmarks Verification**

📌 **Purpose**: Determine where an image or video was taken using buildings, signs, and terrain.

⬜ **Tools:**

- **Google Earth Pro** → earth.google.com
- **Mapillary (Street-Level Views)** → mapillary.com
- **PeakFinder (Mountain Identification)** → peakfinder.org

📌 **Example**: A viral tweet claimed to show a warzone in Ukraine, but a building in the background matched a street in Libya, exposing the fake claim.

🖐 4⬜⬜ Metadata & File Analysis

📌 **Purpose**: Check if an image/video has been edited or altered.

⬜ **Tools:**

- **FotoForensics (ELA & metadata extraction)** → fotoforensics.com
- **ExifTool (detailed metadata analysis)** → exiftool.org

📌 **Example**: A political video was flagged as AI-generated when metadata revealed it was created with DeepFaceLab.

⬜⬜ 5⬜⬜ Social Media Analysis

📌 **Purpose**: Track down the original source of viral posts.

⬜ **Tools**:

- **TweetDeck** (Tracking Twitter trends & accounts)
- **Hoaxy** (Misinformation tracking on social media) → hoaxy.iuni.iu.edu
- **CrowdTangle** (Facebook & Instagram post analysis)

📌 **Example**: A "breaking news" tweet about a celebrity's death was traced back to a known hoax account.

8.6.3 Case Study: Debunking a Viral Hoax

🚨 **Case Study**: "The Shark in the Flooded Highway"

The Claim:

- A viral image circulated after Hurricane Ian (2022), showing a shark swimming on a flooded highway.
- Social media users believed it was real, with news outlets even reporting on it.

OSINT Investigation Steps:

1️ Reverse Image Search

✅ **Finding**: A search on Google Reverse Image Search revealed the same shark image from a 2011 National Geographic article.

2️ Metadata Analysis

✅ **Finding**: The image had no EXIF data, suggesting it was edited.

3️ Geolocation Check

✅ **Finding**: The highway's street signs matched Florida, confirming the flood was real, but the shark was fake.

Conclusion:

🚨 **Hoax Confirmed** – The image was a Photoshop fake, using a real flood photo combined with a stock shark image.

8.6.4 Challenges & Limitations in Fact-Checking

✗ **Metadata can be stripped** – Many platforms remove metadata, making analysis harder.
✓ **Solution**: Use multiple OSINT tools (reverse search, ELA, geolocation).

✗ **AI-generated fakes are improving** – Deepfake videos and AI-generated text are harder to detect.

✔ **Solution**: Cross-check multiple forensic & AI-detection tools.

✘ **Misinformation spreads faster than fact-checking** – Once content is viral, it's hard to control.

✔ **Solution**: Public awareness & real-time fact-checking teams are essential.

📌 **Future Solution**: Blockchain verification & digital watermarks could help prevent media manipulation.

Fact-checking viral content requires a multi-step OSINT approach, combining reverse image search, metadata analysis, geolocation verification, and social media tracking. In a digital world where fake news spreads faster than the truth, OSINT investigators play a critical role in exposing disinformation.

◆ "Before you share, verify. The truth depends on it."

9. Geolocation & Mapping Basics

Geolocation is a powerful OSINT technique that allows analysts to pinpoint locations, track movements, and verify the authenticity of images or videos. By analyzing landmarks, weather patterns, shadows, and publicly available mapping tools, investigators can uncover crucial details hidden in visual content. This chapter introduces fundamental geolocation techniques, including satellite imagery analysis, street view comparisons, and metadata extraction. Whether verifying a social media post, identifying an unknown location, or tracking digital footprints, mastering geolocation and mapping skills will enhance your ability to gather and validate open-source intelligence.

9.1 The Role of Geolocation in OSINT Investigations

Geolocation plays a critical role in Open-Source Intelligence (OSINT) investigations by allowing analysts to determine the physical location of an image, video, or event using open-source data. Whether it's verifying the origin of viral content, tracking criminal activity, or analyzing battlefield footage, geolocation techniques help corroborate or debunk information.

This chapter will cover:

- What geolocation is and why it matters
- Common geolocation techniques & tools
- Real-world applications of geolocation in OSINT
- Challenges & limitations

9.1.1 What is Geolocation in OSINT?

Geolocation refers to the process of identifying the physical location of an object, person, or event using available digital data such as:

✅ **Images & videos** (landmarks, metadata, shadows)
✅ **Social media posts** (geo-tags, timestamps, user mentions)
✅ **Maps & satellite imagery** (Google Earth, OpenStreetMap)
✅ **IP addresses & network data** (tracing online activity)

Why Geolocation Matters in OSINT

📌 **Fact-Checking Viral Content** – Verifying where and when an event actually occurred.

📌 **Investigating Criminal Activity** – Identifying locations used for scams, trafficking, or cybercrime.

📌 **Military & Conflict Analysis** – Analyzing battlefield images & verifying troop movements.

📌 **Missing Persons & Rescue Missions** – Finding people based on background details in images.

📌 **Corporate & Threat Intelligence** – Tracking fraud networks & competitor activities.

9.1.2 Common Geolocation Techniques

1️ Reverse Image & Video Search

✅ **Purpose**: Identify if an image has been previously posted online.

🔲 **Tools**:

- **Google Reverse Image Search** → images.google.com
- **Yandex Image Search** → yandex.com/images
- **TinEye** → tineye.com
- **InVID WeVerify (for video analysis)** → invid-project.eu

📌 **Example**: A viral earthquake photo was geolocated to a 2008 event in China, debunking its claim of being from Turkey's 2023 earthquake.

2️ Analyzing Landmarks & Terrain

✅ **Purpose**: Identify a location by comparing buildings, mountains, or coastlines.

🔲 **Tools**:

- **Google Earth Pro** → earth.google.com
- **PeakFinder (Mountain Identification)** → peakfinder.org
- **Mapillary (Street-Level Views)** → mapillary.com

📌 **Example**: Investigators geolocated a terrorist training camp by matching mountains in a video to satellite imagery in Afghanistan.

3️⃣ Extracting Metadata from Images & Videos

✅ **Purpose**: Retrieve hidden GPS coordinates, timestamps, and camera details.

🛠 **Tools**:

- ExifTool (metadata extraction) → exiftool.org
- FotoForensics (Error Level Analysis & Metadata) → fotoforensics.com

📌 **Example**: A kidnapping ransom photo contained GPS metadata, leading authorities to the victim's exact location.

! **Warning**: Many platforms (Twitter, Instagram) strip metadata from uploaded images.

4️⃣ Cross-Referencing Social Media & Online Posts

✅ **Purpose**: Identify where a post was made based on user behavior, hashtags, and geo-tags.

🛠 **Tools**:

- TweetDeck (Twitter analysis)
- Echosec (Social media & location-based searches)
- Wikimapia (User-generated location data) → wikimapia.org

📌 **Example**: A missing person was found when investigators tracked recent Instagram posts with location tags.

5️⃣ Shadow Analysis for Time & Location Estimation

✅ **Purpose**: Estimate the time of day and location based on shadows cast in an image.
🛠 **Tools**:

- SunCalc (Sun & shadow angle analysis) → suncalc.org
- Shadow Calculator (Astronomical calculations)

📌 **Example**: A video of an execution was timestamped and geolocated by matching the sun's position to the local time zone.

9.1.3 Real-World Geolocation Applications in OSINT

📌 **Case Study 1: Identifying a Warzone**

The Claim: A viral image claimed to show a missile strike in Syria (2022).

OSINT Geolocation Steps:

1️⃣ **Reverse Image Search**: Found similar images from 2016 in Aleppo.

2️⃣ **Satellite Comparison**: Google Earth analysis showed identical buildings, confirming the location.

3️⃣ **Metadata Check**: No original metadata was available, suggesting it was downloaded and re-used.

🔍 **Conclusion**: The claim was false. The image was from an old conflict, not a new attack.

📌 **Case Study 2: Tracking a Kidnapped Journalist**

The Situation: A journalist was kidnapped, and authorities received an anonymous image as proof of life.

OSINT Geolocation Steps:

1️⃣ **Extract Metadata**: Used ExifTool to find GPS coordinates in the photo.

2️⃣ **Satellite Imagery Comparison**: Matched the surrounding terrain with Google Earth Pro.

3️⃣ **Social Media Analysis**: Checked for local reports of unusual activity near the suspected area.

🔍 **Conclusion**: Authorities raided the identified location and rescued the journalist.

9.1.4 Challenges & Limitations of Geolocation in OSINT

✖ Metadata is Often Stripped

- **Problem**: Most social media platforms remove GPS data from images.
- **Solution**: Cross-reference landmarks, weather conditions, and satellite images.

✖ AI-Generated & Deepfake Media

- **Problem**: AI can generate fake locations or synthetic backgrounds.
- **Solution**: Use forensic tools like FotoForensics & Deepware Scanner to detect manipulation.

✖ Limited Access to Real-Time Data

- **Problem**: Not all locations have high-resolution satellite imagery available.
- **Solution**: Use multiple mapping services (Google Earth, Sentinel Hub, OpenStreetMap).

✖ Time-Sensitive Information May Be Deleted

- **Problem**: Users delete posts or modify captions after exposure.
- **Solution**: Archive content using Wayback Machine or Archive.today.

9.1.5 The Future of Geolocation in OSINT

◆ **AI-Assisted Geolocation** – Machine learning models will improve automated location matching.

◆ **Blockchain-Based Verification** – Digital signatures could help verify authentic media sources.

◆ **Better Satellite Imaging** – Increased access to real-time satellite data for analysts.

◆ **Crowdsourced Verification** – Platforms like Bellingcat will enhance collaborative OSINT investigations.

Geolocation is a powerful OSINT technique used to verify information, track threats, and investigate criminal activities. By combining reverse image searches, satellite imagery, metadata extraction, and social media analysis, investigators can accurately determine the where & when of an event. However, challenges like metadata stripping, AI-generated fakes, and limited real-time data require OSINT professionals to stay adaptable and use multiple verification methods.

◆ "Every image tells a story—geolocation helps uncover the truth."

9.2 Extracting Location Data from Photos & Social Media

Extracting location data from photos and social media is a crucial skill in Open-Source Intelligence (OSINT). Whether investigating a crime, verifying a viral post, or tracking a missing person, geolocation techniques help analysts determine where an image or video was taken.

This chapter will cover:

- How to extract metadata from photos
- Using social media to track location data
- Reverse image & video search for geolocation
- Real-world case studies
- Challenges & ethical considerations

9.2.1 Extracting Metadata from Photos

What is Metadata?

Metadata is hidden data stored in digital files, including:

🖈 **GPS Coordinates** – Latitude & longitude of where the image was taken
▦ **Timestamps** – Date & time the photo was captured
📷 **Camera Details** – Model, lens, resolution, and settings
☐ **Editing History** – If the image was modified with Photoshop or filters

Extracting Metadata from Images

☐ **Tools:**

- **ExifTool** → exiftool.org (Command-line metadata extraction)

- **Jeffrey's Image Metadata Viewer** → metapicz.com
- **FotoForensics** → fotoforensics.com

📌 Example: Finding GPS Data in an Image

1☐ Download an image from a suspect's social media.

2☐ Run exiftool image.jpg in the command line.

3☐ If GPS coordinates appear, paste them into Google Maps to get the exact location.

🏛 **Real Case**: A criminal was caught when a ransom photo contained GPS metadata, leading authorities directly to the suspect's hideout.

Limitations of Metadata Extraction

✗ **Social media strips metadata** – Twitter, Instagram, and Facebook remove GPS data from uploaded photos.
✓ **Solution**: Ask for the original image or check file-sharing platforms like Google Drive & Dropbox, which may retain metadata.

9.2.2 Using Social Media to Track Location Data

Even if metadata is removed, social media posts contain clues about location, such as:

- ◆ **Geotags** – Location data attached to posts (Instagram, Twitter, TikTok)
- ◆ **User Mentions & Hashtags** – Users tagging a location (e.g., #TimesSquare)
- ◆ **Background Details** – Landmarks, signs, or weather conditions
- ◆ **EXIF Data in Attachments** – Some platforms (Telegram, Discord) retain metadata in file uploads

1☐ Finding Location Clues in Social Media Posts

☐ **Tools:**

- **TweetDeck** (Advanced Twitter searches)
- **Echosec** (Social media monitoring & geolocation)
- **OSINT Combine Geolocation Tool** (osintcombine.com)

📌 **Example: Tracking a Protest Organizer**

1️⃣ Search Twitter for protest-related hashtags (e.g., #NYCProtest).

2️⃣ Filter posts by date & location using TweetDeck.

3️⃣ Identify users frequently posting from that area.

4️⃣ Cross-check their Instagram posts for geotags or background details.

🏛 **Real Case**: Authorities tracked down a fugitive in Brazil after he accidentally geotagged a beach selfie on Instagram.

9.2.3 Reverse Image & Video Search for Geolocation

🔍 **Reverse Image Search**

✅ **Purpose**: Find where an image was first published & detect out-of-context or recycled images.

☐ **Tools**:

- Google Reverse Image Search → images.google.com
- Yandex Image Search → yandex.com/images
- TinEye → tineye.com

📌 **Example: Debunking a Fake War Photo**

1️⃣ A viral image claimed to show a 2023 missile attack in Ukraine.

2️⃣ A reverse image search on Yandex revealed it was from Syria, 2016.

3️⃣ Conclusion: The image was misleading propaganda.

🎥 **Reverse Video Search & Frame Extraction**

✅ **Purpose**: Identify a video's origin & location by analyzing frames.

☐ **Tools**:

- InVID WeVerify Plugin (invid-project.eu) – Extracts keyframes for reverse image search.
- FFmpeg (Command-line tool to extract frames from videos).

📌 Example: Verifying a Terrorist Video

1️⃣ A terrorist group released a video claiming to be from Iraq.

2️⃣ Investigators used InVID to extract frames & ran a reverse search.

3️⃣ The background matched a location in Somalia, exposing the false claim.

🚨 **Conclusion**: The group was using old footage to spread disinformation.

9.2.4 Case Study: Tracking a Kidnapping Victim Using Social Media

📌 The Case:

A missing teenager posted a Snapchat story with a blurry background.

OSINT Investigation Steps:

1️⃣ Reverse image search of any objects visible in the background.

2️⃣ Cross-referencing Instagram hashtags to find similar locations.

3️⃣ Analyzing shadows & sun position to determine time of day.

4️⃣ Checking Google Street View to match buildings & street signs.

🚨 **Result**: The victim was found within 24 hours in a nearby abandoned warehouse, based on the street signs in the background.

9.2.5 Challenges & Ethical Considerations

✖ Challenges in Extracting Location Data

- **Metadata is often removed** → Solution: Use indirect clues (landmarks, social media tags).
- **Images may be altered** → Solution: Use FotoForensics for manipulation analysis.

- **Some tools are restricted** → Solution: Combine multiple OSINT methods for verification.

⚖ Ethical Considerations

🚫 **Avoid Doxxing**: Publishing private location data without consent is illegal & unethical.
🚫 **No Unauthorized Tracking**: Stalking or unauthorized surveillance violates laws in most countries.
🚫 **Respect Privacy Laws**: OSINT investigators should follow GDPR, CCPA & local laws when analyzing data.

Extracting location data from photos & social media is a powerful OSINT skill, used in:

✔ Fact-checking misinformation

✔ Tracking criminals & missing persons

✔ Military intelligence & geopolitical analysis

By combining metadata extraction, reverse searches, social media monitoring, and geolocation techniques, OSINT professionals can accurately determine the "where" behind digital content.

◆ "Every image tells a story—OSINT helps reveal the truth."

9.3 Using Google Maps & Street View for OSINT

Google Maps and Street View are powerful tools in Open-Source Intelligence (OSINT) investigations. Whether you're tracking a suspect, verifying the location of an event, or analyzing geographic clues from an image, these tools allow you to conduct remote reconnaissance and confirm details without being physically present.

In this chapter, we'll cover:

- How to use Google Maps for OSINT investigations
- Street View techniques for identifying locations
- Historical imagery & satellite view for analysis

- Real-world OSINT case studies
- Challenges & limitations of using Google Maps for OSINT

9.3.1 How to Use Google Maps for OSINT

Google Maps is more than just a navigation tool—it provides real-time traffic, business information, historical images, and street-level views that can assist in investigations.

☐ Key Google Maps Features for OSINT

◆ **Satellite View** – Provides high-resolution aerial imagery of locations.
◆ **Street View** – Allows you to virtually explore an area as if you were there.
◆ **Timeline & Historical Images** – Lets you see how a location changed over time.
◆ **Business & Place Reviews** – Reveals hidden connections & intelligence from user reviews.
◆ **Coordinates Extraction** – Converts visual locations into precise latitude/longitude data.

🔎 Example: Verifying a Kidnapping Location

1☐ A ransom video was filmed inside a warehouse with a small visible window.

2☐ Investigators identified a large sign in the background.

3☐ They searched Google Maps using keywords from the sign.

4☐ Using Street View, they confirmed the location and rescued the victim.

9.3.2 Using Google Street View for OSINT Investigations

Google Street View offers a ground-level perspective of locations worldwide, allowing OSINT investigators to:

✔ Identify landmarks, businesses, and addresses.

✔ Match background objects in images or videos.

✔ Analyze security vulnerabilities of buildings.

✔ Reconstruct a suspect's movements.

🔍 Key OSINT Techniques with Street View

1️⃣ Reverse-Engineering a Location from a Photo

🔲 **Steps:**

1️⃣ Look for street signs, landmarks, and unique objects in the image.

2️⃣ Use Google Maps to search for those keywords.

3️⃣ Drag the Street View pegman onto the map to confirm the location visually.

📌 **Example**: A social media influencer posted a selfie with a unique mural in the background. Investigators found the exact mural using Street View and confirmed their location.

2️⃣ **Tracking a Suspect's Movement**

🔲 **Steps:**

1️⃣ Identify any visible roads, store names, or bus stops.

2️⃣ Search those names on Google Maps.

3️⃣ Use Street View to follow possible exit routes.

📌 **Example**: Law enforcement tracked a bank robbery suspect who was seen entering a subway station in security footage. Using Street View, they analyzed all exits and predicted where the suspect might resurface.

3️⃣ **Identifying Military & Restricted Locations**

🔍 **Warning**: Some locations (e.g., military bases, government buildings) blur their images on Google Maps.

🔲 **Alternative Methods:**

✅ Use Bing Maps or OpenStreetMap for different imagery.

✅ Check historical satellite images before restrictions were applied.

✅ Look for civilian reviews or geo-tagged social media posts.

📌 **Example**: OSINT researchers identified a secret military base in the Middle East using historical Street View images that were later blurred.

9.3.3 Using Historical Imagery & Satellite View for OSINT

Google Maps lets you view older images of locations, which is useful for:

✅ Tracking construction & infrastructure changes over time.

✅ Verifying if a crime scene was altered.

✅ Analyzing before/after disaster images.

◻ **How to Access Historical Images:**

1◻ Open Google Earth Pro (desktop version).
2◻ Click on the Clock Icon (Historical Imagery).
3◻ Scroll through different timestamps to compare past images.

📌 **Example**: Investigators proved that a factory fire was staged by showing an older satellite image of abandoned buildings, contradicting the company's insurance claims.

9.3.4 Real-World OSINT Case Studies Using Google Maps & Street View

📌 **Case Study 1: Exposing a Fake War Video**

The Claim: A viral video claimed to show a recent airstrike in Syria.

OSINT Investigation:

1◻ Analysts extracted a frame from the video.
2◻ Using Street View, they matched a building's unique structure.
3◻ Google Maps confirmed the footage was from a past incident in 2015.

🔎 **Result**: The video was misleading propaganda, not new footage.

📌 **Case Study 2: Finding a Human Trafficking Victim**

The Case: A missing girl posted a TikTok video with no geotag but a unique billboard in the background.

OSINT Investigation:

1☐ Investigators searched Google Maps for the billboard's name.

2☐ Street View matched the surroundings to a city in Mexico.

3☐ Authorities raided the location and rescued her.

🚨 **Result**: OSINT helped locate the victim in under 48 hours.

9.3.5 Challenges & Limitations of Google Maps for OSINT

✘ Blurred or Restricted Areas

🚫 Some locations (e.g., government buildings, private properties) blur their imagery.
✅ **Solution**: Use Bing Maps, OpenStreetMap, or Sentinel Hub for alternative views.

✘ Time Delays in Satellite Images

🗓 Google Maps updates are not always real-time.
✅ **Solution**: Use real-time satellite services like Sentinel-2 or PlanetScope.

✘ Altered or Removed Locations

🚫 Businesses & individuals can request location removals.
✅ **Solution**: Look for cached versions on Archive.org or older Street View images.

Google Maps & Street View are essential tools for OSINT investigations, providing:

✅ Remote verification of locations

✅ Historical imagery for timeline analysis

✅ Identification of key landmarks & pathways

By combining satellite view, business reviews, reverse image searches, and historical imagery, OSINT analysts can fact-check viral claims, track suspects, and gather intelligence effectively.

◆ "The world is mapped—OSINT helps you read between the lines."

9.4 Analyzing Satellite Imagery for Intelligence Gathering

Satellite imagery is a powerful tool in Open-Source Intelligence (OSINT), providing a bird's-eye view of locations worldwide. It allows analysts to track military movements, environmental changes, infrastructure projects, and crisis zones—all without being physically present.

This chapter will cover:

- How to access and analyze satellite imagery
- Key OSINT tools for satellite analysis
- Real-world case studies
- Limitations & challenges of satellite imagery in OSINT

9.4.1 How to Access & Use Satellite Imagery for OSINT

Satellite imagery is widely available from public and commercial sources. OSINT analysts use these images to:

✓ Verify military operations & troop movements

✓ Detect illegal deforestation & environmental damage

✓ Monitor construction projects & infrastructure changes

✓ Assess natural disasters & humanitarian crises

📡 **Sources of Satellite Imagery**

Source	Features	Website
Google Earth	Free access, historical imagery, 3D maps	earth.google.com
Sentinel Hub	Real-time imagery, vegetation & climate data	sentinel-hub.com
NASA Worldview	Weather & environmental monitoring	worldview.earthdata.nasa.gov
PlanetScope	High-resolution commercial imagery	planet.com
Bing Maps	Alternative to Google Maps, aerial views	bing.com/maps

9.4.2 OSINT Techniques for Satellite Image Analysis

1⃣ Identifying Military Bases & Troop Movements

Satellite imagery is frequently used to track military installations, aircraft, naval ships, and vehicle movements.

🔲 Steps for OSINT Analysis:

1⃣ Compare historical satellite images to detect changes over time.

2⃣ Look for runways, barracks, vehicle convoys, or bunkers.

3⃣ Use AI-powered tools to highlight newly constructed facilities.

📌 **Example**: Analysts discovered a new missile base in North Korea by comparing older Google Earth images with recent Sentinel-2 imagery.

2⃣ Verifying Crisis Zones & Natural Disasters

Satellite images can confirm damage assessments after earthquakes, hurricanes, or wildfires.

🔲 Tools for Disaster Monitoring:

- **NASA FIRMS** – Detects wildfires in real time.
- **UNOSAT** – Provides satellite imagery for humanitarian relief.
- **Google Crisis Map** – Maps disasters with real-time updates.

📌 **Example**: After the Beirut explosion (2020), satellite images helped verify the exact blast radius and damage.

3️⃣ Tracking Illegal Activities (Deforestation, Mining, Smuggling)

Satellite imagery exposes illegal deforestation, unregulated mining, and human trafficking routes.

🔲 Techniques for Tracking Environmental Crimes:

✅ Compare past & current satellite images to detect tree loss.

✅ Look for unregistered roads leading into protected forests.

✅ Use thermal imaging & night vision satellites for detecting smuggling operations.

📌 **Example**: OSINT investigators used PlanetScope imagery to reveal illegal gold mining in the Amazon rainforest, leading to government intervention.

4️⃣ Monitoring Large-Scale Construction & Infrastructure Projects

Governments and corporations often build secret projects—including nuclear facilities, underground tunnels, or ghost cities.

🔲 How to Identify Construction Projects:

1️⃣ Look for new roads, excavation sites, or large cranes.
2️⃣ Use historical images to track progress over time.
3️⃣ Check for water sources, power lines, or defensive structures.

📌 **Example**: Analysts discovered China's secret airstrip construction in the South China Sea by comparing historical images with new high-resolution satellite photos.

9.4.3 Real-World Case Studies Using Satellite Imagery for OSINT

📌 Case Study 1: Tracking Russian Troop Movements in Ukraine

The Situation: Before the 2022 Russian invasion of Ukraine, OSINT analysts detected unusual military activity near the border.

OSINT Investigation:

1☐ Satellite images from Maxar Technologies showed large convoys of tanks & artillery.

2☐ Sentinel Hub imagery confirmed the troop buildup near Ukraine's borders.

3☐ Google Earth comparisons showed new trenches and field hospitals—signs of an imminent invasion.

🔘 **Conclusion**: OSINT analysts predicted the invasion weeks before official government announcements.

📌 **Case Study 2: Uncovering North Korean Nuclear Tests**

The Situation: North Korea denied ongoing nuclear tests, but satellite imagery suggested otherwise.

OSINT Investigation:

1☐ Thermal satellite imaging showed unusual heat patterns at Punggye-ri Nuclear Test Site.

2☐ Satellite images revealed new tunnel entrances and heavy machinery.

3☐ A sudden increase in vehicle traffic & excavation work suggested preparations for a test.

🔘 **Conclusion**: Satellite analysis helped confirm North Korea's underground nuclear detonation before official reports.

9.4.4 Challenges & Limitations of Satellite OSINT

✖ Limited Image Resolution

- Free satellite images (e.g., Google Earth) lack high resolution for detailed analysis.

✅ **Solution**: Use commercial providers like Maxar, PlanetScope, or Airbus for higher quality.

✗ Time Delays

- Google Earth updates are not real-time; images can be months or years old.

✓ **Solution**: Use Sentinel Hub for fresher images (updated every few days).

✗ Cloud Cover & Weather Obstructions

Satellite images can be blocked by clouds or nighttime darkness.

✓ **Solution**: Use Synthetic Aperture Radar (SAR) technology, which penetrates clouds.

✗ Ethical & Legal Considerations

- Using satellite images for surveillance or invasion of privacy raises ethical concerns.

✓ **Solution**: Follow local laws & ethical OSINT guidelines when analyzing imagery.

Satellite imagery is a game-changer for OSINT investigations, enabling analysts to:

✓ Monitor military & geopolitical events

✓ Track environmental changes & illegal activities

✓ Verify crisis events & disasters in real time

By combining Google Earth, Sentinel Hub, PlanetScope, and AI-powered analysis, OSINT professionals can uncover hidden intelligence from above.

◆ "The sky isn't the limit—OSINT sees beyond borders."

9.5 Identifying Hidden Clues in Videos & Images for Location Tracking

Images and videos often contain hidden clues that can reveal where they were taken. Open-Source Intelligence (OSINT) investigators use a combination of visual forensics, metadata analysis, and geolocation techniques to track locations, verify claims, and uncover critical intelligence.

This chapter will explore:

- Key OSINT techniques for identifying locations in images/videos
- How to extract and analyze metadata
- Using background objects and environmental clues
- Real-world case studies
- Challenges & limitations of image/video analysis in OSINT

9.5.1 Extracting & Analyzing Metadata

Metadata (EXIF data) stores hidden details about an image or video, such as:

✓ GPS coordinates (if enabled)

✓ Date & time the media was created

✓ Camera model & settings

✓ Editing software used

☐ Tools for Extracting Metadata

Tool	Features	Website
ExifTool	Extracts & edits metadata from images/videos	exiftool.org
FotoForensics	Reveals metadata & error-level analysis	fotoforensics.com
Jeffrey's EXIF Viewer	Online metadata extractor	exif.regex.info
Metadata2Go	Free online metadata viewer	metadata2go.com

☐ How to Extract Metadata from an Image:

1☐ Upload the image to ExifTool or an online metadata extractor.

2☐ Look for GPS coordinates and plug them into Google Maps.

3☐ Check the date/time to establish a timeline.

4️⃣ If metadata is missing, analyze visual clues manually (see next section).

📌 **Example**: Investigators tracked an Instagram influencer's exact location by extracting GPS metadata from an uploaded photo.

📷 **Limitations**: Many social media platforms strip metadata to protect user privacy, so OSINT analysts must rely on visual geolocation techniques.

9.5.2 Using Visual Clues for Geolocation

Even without metadata, images and videos contain hidden clues that reveal where they were taken.

🔍 **Key Elements to Analyze**

Clue Type	Details
Street Signs	Language, road numbers, city names
Shadows & Sun Position	Helps estimate time & hemisphere
Building Architecture	Regional styles can narrow down location
Vegetation & Landscapes	Unique plants & terrain help with identification
License Plates & Vehicles	Country-specific designs & models
Storefronts & Billboards	Business names can be searched online
Skyline & Landmarks	Distinctive structures aid in geolocation

📌 **Example**: Analysts identified the location of a hostage video by analyzing a mountain range in the background, matching it with Google Earth's 3D terrain.

9.5.3 Using Reverse Image Search for Geolocation

Reverse image search helps find similar images online, leading to location verification.

🔲 **Reverse Image Search Tools**

Tool	Features	Website
Google Images	Basic reverse image search	images.google.com
Yandex	Powerful for face & location matching	yandex.com/images
TinEye	Finds older versions of an image	tineye.com
Bing Image Search	Alternative to Google	bing.com/visualsearch

☐ How to Use Reverse Image Search for OSINT:

1☐ Upload the image to Google, Yandex, or TinEye.

2☐ Check if the same image appears elsewhere online.

3☐ If it does, note the location, date, or other context.

4☐ If not, crop and enhance the background before re-uploading.

📌 **Example**: OSINT analysts debunked a viral war image by tracing it back to a different conflict in 2015 using Yandex.

9.5.4 Tracking Locations from Videos

Videos provide additional motion-based clues, such as:

✓ **Background sounds** (accents, call-to-prayer, train horns)
✓ **Weather conditions** (matching real-time forecasts)
✓ **Camera movements** (helping estimate distances & angles)

☐ Steps for Video Geolocation Analysis

1☐ **Extract Frames**: Use VLC Media Player or FFmpeg to convert video to individual frames for analysis.

2☐ **Listen to Audio**: Identify languages, sirens, or local sounds.

3☐ **Check Clothing & Signage**: Match regional styles and text fonts to specific areas.

4☐ **Compare with Street View**: Cross-check buildings, streetlights, and landscapes on Google Maps.

5☐ **Use AI-Powered Search**: Tools like PimEyes can recognize faces, while Sensity AI detects deepfakes.

📌 **Example**: Investigators confirmed the authenticity of a terrorist training camp video by matching fence designs and road layouts with Google Earth satellite imagery.

9.5.5 Case Studies: Using OSINT to Track Locations from Media

📌 **Case Study 1: Exposing a Fake Protest Photo**

A widely shared Twitter post claimed to show a massive protest in 2023.

🔍 **OSINT Analysis:**

✅ Reverse image search revealed the same image was from a 2011 protest in Egypt.

✅ Street signs and vehicle models did not match the alleged protest location.

✅ The viral claim was debunked as misinformation.

⚖ **Conclusion**: OSINT helped prevent the spread of fake news.

📌 **Case Study 2: Finding a Missing Person via TikTok**

A missing teenager posted a TikTok video but did not disclose their location.

🔍 **OSINT Investigation:**

✅ Investigators identified a gas station sign in the background.

✅ Using Google Street View, they matched the store layout to a location in Nevada.

✅ Law enforcement found the teenager within 24 hours.

⚖ **Conclusion**: OSINT saved a life by tracking location clues in a video.

9.5.6 Challenges & Limitations of Location Tracking from Media

✖ Blurred or Edited Content

◆ Some images/videos are intentionally altered to mislead investigators.

✓ **Solution**: Use Error Level Analysis (ELA) to detect manipulation (FotoForensics).

✗ Metadata Stripping

◆ Social media platforms remove EXIF metadata to protect user privacy.
✓ **Solution**: Focus on visual and environmental clues instead.

✗ Similar-Looking Locations

◆ Some places look identical, making verification difficult.
✓ **Solution**: Cross-check with multiple sources (Google Earth, Street View, social media posts).

Analyzing images and videos for location tracking is a critical skill in OSINT investigations. By leveraging metadata extraction, reverse image search, environmental clues, and video frame analysis, analysts can verify events, track people, and debunk misinformation.

◆ "A single image holds more secrets than meets the eye—OSINT helps you uncover them."

9.6 Real-World OSINT Geolocation Exercises

Geolocation is one of the most powerful Open-Source Intelligence (OSINT) techniques, allowing investigators to pinpoint locations using only publicly available images, videos, and data. Whether tracking criminal activities, verifying news reports, or finding missing persons, OSINT geolocation requires a combination of logical deduction, technical tools, and deep observation skills.

This chapter presents real-world OSINT geolocation exercises, showcasing practical techniques to train your investigative skills.

🔎 **Key Skills Covered in This Chapter:**

✓ Analyzing landmarks, signs, and vegetation

✓ Using Google Maps, Earth, and Street View

✓ Applying metadata and satellite imagery

✓ Leveraging social media and weather patterns

✓ Verifying geolocation using OSINT tools

9.6.1 Exercise 1: Finding a Location from a Single Image

☐ Scenario:

You receive this mystery image (hypothetical example):

- A cityscape with a river and several bridges
- A large glass skyscraper in the center
- A red-and-white tram visible in the street
- A signpost with text in an unknown language

🔍 Step-by-Step OSINT Approach:

1☐ Identify Major Landmarks

- Look for unique skyscrapers, bridges, or monuments that can be matched with Google Images or Wikipedia.

2☐ Analyze Public Transport Clues

- Research cities that use red-and-white trams (e.g., Prague, Vienna, Toronto).
- Check for tram network maps to match routes.

3☐ Use Reverse Image Search

- Upload the image to Google Images, Yandex, and TinEye to see if similar images exist online.

4☐ Translate Street Signs

- Use Google Lens or Google Translate to detect the language and identify potential countries.

5️⃣ Confirm with Google Earth & Street View

- Match the skyline, bridges, and roads with Google Earth's 3D maps.

📌 Expected Outcome:

With these clues, an analyst could likely identify the city as Prague, Czech Republic, by recognizing the Vltava River, Prague's iconic skyscrapers, and the distinctive trams.

9.6.2 Exercise 2: Tracking a Person's Location from a Video

🗒 Scenario:

A Twitter user posts a short video claiming to be in New York City, but something seems off. The video contains:

- A yellow taxi (with an unfamiliar license plate)
- A road sign with a non-English language
- A McDonald's restaurant in the background
- A large TV screen billboard

🔍 Step-by-Step OSINT Approach:

1️⃣ Analyze Vehicles & License Plates

- U.S. taxi license plates usually follow a standard format.
- Check if the vehicle models match those used in NYC.

2️⃣ Look at Road Signs & Language

- If signs are in Chinese, Arabic, or Cyrillic, the location is not New York City.

3️⃣ Identify Storefronts & Billboards

- Check McDonald's branch designs—some are region-specific.
- Identify advertisements on billboards using reverse image search.

4️⃣ Check the Time of Day & Weather

- If the video claims to be from NYC in winter, but trees are green, the claim is suspicious.
- Compare with historical weather data.

5️⃣ Confirm with Google Street View

- Match McDonald's storefront, roads, and landmarks with Google Maps & Earth.

📌 Expected Outcome:

Using these techniques, you might determine the video is actually from Hong Kong, where yellow taxis, Chinese-language signs, and McDonald's storefronts match the evidence.

9.6.3 Exercise 3: Using Satellite Imagery to Monitor Changes Over Time

🔲 Scenario:

You suspect that a foreign country is building a new airbase, but no official reports exist.

🔍 Step-by-Step OSINT Approach:

1️⃣ Use Historical Satellite Imagery

- Compare past and current images on Google Earth Pro, Sentinel Hub, or Maxar Technologies.
- Look for changes in terrain, new construction, or cleared land.

2️⃣ Check for New Roads or Infrastructure

- Military bases require access roads, fuel depots, and security fencing.
- Compare before-and-after satellite images.

3️⃣ Monitor Airplane Activity

- Use flight tracking sites like Flightradar24 or ADS-B Exchange to see if unusual military aircraft activity is happening.

4️⃣ Look for Local News Reports

- Search in native languages using Google Translate to find leaked reports.

5️⃣ Verify with AI-Powered Analysis

- Use automated detection tools to highlight new buildings or military installations.

📌 Expected Outcome:

By comparing satellite imagery and monitoring local aviation activity, you could confirm the construction of a secret airbase before the media reports it.

9.6.4 Exercise 4: Verifying a Viral Social Media Post

▢ Scenario:

A viral social media post claims a natural disaster just struck a major city. However, you suspect the image is old or taken from a different event.

🔍 Step-by-Step OSINT Approach:

1️⃣ Perform a Reverse Image Search

Check Google Images, Yandex, and TinEye to see if the image appears in older news reports.

2️⃣ Check Social Media Metadata

Look at the post's timestamp—if it was uploaded years ago and reshared, it may be misinformation.

3️⃣ Analyze Weather & Lighting Conditions

If the image shows snow, but the disaster allegedly happened in summer, it's likely fake. Check historical weather data on timeanddate.com.

4️⃣ Find Other Witnesses

Search Twitter, Facebook, and Instagram for real-time posts from users in the city.

5️⃣ Verify Landmarks & Compare with Old Images

If the city has distinctive buildings, bridges, or monuments, check them against older images of the area.

📌 Expected Outcome:

You discover that the image is actually from a 2010 earthquake in Chile, proving that the viral post is fake news.

9.6.5 Challenges & Limitations of Geolocation Exercises

✖ Image Manipulation & Deepfakes

- Some images and videos are edited or AI-generated to mislead investigators.
- ✅ Solution: Use FotoForensics or Sensity AI to detect tampering.

✖ Missing Metadata

Social media platforms strip EXIF metadata for privacy reasons.

✅ **Solution**: Rely on background details and contextual clues instead.

✖ Similar-Looking Locations

Some cities and landscapes look almost identical (e.g., Miami vs. Dubai).

✅ **Solution**: Use Street View, vegetation analysis, and business names for confirmation.

Mastering geolocation OSINT exercises enhances your investigative skills, whether for journalism, cybersecurity, law enforcement, or fact-checking. By combining reverse image search, metadata analysis, visual observation, and satellite imagery, you can accurately verify locations and uncover hidden truths.

◆ "A single photo can tell a thousand lies—but OSINT helps you find the truth."

10. OSINT Report Writing & Documentation

Collecting intelligence is only half the battle—effectively communicating your findings is just as crucial. A well-structured OSINT report ensures that your insights are clear, actionable, and verifiable. This chapter covers best practices for documenting your research, structuring reports for different audiences, and maintaining proper source attribution. Whether you're writing for law enforcement, cybersecurity teams, or investigative journalism, mastering the art of OSINT reporting will help you present intelligence in a professional and impactful manner.

10.1 The Importance of Clear OSINT Reporting

Gathering Open-Source Intelligence (OSINT) is only half the battle—communicating findings clearly, concisely, and accurately is just as important. Without proper reporting, even the most valuable intelligence can be misinterpreted, ignored, or misused. Whether you're working in cybersecurity, law enforcement, journalism, or corporate investigations, effective OSINT reporting ensures that decision-makers can act on your intelligence.

This chapter explores:

✅ Why clear OSINT reporting matters

✅ The key components of a good OSINT report

✅ Common mistakes to avoid

✅ How to tailor reports for different audiences

✅ Real-world examples of effective OSINT reports

10.1.1 Why Clear OSINT Reporting Matters

🔍 **Intelligence Is Useless If No One Understands It**

A report filled with technical jargon, excessive details, or vague conclusions can confuse readers. Intelligence needs to be actionable and easy to interpret.

💡 **Decision-Makers Need Actionable Insights**

Executives, law enforcement, cybersecurity teams, and journalists don't just want data—they need clear findings and recommendations to take action.

🚨 Preventing Misinformation & Legal Risks

A poorly written OSINT report can:

✗ Lead to wrongful accusations

✗ Cause legal consequences (if private data is misused)

✗ Spread misinformation if not verified correctly

📌 **Example**: In 2020, false OSINT analysis led to a person being wrongly accused of arson during protests, resulting in legal and reputational damage.

🎯 The Goal of OSINT Reporting:

✅ Present facts objectively

✅ Support decision-making

✅ Avoid bias and speculation

✅ Ensure information is verifiable and repeatable

10.1.2 Key Components of an OSINT Report

A well-structured OSINT report should include:

📌 1. Executive Summary

⬥ A brief overview of key findings in plain language.
⬥ Ideal for non-technical decision-makers.

◆ Example:

"This report identifies three phishing domains targeting government employees. The domains are hosted in Russia and have been active since January 2024. Immediate blocking is recommended."

📌 2. Scope & Objective

- ◈ Clearly state what the investigation aimed to find.
- ◈ Define the timeframe, tools, and limitations.

◆ Example:

"This investigation analyzes social media posts from February 1–10, 2024, to verify the authenticity of viral protest videos."

📌 3. Data Collection Methods

- ◈ Explain how and where the intelligence was collected.
- ◈ Ensure legality and transparency.

◆ Example:

"Data was collected using Google Dorking, reverse image search (Yandex, Google Images), and Twitter advanced search. No private or hacked data was accessed."

📌 4. Findings & Analysis

- ◈ Present verified facts with supporting evidence (screenshots, metadata, links).
- ◈ Provide context and relevant patterns.

◆ Example:

"The phishing domains use SSL certificates from Let's Encrypt and mimic government login pages. Whois records link them to past cyberattacks by Group X."

📌 5. Conclusion & Recommendations

- ◈ Summarize key findings.
- ◈ Provide clear next steps (e.g., block domains, alert authorities, continue monitoring).

◆ Example:

"We recommend blocking the phishing domains at the firewall level and alerting all employees to avoid clicking on suspicious links."

📌 6. Appendices & Sources

- ◆ Include screenshots, links, and additional context.
- ◆ Ensure all sources are properly cited.

10.1.3 Common Mistakes in OSINT Reporting

🏮 Avoid these errors that can reduce the credibility of your OSINT report:

✘ 1. Overloading with Technical Jargon

Keep reports concise and understandable.
Use layman's terms where possible.

Example:

✘ "This domain exhibits high entropy SSL configurations."

✔ "This domain uses an SSL certificate commonly seen in phishing attacks."

✘ 2. Failing to Verify Information

Always cross-check sources to prevent spreading false intelligence.

Example:

✘ "A Twitter user claims this video shows a bombing in Kyiv."

✔ "A reverse image search confirms this video is from a 2018 event in Syria, not Kyiv."

✘ 3. No Clear Recommendations

A report should always answer: "What should we do next?"

Example:

✘ "Phishing attacks have increased by 50%."

✓ "Phishing attacks have increased by 50%. We recommend enabling multi-factor authentication and blocking high-risk domains."

✘ 4. Ignoring the Audience

- A CEO needs a summary, while a cybersecurity team needs technical details.
- Tailor your report to the reader.

10.1.4 Adapting OSINT Reports for Different Audiences

A good OSINT report changes based on who reads it.

Audience	What They Need	Example Report Format
Executives (C-suite, decision-makers)	Brief summary & risk assessment	1-page executive summary
Law Enforcement	Detailed findings, sources, legal considerations	Full report + evidence attachments
Cybersecurity Teams	Technical details (IPs, attack vectors, IOCs)	Threat intelligence brief
Journalists	Context, verifiable sources, fact-checking	Investigative report with citations

📌 **Example:**

Scenario: You discover a cybercriminal group is running a fake banking website.

1️⃣ **For the CEO:**

"A fraudulent banking website is actively targeting our customers. We recommend issuing a public warning and taking legal action."

2️⃣ **For the Cybersecurity Team:**

"The malicious domain uses Cloudflare obfuscation, hosts phishing pages on 185.244.31.22, and was registered via Namecheap. IOCs are included in the appendix."

3️⃣ For Law Enforcement:

"Attached are WHOIS records, hosting data, and historical screenshots linking this phishing site to known cybercriminals."

10.1.5 Real-World OSINT Report Example

Scenario: Investigating a Disinformation Campaign

- ◆ **Objective**: Verify if viral Twitter accounts spreading election misinformation are bots.
- ◆ **Methods Used**: Social media analysis, reverse image search, metadata extraction.
- ◆ Findings:

  - 90% of accounts were created in the last two months.
  - Profile photos were AI-generated (deepfake detection).
  - Tweets followed a strict posting schedule (bot behavior).

◆ Conclusion & Actionable Steps:

✓ Flag accounts for platform moderation.

✓ Inform news agencies to prevent misinformation spread.

Clear, structured OSINT reporting is essential for making intelligence actionable. A well-crafted report should be:

✓ Concise & easy to understand

✓ Free from speculation & bias

✓ Tailored to the right audience

✓ Backed by verified evidence

◆ "Good OSINT reporting doesn't just present information—it turns intelligence into action."

10.2 Structuring an OSINT Report: Key Elements

Gathering Open-Source Intelligence (OSINT) is just the first step. The next challenge is structuring your findings into a clear, actionable report that helps decision-makers take the right steps. A poorly structured report can lead to confusion, misinterpretation, or even legal consequences.

This chapter explains:

✅ The essential sections of an OSINT report

✅ How to structure reports for different audiences

✅ The best formats for presenting intelligence

✅ Common pitfalls to avoid

10.2.1 Why Structure Matters in OSINT Reporting

◆ **Clarity & Comprehension** → Decision-makers can understand findings quickly

◆ **Actionability** → Reports should lead to concrete actions

◆ **Credibility** → A structured report shows professionalism & accuracy

◆ **Legal & Ethical Compliance** → Clear documentation prevents misuse of intelligence

📌 **Example:**

Imagine a cybersecurity team receives an OSINT report about a phishing attack. A poorly structured report might contain:

✖ **Unclear conclusions** → No clear next steps

✖ **Disorganized evidence** → Difficult to verify findings

✖ **No prioritization** → Critical threats buried under minor details

A well-structured OSINT report, however, would:

✅ Summarize the threat clearly

✓ Provide supporting evidence

✓ Recommend actionable security measures

10.2.2 Key Elements of an OSINT Report

A strong OSINT report should contain the following sections:

1️ Executive Summary (For Decision-Makers & Non-Technical Audiences)

- Brief overview of the investigation
- Key findings & conclusions
- Recommended actions

◆ Example:

"This report investigates a suspected disinformation campaign on Twitter. Analysis of 500 accounts shows that 80% were created in the past three months, with bot-like behavior. We recommend flagging these accounts and informing relevant fact-checking organizations."

2️ Scope & Objectives (Defining the Investigation's Purpose)

- Why was this report created?
- What specific questions or problems does it address?
- Timeframe & limitations of the research

◆ Example:

"This report examines social media activity from February 1–15, 2024, to verify the authenticity of viral protest videos."

3️ Data Collection & Methodology (Ensuring Transparency & Repeatability)

- Sources used (e.g., social media, public records, news archives)
- Tools & techniques (e.g., reverse image search, Google Dorking)
- Legal & ethical considerations (e.g., no unauthorized access to private data)

◆ Example:

"Data was collected using Google Dorking, WHOIS lookups, and Twitter API analysis. No private accounts or unauthorized sources were accessed."

4⃣ Findings & Analysis (Presenting Verified Information Clearly)

- What was discovered?
- Supporting evidence (screenshots, URLs, metadata)
- Pattern analysis (e.g., bot activity, repeated disinformation themes)

📌 **Example (Cybersecurity OSINT Report):**

Finding: Malicious domains targeting banking customers

Evidence:

- **Domain**: fakebank-login[.]com
- **Hosting Provider**: Namecheap
- **Creation Date**: January 2024
- **Pattern**: Uses a similar design to past phishing sites

📌 **Example (Disinformation Analysis):**

Finding: Fake news article shared 10,000+ times on Twitter

Evidence:

- The article's image is from a 2017 earthquake, not a recent event
- Social media accounts sharing it were created in the last 48 hours

📌 **Important:**

✓ Use visuals (charts, tables, timelines) to enhance readability

✓ Cite sources properly to maintain credibility

5⃣ Threat Assessment & Impact Analysis (Why This Matters)

- Who is affected?

- What are the risks?
- Potential consequences if no action is taken?

◆ Example (Cyber Threat Report):

"Failure to block these phishing domains could result in financial fraud affecting up to 10,000 customers."

◆ Example (Disinformation OSINT Report):

"If this false news continues spreading, it may lead to public unrest and misinformation about election results."

6️ Recommendations & Next Steps (Turning Intelligence into Action)

- What actions should be taken?
- Who should be informed?
- Short-term & long-term recommendations

◆ Example:

"We recommend immediately blocking the identified phishing domains at the firewall level. Additionally, a cybersecurity awareness campaign should be launched to educate users about phishing risks."

📌 **Best Practice**: Make recommendations specific & actionable, not vague.

✖ **Bad**: "More monitoring is needed."
✅ **Good**: "Monitor all Twitter accounts that share this disinformation using keyword tracking tools."

7️ Appendices & Supporting Evidence (Backing Up Your Claims)

- Screenshots of findings
- Raw data (URLs, timestamps, WHOIS records, metadata)
- List of tools & sources used

◆ Example:

📎 Screenshot of a tweet spreading false information
📎 WHOIS lookup results of a phishing website
📎 Timeline chart of bot activity

10.2.3 Formatting & Presentation: Making Reports Easy to Read

✅ **Best Practices for Formatting:**

✔ Use bullet points for clarity

✔ Highlight key findings in bold

✔ Include visual aids (graphs, maps, screenshots)

✔ Keep paragraphs short & concise

📌 **Example Layout of an OSINT Report**

◆ **Executive Summary**

- This report analyzes a network of fake Twitter accounts spreading misinformation.
- 80% of accounts were created within the last two months.
- Recommended action: Report accounts to platform moderators.

◆ **Scope & Objectives**

- Investigate claims of election fraud on social media.
- Identify fake accounts & misinformation patterns.

◆ **Data Collection & Methodology**

- Used Twitter API, reverse image search, WHOIS lookups.
- Analyzed 500 accounts & 10 viral posts.

◆ **Findings & Analysis**

Pattern: Accounts repeatedly used the same hashtags and phrases.

Evidence:

- Account @FakeNewsBot123 posted the same message 100+ times.
- The attached image is actually from a 2016 protest, not a recent event.

◆ Threat Assessment

- Risk: Misinformation could influence public perception & voter behavior.
- Impact: Over 500,000 people have seen the misleading content.

◆ Recommendations

✓ Flag fake accounts for removal

✓ Issue a public fact-check statement

✓ Monitor emerging misinformation trends

◆ Appendices

📎 Screenshots of bot activity
📎 Reverse image search results
📎 Raw Twitter data CSV

A well-structured OSINT report is clear, credible, and actionable. By organizing findings into distinct sections, investigators ensure that their intelligence is useful and impactful.

📌 Key Takeaways:

✓ Use a standardized structure (summary → methods → findings → recommendations)

✓ Make reports concise & easy to scan

✓ Provide clear evidence & cite sources

✓ Tailor the report to your audience

◆ "Good OSINT isn't just about finding information—it's about making it actionable."

10.3 OSINT Note-Taking & Data Organization

Successful Open-Source Intelligence (OSINT) investigations rely on more than just collecting data—how you record, structure, and organize that data is equally important. Poor note-taking and disorganized data can lead to missed connections, inaccurate reports, or legal risks.

This chapter explores:

✅ Best practices for OSINT note-taking

✅ Tools & methods for organizing intelligence

✅ How to track sources & maintain credibility

✅ Ensuring operational security (OPSEC) while handling data

10.3.1 Why OSINT Note-Taking & Data Organization Matters

🔍 Intelligence Is Only Useful If It's Well-Documented

Gathering OSINT without proper note-taking is like collecting puzzle pieces but never assembling the full picture.

⚖️ Legal & Ethical Considerations

- Poor record-keeping can result in legal issues (e.g., GDPR, CCPA violations).
- Failure to track sources can make intelligence inadmissible in legal cases.

☐ Saves Time & Improves Efficiency

- Investigators often revisit past cases—well-organized notes speed up future research.
- Structured data makes reporting & presentations much easier.

📌 Example:

A journalist investigating a disinformation campaign collects hundreds of tweets, images, and links. Without proper note-taking & categorization, crucial evidence gets lost, making verification impossible.

10.3.2 Best Practices for OSINT Note-Taking

📝 1. Use a Standardized Note-Taking Format

To ensure consistency & clarity, every OSINT note should include:

✅ **Date & Time** → When was the data collected?

✅ **Source URL** → Where did the information come from?

✅ **Data Collected** → What was found? (e.g., text, images, metadata)

✅ **Observations & Analysis** → Why is this important?

✅ **Verification Status** → Is the data confirmed or still under review?

📌 **Example** OSINT Note Template (Cybersecurity Investigation)

Date	Source	Data Collected	Observations	Verification
16-Feb-2025	WHOIS Lookup	IP: 192.168.1.1	Linked to past phishing attacks	Verified
16-Feb-2025	Twitter (@FakeNews123)	Tweet: "Election fraud proof!"	Uses fake images from 2016	Unverified

💼 2. Categorizing OSINT Data for Quick Retrieval

Proper categorization helps in quickly retrieving relevant information when needed.

📌 **Suggested OSINT Categories:**

💼 **Threat Actors** → Cybercriminals, Disinformation Networks

💼 **Social Media Profiles** → Fake Accounts, Influencers, Trolls

💼 **Domains & Websites** → WHOIS Data, IP Addresses, Malicious Sites

💼 **Images & Videos** → Metadata, Reverse Image Search Results

💼 **News & Articles** → Misinformation, Media Sources

💼 **Raw Data Dumps** → Leaked Databases, Open Directories

◆ **Example**: A disinformation investigator tags a new Twitter account as:

✅ Fake Profile

✅ Election Misinformation

✅ Created in Feb 2025

Later, they search "Fake Profile + Feb 2025" and find all similar cases, helping establish a pattern.

👓 3. Tracking OSINT Sources for Verification

💡 Every OSINT investigation must track sources properly to maintain credibility.

✅ Best Practices for Source Tracking:

✔ Always save the original URL (webpage links, social media posts).

✔ Use Wayback Machine (archive.org) or permalinks to archive sources.

✔ Screenshot key findings to preserve disappearing content.

✔ Label sources as Primary (direct evidence) or Secondary (reports, news articles).

📌 Example:

❌ **Bad**: "I found a phishing website on Google."
✅ **Good**: "As of 16-Feb-2025, fakebank-login[.]com was active, hosted on Namecheap, and linked to IP 192.168.1.1 (screenshot attached)."

10.3.3 Tools for OSINT Note-Taking & Data Organization

📓 Note-Taking & Documentation Tools

Tool	Use Case	Pros	Cons
Obsidian	Secure, local OSINT notes	Offline, markdown-based	No built-in cloud sync
Evernote	General OSINT note storage	Cloud sync, tagging	Privacy concerns (stores data online)
Joplin	Secure, encrypted note-taking	Open-source, privacy-focused	Basic UI
OneNote	Visual note-taking	Free, easy to use	Lacks encryption

📌 **Best Practice**: Use encrypted note-taking tools (e.g., Joplin, Obsidian) for sensitive OSINT investigations.

🏛 OSINT Data Organization & Search Tools

Tool	Use Case	Pros	Cons
Hunchly	Web browsing evidence collection	Auto-captures pages	Paid tool
Zotero	OSINT source management	Citation tracking	Can be complex
Maltego	Link analysis & visualization	Great for threat mapping	Steep learning curve
Airtable	OSINT database organization	Customizable tables	Requires setup

📌 Example:

A researcher investigating fake news networks:

✓ Uses Hunchly to automatically archive web pages.

✓ Tags sources in Zotero for future reference.

✓ Maps connections using Maltego.

🔒 10.3.4 Ensuring OPSEC (Operational Security) in OSINT Note-Taking

📌 Top Risks:

🚨 Storing OSINT data on unprotected platforms (Google Docs, unencrypted notes)
🚨 Accidentally leaking sources or investigations
🚨 Using cloud-based tools that lack strong security

◆ Best OPSEC Practices for OSINT Data Storage:

✓ Use encrypted note-taking tools (Joplin, Standard Notes)

✓ Avoid storing sensitive OSINT on cloud services unless encrypted

✓ Keep physical backups of crucial intelligence

✓ Use separate, secure accounts for OSINT work

📌 Example:

A cybersecurity investigator keeps phishing URLs in an offline encrypted database instead of using Google Sheets, reducing exposure to leaks.

10.3.5 Real-World OSINT Note-Taking Example

Scenario: Tracking a Malicious Website

◆ Step 1: Initial Note

- **Date**: 16-Feb-2025
- **Source**: WHOIS Lookup
- **Finding**: fakebank-login[.]com is hosted on Namecheap.

◆ Step 2: Screenshot & Metadata

Action: Took a screenshot of the login page and checked metadata.

◆ Step 3: Categorization

✓ Phishing Domain

✓ Financial Scam

✓ Active since Jan 2025

◆ Step 4: Linking to Other Cases

📎 Found a related domain (fakebank-secure[.]com) with the same IP address.

◆ Step 5: Report & Next Steps

🗎 Saved all findings in an encrypted document for reporting to law enforcement.

Good OSINT note-taking & data organization turns raw information into actionable intelligence. Without a structured approach, investigations can become messy, unreliable, and legally questionable.

📌 Key Takeaways:

✅ Use a standardized note-taking format (Date, Source, Data, Observations).

✅ Categorize intelligence properly for easy retrieval.

✅ Track sources carefully to maintain credibility.

✅ Use encrypted & secure tools to protect OSINT data.

✅ Regularly review & update your notes to keep investigations current.

♦ "A well-organized OSINT investigator is a more effective investigator." 🚀

10.4 Writing Non-Biased & Fact-Based Intelligence Reports

In Open-Source Intelligence (OSINT), gathering information is only part of the job. The real challenge lies in presenting intelligence in a neutral, fact-based manner without bias, speculation, or misinformation. An intelligence report that lacks objectivity can lead to misinterpretation, faulty decisions, and reputational damage.

This chapter will cover:

✅ What bias is and how it affects OSINT reports

✅ Best practices for writing fact-based intelligence

✅ How to structure non-biased conclusions

✅ Techniques for verifying and cross-checking data

10.4.1 The Importance of Objectivity in OSINT Reports

A non-biased OSINT report ensures:

◆ **Credibility** – Decision-makers trust intelligence that is fact-driven.
◆ **Legal & Ethical Integrity** – Bias in reporting can lead to misjudgments or legal consequences.
◆ **Actionability** – Reports based on verified facts provide clearer insights for action.

📌 **Example of Biased vs. Non-Biased Reporting:**

✖ **Biased Report:**

"It is clear that this group is engaged in criminal activity, as they were seen on social media discussing sensitive topics."

✅ **Non-Biased Report:**

"Multiple social media posts from this group reference discussions on encrypted messaging platforms. However, no direct evidence confirms illegal activity."

10.4.2 Recognizing & Avoiding Bias in OSINT Reports

☐ **Types of Bias That Affect Intelligence Reporting**

Bias Type	Definition	Example in OSINT
Confirmation Bias	Interpreting data in a way that confirms preexisting beliefs.	Only selecting data that supports a theory while ignoring contradicting evidence.
Selection Bias	Relying on a limited or unrepresentative dataset.	Using only one news outlet's reporting while ignoring other perspectives.
Narrative Bias	Creating a story that connects facts, even if the connections are weak.	Suggesting a political conspiracy without solid proof.
Anchoring Bias	Relying too heavily on an initial piece of information.	Assuming a suspect is guilty based on past accusations.

📌 **Example:**

An OSINT investigator tracking disinformation campaigns may assume that all anonymous accounts promoting a topic are bots. However, without verifying activity patterns and metadata, this assumption could be misleading.

10.4.3 Structuring a Fact-Based Intelligence Report

A structured approach helps maintain objectivity. Below is an ideal OSINT report format that ensures a neutral and fact-driven presentation:

1️ Executive Summary (Brief & Neutral Overview)

- A short, non-speculative summary of key findings.
- Avoid subjective language (e.g., "It is obvious that…").
- Stick to facts: Who, What, Where, When, and How.

📌 Example:

"This report examines the spread of misinformation regarding Election 2025. The analysis is based on 500+ social media accounts and 2,000+ posts."

2️ Scope & Methodology (Ensuring Transparency)

- Define the scope (timeframe, platforms analyzed, focus).
- Explain how data was collected (without revealing sensitive OPSEC methods).
- Clearly state any limitations of the research.

📌 Example:

"This analysis covers Twitter and Facebook activity from January 1–30, 2025. Data was collected using open-source tools and cross-verified with multiple sources."

3️ Data Collection & Source Verification (Cross-Checking for Accuracy)

◆ Best Practices for Source Verification:

✓ Use multiple independent sources to confirm data.

✓ Differentiate between primary sources (direct evidence) and secondary sources (news, blogs, reports).

✓ Archive original URLs & screenshots in case of later disputes.

📌 **Example:**

"Reverse image searches confirm that the viral protest photo was originally taken in 2016 and does not depict recent events."

4️⃣ Findings & Analysis (Presenting Facts, Not Assumptions)

- Describe what the data shows, without speculation.
- Use statistics & evidence-based comparisons.
- Clearly separate data from interpretation.

✗ **Biased**: "This group is likely involved in criminal activity."
✓ **Non-Biased**: "Members of this group frequently share content linked to known extremist forums."

📌 **Example:**

Finding:

- "Analysis of 100+ Twitter accounts shows that 80% were created in the last two months and frequently use identical phrases."

Supporting Evidence:

✓ Metadata from account profiles

✓ Screenshots of posts & engagement patterns

✓ Comparison with known bot activity

5️⃣ Conclusion & Threat Assessment (Avoiding Speculation)

- Summarize findings without drawing conclusions beyond the data.
- If an assumption is made, state it as a hypothesis, not a fact.

📌 **Example:**

"While this network exhibits bot-like behavior, further analysis is required to determine whether these accounts are fully automated."

6️ Recommendations & Next Steps (Fact-Based Actions, Not Opinions)

- Provide clear, actionable next steps based on evidence.
- Avoid emotionally driven suggestions (e.g., "Authorities must act immediately!").

📌 **Example:**

"Further monitoring of these accounts is recommended, including linguistic analysis and engagement tracking."

10.4.4 Tools & Techniques for Fact-Checking OSINT Reports

🔍 **Fact-Checking & Verification Tools**

Tool	Purpose
Google Reverse Image Search	Check if an image is used out of context.
Yandex & Bing Reverse Search	Find image origins in non-Western sources.
Wayback Machine	View archived versions of altered/deleted pages.
Snopes & FactCheck.org	Verify common misinformation claims.
InVID	Analyze video metadata & detect deepfakes.

📌 **Example:**

An OSINT investigator verifies a viral image of a conflict zone and finds it was actually taken years ago in a different country.

10.4.5 Common Pitfalls & How to Avoid Them

☐ **Common Mistakes in OSINT Reports:**

🚫 **Overgeneralization** → "All accounts supporting X are bots."

⊘ **Lack of Source Verification** → Using one source instead of cross-checking.

⊘ **Emotional Language** → "The attack was horrific and unjustified."

⊘ **Unstated Assumptions** → Presenting opinions as facts.

✅ **Best Practices:**

✓ Cross-check sources before concluding.

✓ Use neutral, precise language.

✓ Avoid speculating beyond the evidence.

✓ Clearly distinguish between data, analysis, and opinion.

Writing fact-based, non-biased OSINT reports is crucial for credibility, decision-making, and legal compliance. By following structured reporting methods, verifying sources, and avoiding speculation, OSINT investigators can ensure their reports are trusted and actionable.

📌 **Key Takeaways:**

✅ Recognize & eliminate bias in reporting.

✅ Use structured formats for clarity & objectivity.

✅ Verify sources using multiple fact-checking tools.

✅ Avoid speculation & emotional language.

✅ Ensure transparency in data collection methods.

◆ "An intelligence report should inform, not persuade." 🚀

10.5 Redacting & Protecting Sensitive OSINT Findings

Open-Source Intelligence (OSINT) investigations often uncover sensitive data that, if mishandled, could lead to privacy violations, legal consequences, or security risks. Whether working in cybersecurity, law enforcement, corporate intelligence, or journalism, knowing how to redact and protect sensitive findings is crucial.

This chapter will cover:

✅ What constitutes sensitive OSINT data

✅ Best practices for redacting information

✅ Secure storage & data protection methods

✅ Ethical & legal considerations

10.5.1 Understanding Sensitive OSINT Data

🔍 What Data Needs Protection?

Sensitive OSINT findings can include:

Category	Examples	Risk if Exposed
Personal Identifiable Information (PII)	Names, addresses, phone numbers, email addresses	Identity theft, harassment, privacy violations
Financial Data	Bank account details, credit card information, cryptocurrency wallets	Fraud, financial exploitation
Operational Security (OPSEC) Data	Internal communications, employee lists, VPN/IP addresses	Cyberattacks, doxxing, unauthorized access
Law Enforcement & Government Data	Surveillance logs, informant identities, case details	Compromised investigations, national security risks
Corporate Intelligence	Trade secrets, competitor analysis, legal documents	Industrial espionage, legal disputes

📌 Example:

If an OSINT investigator uncovers an unprotected government database with citizen records, disclosing or sharing raw data could violate privacy laws (e.g., GDPR, CCPA) and pose serious security threats.

10.5.2 Redacting Sensitive OSINT Findings

Redaction is the process of concealing or removing sensitive information before sharing an OSINT report.

◆ Best Practices for Effective Redaction

✓ **Use Proper Redaction Tools** – Do NOT simply "black out" text in a document or image (text can be recovered).

✓ **Ensure Metadata is Also Removed** – Hidden metadata can still contain redacted details.

✓ **Test Redactions Before Sharing** – Double-check redacted files to ensure they are secure.

🔧 Tools for Redacting OSINT Reports

Tool	Purpose	Platform
Adobe Acrobat Pro	Secure PDF redaction	Windows, Mac
PDF Redact Tools	Open-source redaction tool for PDFs	Linux, Windows, Mac
EXIF Purge	Removes metadata from images	Windows, Mac
MAT2 (Metadata Anonymization Toolkit)	Strips metadata from images, PDFs, office files	Linux

📌 Example:

An OSINT investigator is preparing a report on a criminal network. Before sharing, they must remove names, phone numbers, and metadata from images to protect individuals involved.

10.5.3 Secure Storage & Data Protection

Sensitive OSINT findings should be stored securely to prevent unauthorized access.

🗄 Best Practices for Secure OSINT Data Storage

✓ **Use Encrypted Storage** – Store findings on encrypted drives (e.g., VeraCrypt, BitLocker).

✓ **Avoid Cloud Storage for Sensitive Data** – Public cloud services (e.g., Google Drive) may not be secure enough.

✓ **Use Strong Access Controls** – Limit who can access raw data and reports.

✓ **Secure Physical Devices** – Lock computers, use two-factor authentication (2FA), and avoid storing data on unprotected USB drives.

📌 **Example:**

An OSINT researcher analyzing threat actor activity stores their findings in a VeraCrypt-encrypted drive, ensuring data is protected from leaks or cyber threats.

10.5.4 Ethical & Legal Considerations in OSINT Data Protection

🔭 **Key Legal Regulations**

Law/Regulation	Applies To	Key Requirement
GDPR (Europe)	Personal data of EU citizens	Data must be anonymized & protected
CCPA (California, USA)	Personal data of CA residents	Individuals have the right to request data deletion
HIPAA (USA)	Medical & health data	Prohibits unauthorized disclosure of patient data
FOIA/Privacy Acts	Government documents	Protects sensitive government & personal records

⚖ Violating these laws can result in fines, lawsuits, and criminal charges.

📌 **Example:**

If an OSINT investigator uncovers a leaked hospital database, they must ensure any shared findings do not expose patients' personal health information (PHI) to comply with HIPAA laws.

10.5.5 Securely Sharing OSINT Reports

If sharing OSINT findings is necessary, it must be done securely to protect sources, individuals, and organizations.

📌 **Best Practices for Secure Sharing**

✓ **Use Encrypted Communication** – Tools like ProtonMail, Tutanota, or Signal provide end-to-end encryption.

✓ **Apply Watermarking** – Helps track unauthorized leaks of sensitive OSINT reports.

✓ **Share Only What's Necessary** – Avoid oversharing raw data when a summary suffices.

✓ **Use Secure File Transfer** – Services like OnionShare, SecureDrop, or Tresorit ensure safe transfers.

📌 **Example:**

A journalist working on an OSINT investigation uses SecureDrop to share findings with a news organization while keeping sources anonymous.

10.5.6 Case Study: A Real-World OSINT Redaction Failure

🔎 **Case: 2019 Australian Government Redaction Failure**

📌 **What Happened?**

- The Australian government released a redacted intelligence report as a PDF.
- Investigators quickly removed the blacked-out text by copying and pasting the content into another document.
- This led to classified information being exposed, including sensitive national security details.

📌 **Key Lessons Learned:**

✓ Use proper redaction tools (not just black boxes).

✓ Ensure redacted documents cannot be reversed.

✓ Always test before publishing.

Protecting sensitive OSINT findings is as important as collecting the intelligence itself. Mishandling sensitive data can compromise investigations, violate laws, and endanger individuals.

◆ **Key Takeaways:**

✓ Understand what data needs protection (PII, financial info, OPSEC data).

✓ Use proper redaction tools (not basic black bars!)

✓ Store sensitive OSINT findings securely (encryption, access control).

✓ Follow legal regulations (GDPR, CCPA, HIPAA) to avoid violations.

✓ Use secure sharing methods (encrypted emails, SecureDrop, watermarks).

◆ "OSINT without proper protection can become a security risk itself." 🚀

10.6 Tools & Templates for OSINT Documentation

Efficient OSINT investigations require structured documentation to ensure accuracy, consistency, and clarity. Proper documentation helps investigators track findings, verify sources, organize data, and present reports effectively. Without it, intelligence can become disorganized, unreliable, or difficult to analyze.

This chapter will cover:

✓ Why structured OSINT documentation matters

✓ Essential tools for OSINT documentation

✓ Templates for note-taking, reporting, and data organization

✓ Best practices for managing and securing OSINT records

10.6.1 Why Structured OSINT Documentation Matters

Well-organized documentation improves:

◆ **Accuracy & Verification** – Ensures sources are properly recorded for cross-checking.
◆ **Collaboration** – Allows multiple investigators to review and contribute.
◆ **Legal & Ethical Compliance** – Helps prove responsible handling of intelligence.
◆ **Efficiency** – Saves time by preventing duplicate work and lost findings.
◆ **Actionability** – Decision-makers can trust and act on well-documented intelligence.

📌 **Example:**

An OSINT investigator tracking a cybercriminal network uses a structured spreadsheet template to log usernames, IP addresses, timestamps, and patterns of activity. This ensures that all findings remain organized and traceable.

10.6.2 Essential Tools for OSINT Documentation

Different tools serve different documentation needs, from note-taking to structured reporting and collaboration.

📝 **Note-Taking & Information Gathering**

Tool	Purpose	Best For	Platform
Obsidian	Local markdown-based note-taking	Secure, offline documentation	Windows, Mac, Linux
Joplin	Encrypted note-taking	Syncing across devices	Windows, Mac, Linux, Mobile
Evernote	Cloud-based notes	Quick data capture	Windows, Mac, Mobile
CherryTree	Hierarchical note organization	Detailed case notes	Windows, Linux

📌 **Example:**

An OSINT investigator logs all search queries, URLs, and timestamps in Obsidian, ensuring findings are well-organized and locally stored for security.

🗄 **Data Organization & Case Management**

Tool	Purpose	Best For	Platform
Excel / Google Sheets	Tabular data storage	Organizing large datasets	Web, Windows, Mac
AirTable	Visual database organization	Sorting intelligence data	Web, Mobile
Maltego	Link analysis & entity mapping	Network visualization	Windows, Mac, Linux
CaseFile (from Maltego)	Manual graphing & linking of entities	Investigations without online queries	Windows, Mac, Linux

📌 **Example:**

For an investigation into a phishing campaign, an investigator logs email sender addresses, domains, and associated IPs in an Excel sheet for pattern analysis.

📓 **OSINT Report Writing & Formatting**

Tool	Purpose	Best For	Platform
Microsoft Word / Google Docs	Traditional document writing	Formal OSINT reports	Web, Windows, Mac
LaTeX (Overleaf)	Structured technical reports	Formatting professional reports	Web
Notion	Flexible note + report organization	Collaborative reporting	Web, Windows, Mac

📌 **Example:**

A security analyst uses Google Docs to create a detailed incident report on an exposed database, complete with screenshots, findings, and recommendations.

🔍 **Source Verification & Citation Management**

Tool	Purpose	Best For	Platform
Zotero	Source management	Citing and organizing references	Windows, Mac, Linux
Wayback Machine	Archiving web pages	Preserving deleted content	Web
InVID	Verifying videos	Fact-checking media	Web

📌 **Example:**

An OSINT investigator cites archived web pages in Zotero to preserve evidence of disinformation campaigns that might later be deleted.

10.6.3 OSINT Documentation Templates

📝 **OSINT Note-Taking Template**

- ◆ **Case Name**: (Title of investigation)
- ◆ **Date & Time**: (Timestamp of entry)
- ◆ **Investigator**: (Your name/alias)
- ◆ **Sources & URLs**: (List of sources)
- ◆ **Findings**: (Summary of key discoveries)
- ◆ **Next Steps**: (Actions to follow up on)

📌 **Example Entry:**

- • **Case Name**: Phishing Scam Investigation
- • **Date & Time**: Feb 16, 2025 – 14:30 UTC
- • **Investigator**: J. Doe
- • **Sources**: https://phishingdatabase.com/sample123
- • **Findings**: Detected multiple fake login pages targeting financial institutions.
- • **Next Steps**: Reverse image search logos used in scam.

🏛 OSINT Spreadsheet Template (Google Sheets / Excel)

Entity Type	Name / Handle	Source URL	Date Found	Verified?	Notes
Twitter Account	@badactor123	twitter.com/badactor123	2025-02-16	✖ No	Suspicious bot activity
Domain	scam-website.com	whois lookup	2025-02-16	☑ Yes	Registered in Russia
Email Address	fraud@xyz.com	Phishing email	2025-02-15	✖ No	Needs further verification

📑 OSINT Report Template (Word / Google Docs)

📌 **Title**: (OSINT Report on [Subject])

📌 **Date**: (MM/DD/YYYY)

📌 **Author**: (Investigator Name/Alias)

📌 **Scope**: (Define scope, platforms analyzed, timeframes)

📌 **Methodology**: (How was data collected? Tools used?)

📌 **Findings**: (Summarize key intelligence, supported by screenshots/data)

📌 **Verification & Source Analysis**: (How were findings validated?)

📌 **Conclusion & Risk Assessment**: (Summarize key risks and insights)

📌 **Recommendations**: (Next steps, actions needed)

📌 **Example Report Title:**

"OSINT Analysis of a Disinformation Campaign Targeting Election 2025"

10.6.4 Best Practices for OSINT Documentation

✓ Use structured templates for consistency.

✓ Keep raw data and processed intelligence separate.

✓ Timestamp all findings to track updates.

✓ Verify sources before adding them to reports.

✓ Store sensitive OSINT data securely (encryption, offline backups).

✓ Use version control (Google Docs history, Git, etc.) to track changes.

Proper documentation ensures OSINT investigations remain credible, organized, and legally defensible. Using structured templates, verification tools, and secure storage methods, investigators can create actionable intelligence reports with clarity and professionalism.

◆ Key Takeaways:

✓ Structured documentation prevents data loss & improves collaboration.

✓ Use tools like Obsidian, Maltego, and Google Sheets for efficiency.

✓ Templates streamline reporting, note-taking, and source tracking.

✓ Secure OSINT findings with encryption & proper storage methods.

✓ Well-documented OSINT reports are essential for legal & ethical compliance.

🚀 "Good intelligence is only as useful as its documentation."

11. OPSEC for OSINT Practitioners

Practicing OSINT without proper Operational Security (OPSEC) can expose investigators to risks, from digital tracking to unintended exposure of their own identities. As an OSINT practitioner, safeguarding your methods, tools, and personal data is essential to conducting secure and anonymous research. This chapter explores key OPSEC principles, including the use of VPNs, burner accounts, secure browsers, and compartmentalized workflows. By implementing strong security measures, you can minimize digital footprints, protect sensitive investigations, and ensure your safety while conducting open-source intelligence gathering.

11.1 Understanding Operational Security (OPSEC)

Operational Security (OPSEC) is a critical practice for OSINT investigators, cybersecurity professionals, law enforcement, and intelligence analysts. OPSEC involves identifying and protecting sensitive information to prevent adversaries from exploiting vulnerabilities. In OSINT investigations, poor OPSEC can lead to identity exposure, counter-surveillance, or legal risks.

This chapter will cover:

✓ What OPSEC is and why it matters

✓ Common OPSEC risks in OSINT investigations

✓ Best practices for maintaining OPSEC

✓ Essential OPSEC tools and techniques

11.1.1 What is OPSEC?

📌 **Definition**

Operational Security (OPSEC) is a proactive security strategy used to identify and protect sensitive information from adversaries. It involves:

- **Risk assessment** – Identifying information that could be exploited.
- **Threat modeling** – Understanding who the adversaries are and their tactics.

- **Mitigation** – Implementing protective measures to reduce risks.

OPSEC is widely used in:

◆ **Military & intelligence operations** – Concealing troop movements and classified missions.
◆ **Cybersecurity** – Protecting internal data from hackers.
◆ **Law enforcement** – Safeguarding investigations and undercover agents.
◆ **Corporate security** – Preventing industrial espionage.
◆ **OSINT investigations** – Avoiding detection while gathering intelligence.

📌 **Example:**

An OSINT investigator researching cybercriminal groups must mask their real identity, location, and digital footprint to avoid retaliation.

11.1.2 Common OPSEC Risks in OSINT Investigations

OSINT investigators face unique risks due to the public nature of their work. Failing to maintain OPSEC can result in exposure, counter-surveillance, and potential legal issues.

⚫ **Top OPSEC Threats for OSINT Investigators**

Risk	Description	Example
Identity Exposure	Investigators can be traced via their online footprint.	Using a personal account to research a suspect.
IP & Location Leaks	Websites and adversaries can track IP addresses.	Not using a VPN while visiting a target's site.
Metadata Exposure	Images, PDFs, and documents contain hidden data.	Uploading a screenshot that includes EXIF metadata.
Digital Fingerprinting	Websites track unique browser and system configurations.	Using a regular browser instead of a privacy-focused one.
Social Engineering Attacks	Adversaries manipulate investigators to gain info.	A phishing email tricks an investigator into revealing details.

📌 **Real-World Case:**

In 2020, a journalist investigating a hacker forum was doxxed after members traced his IP address and browser fingerprint due to weak OPSEC.

11.1.3 Best Practices for Maintaining OPSEC in OSINT

To reduce OPSEC risks, OSINT investigators must follow strict security protocols.

◆ 1. Protect Your Identity & Online Presence

✓ **Use an Alias** – Never use your real name, email, or personal accounts for OSINT.

✓ **Create Separate Personas** – Maintain different identities for different investigations.

✓ **Avoid Oversharing Online** – Be mindful of what you post on social media.

◆ 2. Hide Your IP Address & Location

✓ **Use a VPN** – Encrypts internet traffic and masks your real IP.

✓ **Use Tor or Tails OS** – Provides stronger anonymity for sensitive investigations.

✓ **Disable Location Services** – Prevents apps and websites from tracking your location.

◆ 3. Manage Your Digital Fingerprint

✓ **Use a Privacy Browser** – Brave, Tor, or Firefox with security add-ons.

✓ **Block Tracking Scripts** – Use uBlock Origin and NoScript.

✓ **Spoof Browser Fingerprint** – Use tools like Chameleon or FireGloves.

◆ 4. Remove Metadata from Files & Images

✓ **Use Metadata Removal Tools** – MAT2, ExifTool, and ImageScrubber.

✓ **Convert Files to Secure Formats** – Convert PDFs to plain text before sharing.

◆ 5. Use Secure Communication Channels

✓ **Encrypted Messaging** – Signal, Session, or Threema.

✔ **Anonymous Email Services** – ProtonMail or Tutanota.

✔ **Secure File Transfers** – OnionShare or Tresorit.

📌 **Example:**

An OSINT investigator researching human trafficking networks uses a separate identity, VPN, Tor browser, and secure email to avoid detection.

11.1.4 Essential OPSEC Tools for OSINT Investigators

🔲 Anonymity & Privacy Tools

Tool	Purpose	Platform
NordVPN / ProtonVPN	Hides IP address	Windows, Mac, Linux, Mobile
Tor Browser	Provides anonymity	Windows, Mac, Linux
Tails OS	Live OS for anonymous browsing	USB Bootable
Whonix	Secure OS with Tor routing	Virtual Machine

📁 Metadata & File Protection

Tool	Purpose	Platform
ExifTool	Removes metadata from images/files	Windows, Mac, Linux
MAT2 (Metadata Anonymization Toolkit)	Strips metadata from documents	Linux
OnionShare	Secure file sharing	Windows, Mac, Linux

✉ Secure Communication

Tool	Purpose	Platform
ProtonMail	Encrypted email	Web, Mobile
Signal	Secure messaging	Windows, Mac, Mobile
SecureDrop	Whistleblower document sharing	Web

📌 **Example:**

An OSINT investigator communicating with a confidential source uses ProtonMail and Signal instead of regular email or WhatsApp.

11.1.5 Case Study: OPSEC Failure in OSINT

📟 **Case**: Dutch Intelligence Officer Exposed (2022)

📌 **What Happened?**

- A Dutch intelligence officer was compromised while investigating cyber threats.
- He used his personal phone and email to register for a forum.
- Hackers traced his IP and digital footprint, revealing his real identity.
- The exposure led to operational failure and security risks.

📌 **Lessons Learned:**

✅ Always use burner accounts and secure devices for investigations.

✅ Never mix personal and professional identities.

✅ Mask your IP address and digital fingerprint at all times.

OPSEC is non-negotiable in OSINT investigations. Without proper security measures, investigators risk exposure, doxxing, cyberattacks, or legal consequences. By implementing strong OPSEC practices, investigators can operate safely, effectively, and anonymously.

◆ **Key Takeaways:**

✅ **Always use an alias** – Never mix personal and OSINT accounts.

✅ **Mask your IP & location** – Use a VPN, Tor, or Tails OS.

✅ **Remove metadata** – Strip files of hidden information before sharing.

✅ **Secure your digital fingerprint** – Use privacy browsers & anti-tracking tools.

✅ **Communicate securely** – Use encrypted email and messaging apps.

🚀 "In OSINT, your best investigation is the one where you remain invisible." 🔍

11.2 Avoiding Digital Fingerprinting While Conducting OSINT

When conducting OSINT investigations, avoiding digital fingerprinting is essential to maintain anonymity, prevent tracking, and protect operational security (OPSEC). Digital fingerprinting refers to the unique identifiable characteristics that websites, online services, and adversaries can use to track and profile an investigator.

In this chapter, we will cover:

✅ What digital fingerprinting is and how it works

✅ Common fingerprinting techniques used by websites and adversaries

✅ Best practices for avoiding digital fingerprinting

✅ Essential tools for protecting your online identity

11.2.1 What is Digital Fingerprinting?

📌 Definition

Digital fingerprinting is the process of collecting unique data points from a user's device, browser, and online behavior to identify and track them across websites. Unlike traditional tracking methods (such as cookies), fingerprinting does not require user consent and can be very difficult to avoid.

🔎 How Digital Fingerprinting Works

Websites and online services collect the following data points to create a unique digital fingerprint:

Fingerprinting Method	Data Collected	Example of Tracking
Browser Fingerprinting	Browser type, version, extensions, fonts, screen size	A site detects that you use a rare browser setup
Device Fingerprinting	Operating system, CPU, GPU, device model	An investigator's MacBook is uniquely identified
IP Address & Location Tracking	Public IP, geolocation, ISP	A website detects your real location
Behavioral Fingerprinting	Typing speed, mouse movements, scrolling patterns	AI detects a user based on typing style
Canvas Fingerprinting	Graphics rendering differences in a browser	Your unique GPU rendering is logged
WebRTC Leaks	Real IP address leaks despite VPN use	A website sees your real IP through WebRTC
Audio & Battery Fingerprinting	Sound card data, battery level	A site identifies your device based on audio signals

📌 Example:

An OSINT investigator uses a VPN but does not prevent WebRTC leaks. A website logs their real IP address, exposing their location.

11.2.2 Why Avoid Digital Fingerprinting?

For OSINT professionals, digital fingerprinting poses several risks:

● Risks of Digital Fingerprinting in OSINT Investigations

✗ **Identity Exposure** – Investigators can be tracked across multiple websites.
✗ **Counter-Surveillance** – Adversaries can detect and log investigator visits.
✗ **Legal & Ethical Risks** – Visiting certain websites with a trackable fingerprint can violate privacy laws.
✗ **Targeted Attacks** – Hackers can track and exploit investigators based on their digital footprint.

📌 Real-World Case:

In 2021, security researchers investigating malware forums were identified by their unique browser fingerprints, leading to counter-surveillance efforts by cybercriminals.

11.2.3 Best Practices to Avoid Digital Fingerprinting

To stay anonymous, OSINT investigators must blend in with normal internet traffic rather than stand out. Below are key strategies to minimize fingerprinting risks.

◆ 1. Use a Secure, Anonymous Browser

✅ **Use**: Tor Browser, Brave with privacy settings, Firefox with hardened configurations.
✖ **Avoid**: Google Chrome, Microsoft Edge, Safari (highly fingerprintable).

📌 Example:

Instead of using a custom browser setup that makes them unique, an investigator uses Tor Browser in its default settings, blending in with millions of other Tor users.

◆ 2. Mask Your IP Address & Location

✅ **Use**: VPN (ProtonVPN, Mullvad), Tor, Tails OS.
✖ **Avoid**: Using your home IP, public Wi-Fi without protection.

📌 Example:

An OSINT analyst uses a VPN with no logs policy to prevent websites from logging their real IP address.

◆ 3. Prevent WebRTC, Canvas, and Audio Fingerprinting

✅ Use:

- **uBlock Origin** – Blocks tracking scripts.
- **CanvasBlocker** – Prevents canvas fingerprinting.
- Disable WebRTC in Browser Settings.
- **Privacy Badger** – Blocks known trackers.

📌 Example:

An investigator disables WebRTC leaks in Firefox to prevent sites from seeing their real IP even when using a VPN.

◆ 4. Use Virtual Machines & Disposable Systems

✅ **Use**: Whonix, Tails OS, or a virtual machine with a burner OS.
✖ **Avoid**: Using your personal computer for sensitive OSINT work.

📌 Example:

An investigator boots into Tails OS on a USB stick to conduct research, leaving no traces on their real device.

◆ 5. Standardize Your Browser & System Setup

✅ **Use**: Default settings in Tor or Brave to blend in.
✖ **Avoid**: Custom fonts, rare screen resolutions, unique browser extensions.

📌 Example:

Instead of using a customized Firefox setup, an investigator sticks to Tor Browser defaults, making them indistinguishable from other users.

◆ 6. Rotate and Manage Online Personas

✅ **Use**: Multiple virtual identities for different investigations.

✖ **Avoid**: Reusing the same account or email across multiple investigations.

📌 Example:

An OSINT investigator creates separate email accounts and usernames for different research cases to prevent cross-tracking.

11.2.4 Essential Tools for Avoiding Digital Fingerprinting

Tool	Purpose	Platform
Tor Browser	Anonymizes web activity	Windows, Mac, Linux
Brave Browser	Blocks trackers and fingerprinting scripts	Windows, Mac, Linux
Firefox (Hardened)	Privacy-focused browsing with custom settings	Windows, Mac, Linux
Tails OS	Live operating system for anonymity	USB Bootable
Whonix	Virtual OS that forces all traffic through Tor	Virtual Machine
Mullvad VPN	Privacy-focused VPN with no logs	Windows, Mac, Linux
uBlock Origin	Blocks ads, scripts, and tracking	Browser Extension
CanvasBlocker	Prevents browser fingerprinting	Browser Extension
Privacy Badger	Blocks invisible trackers	Browser Extension
ExifTool	Removes metadata from files	Windows, Mac, Linux

📌 Example:

An OSINT investigator uses Tor Browser with NoScript, CanvasBlocker, and a VPN to conduct research without leaving a fingerprint.

Avoiding digital fingerprinting is crucial for OSINT investigators to maintain anonymity, security, and operational effectiveness. By understanding how websites track users and implementing privacy-focused tools and techniques, investigators can blend in with normal internet traffic and avoid detection.

◆ Key Takeaways:

✓ Use privacy-focused browsers (Tor, Brave, Firefox with anti-tracking).

✓ Mask your IP & prevent WebRTC leaks (Use a VPN, Tor, Tails OS).

✓ Standardize your browser & device setup (Avoid unique configurations).

✓ Use metadata removal tools (ExifTool, MAT2).

✓ Rotate personas & separate accounts for different investigations.

🚀 "In OSINT, staying invisible is just as important as finding intelligence." 🔍

11.3 Using VPNs, Proxies & Secure Browsers for OSINT

When conducting OSINT investigations, maintaining anonymity and security is crucial. Investigators often interact with potentially malicious websites, track online activities, or gather intelligence without revealing their identities. Using Virtual Private Networks (VPNs), proxies, and secure browsers helps mask digital footprints, protect data, and avoid detection.

This chapter will cover:

✅ Differences between VPNs, proxies, and secure browsers

✅ How each tool protects OSINT investigations

✅ Best practices for using VPNs, proxies, and browsers together

✅ Recommended tools for anonymity and security

11.3.1 Understanding VPNs, Proxies & Secure Browsers

Each tool provides a different level of anonymity, encryption, and security.

Tool	Function	Security Level	Best Used For
VPN (Virtual Private Network)	Encrypts internet traffic and hides IP address by routing through a secure server	●●●○ (High)	General browsing, secure communication, avoiding geolocation tracking
Proxy Server	Redirects traffic through an intermediary server but often lacks encryption	●●○○○ (Medium-Low)	Bypassing geo-restrictions, accessing blocked content
Secure Browser	Blocks trackers, fingerprinting, and enhances privacy settings	●●●●● (Very High)	Anonymous browsing, avoiding surveillance and tracking

📌 **Example:**

An OSINT investigator researching a hacker forum uses a VPN and Tor Browser to hide their IP and prevent tracking by forum admins.

11.3.2 VPNs for OSINT: How They Work & Why They Matter

◆ How a VPN Works

A VPN encrypts internet traffic and routes it through a secure server, replacing the user's real IP address with the VPN server's IP.

◆ Why VPNs Are Essential for OSINT

✓ **Hides real IP address** – Prevents adversaries from tracking investigators.
✓ **Encrypts traffic** – Protects data from surveillance and ISP monitoring.
✓ **Bypasses geo-restrictions** – Allows access to country-specific data.
✓ **Reduces risk of doxxing** – Prevents exposure while engaging with online communities.

☐ Risks of VPNs

✗ **VPN logs can be subpoenaed** – Some providers store connection logs.
✗ **VPNs can be blocked** – Some sites detect and block known VPN IPs.

✓ Best VPNs for OSINT (No-Logs & High Security)

VPN Provider	Logging Policy	Jurisdiction	Multi-Hop?	Best Features
Mullvad	No logs	Sweden	Yes	Anonymous account creation, strong encryption
ProtonVPN	No logs	Switzerland	Yes	Tor over VPN, Secure Core servers
IVPN	No logs	Gibraltar	Yes	Anti-tracking features, WireGuard support
NordVPN	No logs	Panama	Yes	Large server network, Obfuscated servers

📌 Example:

An investigator using Mullvad VPN can browse the web without revealing their IP, ensuring anonymity while collecting data from online sources.

11.3.3 Proxies for OSINT: When & How to Use Them

◆ What is a Proxy?

A proxy server acts as an intermediary between a user's device and the internet. Unlike VPNs, proxies do not encrypt traffic but can still hide the user's IP.

◆ Types of Proxies & Their Uses in OSINT

Proxy Type	Function	Best For	Encryption?
HTTP Proxy	Redirects only web browser traffic	Accessing geo-blocked websites	✕ No
SOCKS5 Proxy	Redirects all traffic, not just web browsing	Torrenting, accessing certain services	✕ No
Residential Proxy	Uses real residential IPs	Scraping websites without detection	✕ No
TOR Proxy	Routes traffic through the Tor network	High anonymity research	☑ Yes

☐ Risks of Using Proxies

✕ **No encryption** – Unlike VPNs, proxies don't secure traffic.
✕ **Proxy logs** – Many free proxies log and sell user data.
✕ **Easily detectable** – Websites can block known proxy IPs.

✓ Best Proxy Services for OSINT

- **Smartproxy** (Residential proxies for web scraping)
- **SOCKS5** Proxies from Mullvad or NordVPN (For secure browsing)
- **TOR Proxy** (Onion Routing) (For anonymous research)

📌 Example:

An investigator uses Smartproxy's residential IPs to scrape a website without triggering bot detection systems.

11.3.4 Secure Browsers for OSINT Investigations

◆ Why Secure Browsers Are Essential

Secure browsers prevent tracking, reduce fingerprinting risks, and protect online activity from surveillance.

✅ Best Secure Browsers for OSINT

Browser	Fingerprint Protection	Default Security Level	Best Use Case
Tor Browser	☑ Strong	●●●●● (Very High)	High-anonymity investigations
Brave	☑ Strong	●●●●○ (High)	Privacy-focused browsing
Firefox (Hardened)	☑ Moderate	●●●○○ (Medium)	General research with privacy settings
Ungoogled Chromium	✗ Weak	●●○○○ (Low)	Avoiding Google tracking

📌 Example:

An OSINT analyst uses Tor Browser in its default settings to investigate a darknet market without revealing their identity.

☐ Browser Fingerprinting & Tracking Risks

✗ Custom browser settings can make investigators unique and trackable.

✗ Logging into personal accounts can link activities to real identities.

✗ Plugins & Extensions may expose user details.

✅ Best Practices for Secure Browsing in OSINT

✓ Use Tor Browser or Brave with privacy settings enabled.

✓ Disable WebRTC to prevent IP leaks.

✓ Avoid browser extensions that add unique fingerprints.

✓ Use private browsing modes (incognito mode isn't enough).

11.3.5 Combining VPNs, Proxies & Secure Browsers for Maximum Anonymity

For OSINT, layering these tools provides the best protection.

● Recommended OSINT Security Setups

Use Case	Setup
General OSINT Research	VPN + Brave or Hardened Firefox
Deep Web/Darknet Research	VPN + Tor Browser
Web Scraping / Mass Data Collection	Residential Proxy + Hardened Firefox
High-Security Investigations	VPN + Virtual Machine + Tor Browser

📌 Example:

A cybersecurity analyst researching cybercrime groups uses:

1️⃣ Tails OS for a clean environment.

2️⃣ Tor Browser for maximum anonymity.

3️⃣ VPN (Mullvad) with multi-hop servers to prevent IP leaks.

Using VPNs, proxies, and secure browsers is essential for OSINT professionals to remain anonymous, protect data, and avoid detection. Each tool serves a different purpose, but combining them provides the best security.

◆ Key Takeaways:

✔ Use a no-logs VPN (Mullvad, ProtonVPN) to hide your IP.

✔ Use proxies (SOCKS5, residential proxies) when scraping or bypassing restrictions.

✔ Use secure browsers (Tor, Brave, hardened Firefox) to avoid fingerprinting.

✔ Never log into personal accounts when conducting OSINT research.

🚀 "In OSINT, your best defense is invisibility." 🔍

11.4 Protecting Personal Identities in OSINT Investigations

One of the biggest risks in OSINT (Open-Source Intelligence) investigations is exposing your own identity while gathering intelligence. Whether you are investigating cybercriminals, corporations, nation-state actors, or social movements, you must ensure that your real name, location, and digital footprint remain protected.

Failing to do so can result in:

✘ Retaliation from targets (doxxing, harassment, or cyberattacks)

✘ Compromised investigations (subjects detecting your presence)

✘ Legal or ethical issues (violating terms of service or privacy laws)

This chapter will cover:

✓ Key identity risks for OSINT investigators

✓ Techniques to separate personal and investigative identities

✓ Best tools for anonymity and secure research

✓ Real-world case studies of identity leaks in OSINT

11.4.1 Why Protecting Your Identity in OSINT Matters

◆ How OSINT Investigators Get Exposed

Risk	How It Happens	Example
IP Address Leaks	Visiting websites without VPN/proxy	A hacker forum logs your real IP
Social Media Cross-Linking	Using personal accounts for research	A fake profile links back to your real identity
Browser Fingerprinting	Unique browser settings expose you	Tracking scripts identify your OS and plugins
Metadata Leaks	Images or documents reveal personal info	EXIF data shows your location
Operational Sloppiness	Using the same username or email	Your alias is linked to your real account

📌 Case Study:

A journalist investigating extremist groups used a fake social media account but logged in from their home IP. The group traced their real location, leading to threats.

11.4.2 Separating Personal & Investigative Identities

◆ Golden Rule: Create a "Burner" Identity

When conducting OSINT, NEVER use your real name, email, or phone number. Instead, build a completely separate identity.

✓ **Fake Name Generator** – Use a random but realistic alias.

✓ **New Email & Phone** – Use ProtonMail & VoIP numbers (Google Voice, MySudo).

✓ **Dedicated OSINT Device** – Keep investigation work off your personal computer.

✓ **Separate Browser Profiles** – One for research, one for personal use.

✓ **New Social Media Accounts** – Create fake but believable profiles.

📌 Example:

An OSINT investigator builds a fake persona:

- **Name**: Emily Carter
- **Email**: emily_c_investigator@protonmail.com
- **Phone**: VoIP number from Hushed app
- **Laptop**: A separate OSINT machine (not personal laptop)
- **Browser**: Uses Firefox with hardened privacy settings

11.4.3 Digital Anonymity: VPNs, Proxies & Secure Browsers

◆ Tools to Hide Your Digital Identity

Tool	Function	Best Use Case
VPN (Virtual Private Network)	Encrypts traffic & hides real IP	General browsing, avoiding geo-tracking
Tor Browser	Routes traffic through onion network	Dark web research, high anonymity work
Tails OS	A portable, privacy-focused operating system	Air-gapped investigations, high-risk research
Whonix	A secure, anonymous OS using Tor	Long-term OSINT investigations
Brave Browser	Blocks tracking, fingerprinting	General OSINT research

📌 **Best VPNs for OSINT:**

◆ **Mullvad** (No logs, anonymous payment options)
◆ **ProtonVPN** (Strong security, Tor integration)
◆ **IVPN** (Multi-hop and WireGuard support)

☐ **DON'T**: Use a free VPN – they often log and sell data!

📌 **Example:**

An OSINT investigator researching cybercriminal networks uses:

✅ Tails OS on a USB drive

✅ Tor Browser for dark web browsing

✅ Mullvad VPN for additional encryption

11.4.4 Avoiding Digital Fingerprinting & Tracking

◆ How Websites & Platforms Track You

- **Cookies & Tracking Scripts** – Sites track login sessions.
- **Device & OS Fingerprinting** – Unique system settings reveal your identity.
- **WebRTC & IP Leaks** – Exposes your real IP even when using a VPN.

◆ How to Block Tracking

✓ Use privacy-focused browsers – Brave, Firefox (hardened), or Tor.

✓ Disable WebRTC – Prevents IP leaks in browser settings.

✓ Clear cookies & cache – Stops tracking persistence.

✓ Use uBlock Origin & Privacy Badger – Blocks fingerprinting.

📌 Example:

An investigator searching for leaked databases disables WebRTC in Firefox and uses Brave with strict fingerprinting protection.

11.4.5 Secure Communication: Emails, Messaging & Calls

◆ Secure Email & Phone Alternatives

Service	Use Case	Best Features
ProtonMail	Secure email	End-to-end encryption, no logs
Tutanota	Anonymous email	Encrypted inbox & metadata protection
Hushed / MySudo	Burner phone numbers	Disposable, anonymous VoIP numbers
Signal	Secure messaging	Encrypted chats & calls
Session	Anonymous messaging	Decentralized, no phone number needed

📌 Example:

An OSINT investigator creates a ProtonMail address and MySudo VoIP number for secure tip-sharing with a journalist.

☐ DON'T:

- **Use Gmail or Yahoo** – They track and log all activity.
- **Use your real phone number** – Even for 2FA verification.

11.4.6 Best Practices for Protecting Personal Identities

◆ Do's & Don'ts of OSINT Identity Protection

☑ DO	✖ DON'T
Use separate devices for OSINT	Use your personal phone or laptop
Always browse with a VPN & secure browser	Visit risky sites without protection
Use fake emails & VoIP numbers	Use your real email or number
Disable tracking & fingerprinting	Log into personal accounts while investigating
Regularly clear cookies & cache	Stay logged into sites while researching

📌 **Example:**

An OSINT researcher working on a corporate investigation keeps all research on a dedicated laptop with Tails OS, ensuring complete separation from personal life.

Conclusion

◆ Protecting your personal identity is the #1 rule in OSINT.
◆ Never mix personal and investigative accounts, devices, or data.
◆ Use VPNs, proxies, secure browsers, and burner accounts.
◆ Be aware of tracking techniques and digital fingerprinting risks.

❗ Final Thought: "An OSINT investigator's best tool is invisibility." □□♂□

11.5 Dealing with Online Threats & Counter-OSINT

Open-Source Intelligence (OSINT) investigators often operate in hostile online environments, where they may become targets of counter-OSINT, doxxing, hacking attempts, or even legal threats. Adversaries, such as cybercriminals, extremist groups, corporate entities, or state actors, may attempt to identify and retaliate against investigators.

This section covers:

✓ Common online threats faced by OSINT practitioners

✓ Counter-OSINT techniques used by adversaries

✓ How to detect and mitigate digital attacks

✓ Best practices for staying anonymous and safe

11.5.1 Understanding Online Threats to OSINT Investigators

◆ Who Might Target an OSINT Investigator?

Threat Actor	Motivation	Potential Risks
Hackers & Cybercriminals	Protecting illegal operations	Hacking, malware, phishing
Terrorist & Extremist Groups	Silencing critics or investigators	Threats, harassment, real-world violence
Corporations & Private Entities	Preventing exposure of unethical practices	Legal threats, smear campaigns, doxxing
Nation-State Actors	Counterintelligence, political motivations	Surveillance, cyberattacks, arrest (if local)
Trolls & Harassers	Retaliation or personal vendettas	Doxxing, online abuse, reputational attacks

📌 Real-World Example:

In 2020, OSINT researchers investigating cybercriminals on dark web forums were targeted by DDoS attacks and phishing attempts after exposing sensitive data leaks.

11.5.2 Common Counter-OSINT Techniques Used by Adversaries

Adversaries use counter-OSINT to detect, track, and retaliate against investigators.

◆ Counter-OSINT Tactics

Tactic	How It Works	Impact
Doxxing	Exposing personal information (name, address, phone)	Threats, harassment, real-world danger
Social Engineering	Tricking you into revealing sensitive data	Identity theft, account compromise
Honeypots	Fake profiles or sites to lure investigators	Data harvesting, exposure
Legal Threats (SLAPP Lawsuits)	Intimidation through lawsuits	Censorship, legal fees
Cyber Attacks	Phishing, malware, DDoS attacks	System compromise, data loss
Misinformation & Deception	Spreading false leads, red herrings	Wasting time, undermining investigations

📌 **Example:**

A fake LinkedIn profile posing as a cybersecurity recruiter was used to gather intel on OSINT researchers by tricking them into connecting and engaging in private discussions.

11.5.3 How to Detect & Mitigate Counter-OSINT Attacks

◆ **How to Recognize an Attack is Happening**

⚠️ Unusual login attempts on your email or social media.
⚠️ Fake friend requests or messages from unknown profiles.
⚠️ Malicious email attachments or phishing links.
⚠️ Sudden increase in online harassment or trolling.
⚠️ Receiving unexpected legal notices or threats.

◆ **Steps to Protect Yourself**

✓ **Enable Multi-Factor Authentication (MFA)** – Prevents account takeovers.

✓ **Use Unique, Complex Passwords** – Use a password manager.

✓ **Monitor Your Digital Footprint** – Google yourself regularly.

✓ **Use Burner Emails & Numbers** – Avoid using personal details.

✓ **Be Cautious of Unverified Sources** – Avoid clicking unknown links.

✓ **Encrypt Your Communications** – Use ProtonMail, Signal, or Session.

✓ **Harden Your Social Media Privacy Settings** – Limit public visibility.

📌 **Case Study:**

An OSINT investigator researching an extremist group received a phishing email disguised as a "journalist request." The attached file contained spyware designed to steal credentials.

✓ **Mitigation**: The investigator used a sandboxed virtual machine to open the email, preventing malware infection.

11.5.4 Protecting Yourself from Doxxing & Harassment

◆ **How to Prevent Doxxing**

✓ Remove Your Personal Data from People Search Engines (e.g., Spokeo, Whitepages, BeenVerified).

✓ Avoid Using Your Real Name on OSINT Platforms.

✓ Use a PO Box or Virtual Address instead of your home address.

✓ Don't Post Personal Information (birthday, location, family details).

✓ Set Social Media Accounts to Private and use alias accounts.

📌 **Example:**

An OSINT researcher had their home address leaked after using their real name on a WHOIS domain lookup.

✓ **Mitigation**: They switched to using privacy protection services on domains and registered everything under an alias.

11.5.5 Secure Your Devices & Online Presence

◆ **Best Tools for OSINT Security**

Tool	Function	Why Use It?
ProtonMail	Secure email	Encrypted, no tracking
Signal / Session	Secure messaging	No metadata logging
Tails OS	Anonymized OS	Runs off USB, leaves no traces
Mullvad / ProtonVPN	VPN for anonymity	No logs, strong encryption
Bitwarden / KeePass	Password manager	Secure, randomized passwords
uBlock Origin & NoScript	Browser security	Blocks tracking & malicious scripts

📌 Example:

A journalist conducting OSINT on government corruption used Tails OS on a burner laptop with ProtonMail to ensure complete anonymity.

11.5.6 What to Do If You Are Targeted?

◆ Immediate Steps to Take

☐ If you suspect you are being targeted:

✓ Change all passwords and enable MFA.

✓ Check if your data has been leaked using Have I Been Pwned?

✓ Monitor your email for unauthorized logins.

✓ Report harassment or threats to authorities/platforms.

✓ Consider a legal consultation if facing lawsuits or serious threats.

◆ When to Go Completely Offline?

If you are dealing with high-risk adversaries (cybercriminals, extremists, or state actors), it may be necessary to:

✓ Deactivate personal social media or use aliases.

✓ Use only encrypted communication (Signal, ProtonMail, Session).

✓ Stop using personal devices and switch to burner phones/laptops.

📌 **Example:**

A security researcher investigating a ransomware gang found their personal data leaked on a dark web forum. They:

✔ Immediately changed all passwords and activated MFA.

✔ Used Mullvad VPN & Tails OS to continue research anonymously.

✔ Notified law enforcement about the threats.

◆ Online threats are a serious risk for OSINT investigators.
◆ Counter-OSINT tactics like doxxing, phishing, and legal intimidation are common.
◆ Using strong OPSEC (operational security) is critical to staying safe.
◆ If you become a target, act quickly to protect your identity and security.

💡 **Final Thought:**

"In OSINT, the best defense is invisibility. Stay hidden, stay secure, and always be one step ahead." 🚀

11.6 Best Practices for Safe & Anonymous OSINT Investigations

Conducting Open-Source Intelligence (OSINT) investigations comes with significant risks, including doxxing, cyberattacks, legal threats, and surveillance. Whether you're researching cybercriminals, extremist groups, corporate entities, or political movements, maintaining anonymity and security is critical.

This section covers:

✅ How to maintain anonymity while conducting OSINT

✅ Best tools for secure and private investigations

✅ How to avoid tracking and counter-OSINT tactics

✅ Common mistakes that can expose your identity

11.6.1 Understanding the Risks of OSINT Investigations

Before diving into best practices, it's important to understand the major risks involved:

◆ **OSINT Investigator Risks**

Risk	How It Happens	Potential Consequences
Doxxing	Personal data gets exposed	Harassment, threats, identity theft
IP Address Leaks	Visiting websites without a VPN/proxy	Tracking, location exposure
Legal Issues	Accessing restricted data	Lawsuits, investigations, fines
Social Engineering Attacks	Trickery, phishing attempts	Account compromise, identity theft
Device Compromise	Malware, spyware, keyloggers	Stolen data, unauthorized access
Browser Fingerprinting	Unique browser settings reveal identity	Tracking across sites, OSINT profile exposure

📌 **Real-World Example:**

An OSINT researcher investigating cybercriminals forgot to use a VPN while visiting a hacker forum. The forum logged their real IP address, exposing their location and internet service provider (ISP).

11.6.2 Essential Tools for Safe & Anonymous OSINT

To stay anonymous, you need the right tools to protect your identity, devices, and data.

◆ **Secure Browsing & Internet Access**

Tool	Purpose	Why Use It?
Mullvad VPN / ProtonVPN	Hide real IP address	No-logs, strong encryption
Tor Browser	Anonymous browsing	Onion routing for privacy
Tails OS	Secure, disposable OS	Leaves no digital traces
Whonix	Virtual machine-based privacy OS	Prevents IP leaks & tracking
Brave / Hardened Firefox	Privacy-focused browsers	Blocks ads, tracking, fingerprinting

📌 Best VPNs for OSINT:

✓ Mullvad (No logs, anonymous payments)

✓ ProtonVPN (Strong encryption, Tor integration)

✓ IVPN (Multi-hop feature for extra anonymity)

◆ Secure Communication & Data Storage

Tool	Purpose	Why Use It?
ProtonMail / Tutanota	Secure email	End-to-end encryption, no tracking
Signal / Session	Encrypted messaging	No metadata logging
VeraCrypt	Encrypt files & data	Protects sensitive OSINT findings
Bitwarden / KeePass	Password manager	Creates & stores strong passwords
Hushed / MySudo	Anonymous phone numbers	Disposable, VoIP numbers for OSINT

📌 Example:

An investigator tracking political disinformation campaigns uses Tails OS, a burner ProtonMail account, and Signal for secure communication.

11.6.3 How to Avoid Tracking & Digital Fingerprinting

Adversaries use browser fingerprinting, tracking scripts, and metadata to identify and monitor OSINT investigators.

◆ How to Reduce Your Digital Footprint

✅ **Use a VPN or Tor** – Prevents IP leaks and geo-tracking.
✅ **Disable JavaScript & Cookies** – Stops tracking scripts.
✅ **Block WebRTC & Fingerprinting** – Prevents IP leaks even with a VPN.
✅ **Use uBlock Origin & NoScript** – Blocks ads, trackers, and fingerprinting scripts.
✅ **Create Separate Browser Profiles** – One for OSINT, one for personal use.

📌 Example:

A researcher analyzing fake social media accounts uses Brave browser with NoScript and a VPN, ensuring their activity isn't tracked.

11.6.4 Setting Up a Secure OSINT Work Environment

◆ Do's & Don'ts of an OSINT Workstation

☑ Do	✕ Don't
Use a dedicated OSINT laptop	Use your personal laptop for OSINT
Run Tails OS or Whonix for research	Use Windows/macOS without security modifications
Use a VPN or Tor for all OSINT activities	Browse OSINT targets from your home IP
Store findings in encrypted folders	Save OSINT data in cloud storage (Google Drive, Dropbox)
Create fake burner accounts	Use your real email for research

📌 Example:

A journalist investigating corporate corruption sets up a dedicated OSINT laptop with Whonix VM, ProtonVPN, and encrypted storage to protect their work.

11.6.5 Managing Online Identities & Burner Accounts

◆ How to Create & Manage Fake Identities

✓ **Use a Fake Name Generator** – Random, realistic alias.
✓ **Create Separate Email & Phone** – ProtonMail & MySudo VoIP number.
✓ **Use Different Profile Pictures** – Reverse image search to check uniqueness.
✓ **Vary Writing Styles** – Prevents linguistic fingerprinting.
✓ **Keep Detailed Notes** – Track aliases, login details, and personas.

📌 Example:

An OSINT analyst tracking dark web activities creates a burner identity with a realistic backstory and a separate ProtonMail account.

11.6.6 Common Mistakes That Can Expose Your Identity

◆ OSINT Mistakes to Avoid

✕ Logging into personal accounts while investigating.

✕ Reusing usernames or emails from personal life.

✕ Forgetting to clear metadata from images or files.

✕ Using the same writing style across different accounts.

✕ Accessing high-risk websites without proper anonymity tools.

📌 Case Study:

An investigator tracking fake social media accounts accidentally logged into their real Twitter account while using a burner profile—exposing their real identity to their target.

✅ **Mitigation**: Always use separate browsers & devices for OSINT and personal use.

- ◆ Anonymity and security are critical in OSINT investigations.
- ◆ Use VPNs, Tor, and hardened browsers to prevent tracking.
- ◆ Set up a separate OSINT workstation with encrypted storage.
- ◆ Create and manage fake burner identities properly.
- ◆ Be mindful of common mistakes that can expose your identity.

💡 Final Thought:

"In OSINT, staying anonymous is not an option—it's a necessity. Protect yourself first, so you can continue uncovering the truth safely." □□♂□🚀

12. Practicing OSINT: Real-World Exercises

Theory alone isn't enough—true mastery of OSINT comes from hands-on experience. This chapter provides practical exercises and case studies to help you apply your skills in real-world scenarios. From identifying digital footprints and verifying online identities to geolocating images and uncovering hidden data, these exercises will challenge you to think like an OSINT analyst. Whether you're a beginner looking to test your knowledge or an aspiring professional refining your techniques, these hands-on challenges will sharpen your investigative abilities and prepare you for real-world intelligence gathering.

12.1 Step-by-Step Beginner OSINT Investigation

Open-Source Intelligence (OSINT) investigations involve collecting, analyzing, and verifying publicly available information to uncover hidden details. Whether you're a journalist, cybersecurity professional, private investigator, or researcher, knowing how to conduct a structured OSINT investigation is essential.

This section will guide you through a step-by-step beginner OSINT investigation, covering:

✓ Defining objectives

✓ Selecting the right tools

✓ Gathering & verifying data

✓ Analyzing and reporting findings

By following these steps, you'll develop a methodical approach to OSINT, ensuring accuracy, efficiency, and security.

Step 1: Define Your OSINT Investigation Goals

Before diving into data collection, ask:

- What are you investigating? (Person, business, cybercrime, event?)
- What key information do you need? (Names, locations, emails, social media?)
- What is your end goal? (Report for cybersecurity, law enforcement, intelligence?)

◆ What are the legal & ethical boundaries? (Ensure compliance with laws like GDPR, CCPA.)

📌 **Example:**

☞ **Case**: You're investigating an anonymous Twitter user suspected of spreading disinformation.
☞ **Goal**: Identify their real name, location, or associated accounts to verify credibility.

Step 2: Gather Initial Data

Start with basic search techniques to collect publicly available information.

◆ **Google Dorking (Advanced Search Operators)**

Use Google search operators to find hidden data:

Search Query	Function	Example
`site:twitter.com "@username"`	Search a Twitter user's mentions	`site:twitter.com "@john_doe"`
`intitle:"index of" confidential`	Find open directories	`intitle:"index of" passwords`
`filetype:pdf "confidential report"`	Search for leaked files	`filetype:xlsx "employee salaries"`
`"John Doe" AND "email"`	Find linked mentions	`"John Doe" AND "@gmail.com"`

📌 **Example:**

☞ Searching site:linkedin.com "John Doe" "New York" finds a LinkedIn profile with company details.

◆ **Reverse Image Search**

Find where else an image appears online using:

🔍 **Google Images** – images.google.com
🔍 **Yandex Images** – yandex.com/images/
🔍 **Bing Visual Search** – bing.com/visualsearch

📌 **Example:**

☞ A suspicious profile picture on Twitter is reverse-searched on Yandex, revealing the same image on a different name's Facebook profile—indicating a fake identity.

Step 3: Expand Your Investigation

Once you have basic information, use advanced OSINT techniques to find hidden connections.

◆ **Social Media OSINT**

Platform	Tool/Technique	Purpose
Twitter	TweetBeaver, Twint	Find linked accounts, hashtags
Facebook	Facebook Graph Search, Stalkscan	Find friends, hidden posts
Instagram	IG tools, Metadata analysis	Track locations, metadata
LinkedIn	LinkedIn Dorks, Hunter.io	Find corporate connections

📌 **Example:**

☞ You find a Twitter user's LinkedIn page by searching their username on Google (site:linkedin.com inurl:profile @username). This reveals their full name and employer.

◆ **WHOIS & Domain Lookups**

Investigate websites with:

☐ **who.is** – Find domain owners
☐ **viewdns.info** – Domain history, IP lookups
☐ **dnslytics.com** – Reverse IP tracking

📌 **Example:**

☞ Searching whois hackerwebsite.com reveals the domain owner's email and links to other sites they own.

Step 4: Verify & Cross-Check Data

◆ How to Verify Data

✅ **Use multiple sources** – Don't trust a single website.
✅ **Check metadata** – Look at timestamps, geolocation in images and videos.
✅ **Corroborate with official sources** – Government databases, court records.
✅ **Identify fake or manipulated content** – Use deepfake detectors and fact-checking tools.

📌 Example:

☞ A suspicious Facebook user claims to be in New York, but their uploaded images contain metadata from Brazil—suggesting deception.

Step 5: Document & Report Your Findings

Once you've collected and verified data, organize it into a report for easy reference.

◆ OSINT Reporting Best Practices

📌 **Use structured formats** – Summarize findings clearly.
📌 **Include screenshots & URLs** – Capture evidence.
📌 **Redact sensitive data** – Protect personal info.
📌 **Cite sources properly** – Ensure credibility.

📌 Example:

☞ You create an OSINT report on a fake social media scammer, including:

✔ Screenshots of their accounts

✔ Timeline of activity

✔ Metadata from uploaded photos

✔ Linked accounts found via WHOIS lookups

Step 6: Maintain Anonymity & Security

Since OSINT investigations can make you a target, always practice strong OPSEC (Operational Security).

◆ Anonymity & Security Tips

✅ Use a VPN & secure browser (Tor, Brave, Mullvad VPN).

✅ Never use your personal email or accounts.

✅ Use burner devices or virtual machines.

✅ Avoid clicking suspicious links (malware risks).

✅ Separate personal & OSINT identities.

📌 Example:

☞ An OSINT investigator tracking cybercriminals uses Tails OS, a VPN, and a fake alias to avoid exposure.

Conclusion

✔ **Step 1**: Define your OSINT investigation goals.

✔ **Step 2**: Gather initial data using search engines & image searches.

✔ **Step 3**: Expand using social media, domain lookups, and metadata analysis.

✔ **Step 4**: Verify & cross-check all data for accuracy.

✔ **Step 5**: Document findings in a structured report.

✔ **Step 6:** Stay anonymous and secure during your investigation.

💡 Final Thought:

"A good OSINT investigation isn't just about finding information—it's about verifying it and staying undetected while doing so." 🚀

12.2 Finding a Person Online with OSINT Techniques

Finding a person online using Open-Source Intelligence (OSINT) is a valuable skill for investigators, journalists, law enforcement, and cybersecurity professionals. Whether tracking a missing person, verifying an online identity, or investigating fraud, OSINT tools can reveal social media profiles, emails, addresses, phone numbers, and more.

This guide will take you through a step-by-step process to locate a person online, covering:

✓ Collecting basic information

✓ Using search engines effectively

✓ Leveraging social media platforms

✓ Performing image and metadata analysis

✓ Finding hidden connections

Step 1: Gather Basic Information

Before searching, collect any details about the target. Even small pieces of information can help connect the dots.

- ◆ Full name or aliases
- ◆ Username or email address
- ◆ Phone number
- ◆ Location (city, country, workplace, school)
- ◆ Photos or profile pictures
- ◆ Known social media accounts

📌 Example:

☞ You are trying to locate John Doe, who previously lived in Chicago and used the email jdoe1990@gmail.com.

Step 2: Search Engines & Google Dorking

Start by using Google, Bing, and DuckDuckGo to search for names, usernames, and emails.

◆ **Google Search Operators**

Search Query	Purpose	Example
`"John Doe" Chicago`	Find exact name in a location	`"John Doe" New York`
`site:linkedin.com "John Doe"`	Search LinkedIn profiles	`site:linkedin.com "Jane Smith"`
`"jdoe1990@gmail.com"`	Search email mentions	`"johnsmith@gmail.com"`
`intitle:"index of" "John Doe"`	Find open directories	`intitle:"index of" "jdoe1990"`
`filetype:pdf "John Doe"`	Find documents	`filetype:xlsx "John Doe"`

📌 **Example:**

☞ Searching "jdoe1990@gmail.com" in Google reveals a forum post where the email was used—possibly linking to a username or additional details.

◆ **People Search Engines**

These sites aggregate public records, addresses, phone numbers, and emails:

🔍 **TruePeopleSearch** – truepeoplesearch.com
🔍 **Spokeo** – spokeo.com
🔍 **PeekYou** – peekyou.com
🔍 **Pipl** – pipl.com (Paid)
🔍 **BeenVerified** – beenverified.com

📌 **Example:**

☞ Searching John Doe's phone number on TruePeopleSearch provides a possible current address.

Step 3: Find Social Media Accounts

People often reuse usernames, emails, and profile pictures across platforms.

◆ Username Search

🔍 **WhatsMyName** – whatsmyname.app (Search username across platforms)
🔍 **Namechk** – namechk.com (Check username availability)
🔍 **Sherlock** – Python tool to find usernames

📌 Example:

☞ You search "johndoe1990" in WhatsMyName and find a Reddit, Twitter, and Instagram account using the same handle.

◆ Social Media OSINT Tools

Platform	Tool/Technique	Purpose
Facebook	Facebook Graph Search	Find hidden friends, posts
Twitter	TweetBeaver, Twint	Search tweets, linked accounts
Instagram	IG tools, Story viewers	Reverse image search, locations
LinkedIn	Hunter.io, LinkedIn Dorks	Find workplace, email address
TikTok	TokSearcher	Locate TikTok profiles

📌 Example:

☞ Searching "jdoe1990" on Instagram reveals a LinkedIn profile using the same username, which includes a company name.

Step 4: Reverse Image & Metadata Search

◆ Reverse Image Search

Find where a profile picture has been used before:

🔍 **Google Images** – images.google.com
🔍 **Yandex Reverse Search** – yandex.com/images
🔍 **Bing Visual Search** – bing.com/visualsearch

📌 Example:

☞ A Twitter profile picture reverse-searched on Yandex leads to a Facebook account with the same image, revealing the person's full name.

◆ **Extract Metadata from Photos**

Check images for hidden metadata (timestamps, location, device info):

🔍 **ExifTool** – Extract EXIF data
🔍 **FotoForensics** – Analyze image integrity
🔍 **Jeffrey's Exif Viewer** – Check geolocation

📌 **Example**:

☞ You download a photo from Instagram, run it through ExifTool, and find GPS coordinates showing where the photo was taken.

Step 5: Investigate Hidden Connections

Finding associates, friends, and relatives can help narrow your search.

◆ **Relationship Mapping**

✅ **Find LinkedIn connections** – site:linkedin.com "John Doe"
✅ Search mutual followers on Twitter & Instagram
✅ Use Facebook Graph Search for friendships

📌 **Example:**

☞ You check who "John Doe" interacts with on Twitter and find his sister's profile, which mentions his location.

◆ **Finding Related Websites**

Use WHOIS & domain lookup tools to find personal websites or email domains:

☐ **who.is** – Find domain owners
☐ **viewdns.info** – Reverse IP lookups

☐ **hunter.io** – Find email addresses

📌 **Example:**

☞ Checking WHOIS data for johndoe.com reveals an email linked to another website he owns.

Step 6: Verify & Cross-Check Data

🔎 Always verify findings before making conclusions!

✅ Check multiple sources – A single mention isn't proof.

✅ Confirm profiles via mutual friends & activity.

✅ Look for inconsistencies in location or timeline.

✅ Cross-reference with government/public databases.

📌 **Example:**

☞ You find John Doe's Twitter account, but the LinkedIn shows a different job history—suggesting it may not be the same person.

Step 7: Maintain OPSEC & Stay Anonymous

☐☐ To protect yourself during OSINT investigations:

✅ Use a VPN & secure browser (Tor, Mullvad, Brave)

✅ Avoid logging into accounts while investigating

✅ Create fake burner accounts for searches

✅ Use virtual machines or Tails OS

✅ Never click suspicious links or download files

📌 **Example:**

☞ An investigator looking into a criminal network uses a burner phone, ProtonMail, and a secure VPN to prevent tracking.

Conclusion

✓ **Step 1**: Gather Basic Info – Name, email, phone, usernames.

✓ **Step 2:** Use Search Engines – Google Dorking, people search sites.

✓ **Step 3**: Find Social Media Accounts – Username search, hidden profiles.

✓ **Step 4:** Reverse Image Search & Metadata – Find linked accounts, locations.

✓ **Step 5**: Investigate Connections – Relatives, associates, business links.

✓ **Step 6:** Verify Everything – Cross-check sources before conclusions.

✓ **Step 7:** Stay Anonymous – Use VPNs, burner accounts, and OPSEC.

💡 **Final Thought:**

"The internet never forgets. With the right OSINT techniques, you can uncover more than people realize they're sharing." □□♂□

12.3 Verifying a Viral News Story Using OSINT

In the age of social media, misinformation and fake news spread rapidly. Viral stories can range from political disinformation to hoaxes and manipulated media. OSINT (Open-Source Intelligence) techniques help verify the accuracy, source, and intent behind viral news before it is shared further.

This guide will walk through a step-by-step process to verify a viral news story using OSINT, covering:

✓ Checking the original source

✓ Using reverse image & video search

✓ Verifying timestamps & metadata

✓ Cross-referencing with official sources

✓ Analyzing language & bias

By following these steps, you can determine whether a viral story is real, misleading, or outright false.

Step 1: Identify the Original Source

Before verifying a story, ask:

- Where did this story originate? (Social media, news site, forum?)
- Who published it? (A reliable journalist or an anonymous account?)
- Are official sources reporting it?

◆ Check Website Credibility

✔ **Examine the website domain** – Is it a legitimate news source?
✔ **Look for typos & poor formatting** – Fake news sites often have errors.
✔ **Check the 'About' page** – Who owns the website?
✔ **Review past articles** – Are they sensationalist or unreliable?

📌 Example:

☞ A viral story claims that a politician was arrested. You check the website and find it was registered just a month ago, with no official contact information—a red flag.

Step 2: Check Reverse Image & Video Searches

Fake news often uses misleading images or old videos taken out of context.

◆ Reverse Image Search

🔍 **Google Reverse Image** – images.google.com
🔍 **Yandex Reverse Search** – yandex.com/images
🔍 **TinEye** – tineye.com

📌 Example:

☞ A viral photo claims to show flooding in New York. You reverse search it and find it was actually taken in Mumbai in 2019.

◆ Reverse Video Search

🔍 **InVID & WeVerify** – Extracts video thumbnails for verification
🔍 **Bing Visual Search** – Can track video frames
🔍 **YouTube DataViewer** – Checks upload timestamps

📌 Example:

☞ A Twitter video claims to show a war crime. Using InVID, you find it was originally uploaded to YouTube in 2015, proving it's outdated.

Step 3: Verify Dates & Locations

Viral stories often misrepresent dates or locations to manipulate narratives.

◆ Checking Metadata & EXIF Data

☐ **ExifTool** – Extracts hidden metadata from images/videos
☐ **Jeffrey's Exif Viewer** – Shows timestamps & GPS locations
☐ **Fotoforensics** – Detects image tampering

📌 Example:

☞ A news article shares an image of a burning city, claiming it's happening now. You check the EXIF data and see the photo was taken five years ago.

◆ Using Maps & Satellite Imagery

☐ **Google Earth & Google Maps** – Verify landmarks and locations
☐ **Yandex Maps & Baidu Maps** – For non-Western regions
☐ **Wikimapia** – Crowdsourced location data

📌 Example:

☞ A news report claims a missile hit a government building. You compare the images with Google Street View and find the building is intact, proving the report is false.

Step 4: Cross-Reference with Official & Reputable Sources

If a story is true, official organizations and credible news agencies will report on it.

◆ Fact-Checking Websites

✅ **Snopes** – snopes.com (Debunks viral stories)
✅ **AFP Fact Check** – factcheck.afp.com (Investigative fact-checking)
✅ **PolitiFact** – politifact.com (Political claims verification)
✅ **BBC Reality Check** – bbc.com/realitycheck (Verifies global news)

📌 Example:

☞ A Facebook post claims a famous actor has died. You check Snopes and find it's a recycled hoax.

◆ Government & NGO Websites

✅ **World Health Organization (WHO)** – For health-related claims
✅ **Interpol & FBI Press Releases** – For criminal investigations
✅ **National Weather Services** – To verify natural disasters

📌 Example:

☞ A viral tweet claims a deadly virus outbreak in London. WHO's website shows no alerts, debunking the claim.

Step 5: Analyze Language & Bias

Fake news often uses emotional language, exaggerations, or misleading statements.

◆ Spot Manipulative Writing

● **Excessive capital letters & exclamation points** – "BREAKING: THE WORLD IS ENDING!!!"
● **Vague sources** – "Experts say…" (Which experts?)
● **Calls to action** – "Share this before it's deleted!"

📌 Example:

☞ A story says, "Top scientists confirm aliens built the pyramids!!!" but no legitimate scientific journal supports the claim.

◆ Use AI-Powered Fake News Detectors

☐ **Hoaxy** – Tracks how misinformation spreads online
☐ **Botometer** – Detects Twitter bots spreading fake news
☐ **NewsGuard** – Rates news sources for reliability

📌 Example:

☞ You check a viral tweet with Botometer and find it's from a bot network spreading propaganda.

Step 6: Look for Pattern Recognition & Past Fake News

Many fake news sites reuse the same tactics over time.

◆ Find Similar Fake Stories

✅ Search previous fact-checking reports

✅ Compare article layouts with known fake news sites

✅ Check archived versions (Wayback Machine)

📌 Example:

☞ A celebrity death hoax is shared. Checking previous Snopes reports reveals the same website falsely reported other celebrity deaths before.

Step 7: Stay Objective & Avoid Spreading Misinformation

◆ Before sharing a news story, ask yourself:

✔ Is this from a credible source?

✔ Can I verify images and videos?

✔ Have official sources confirmed it?

✓ Does this seem emotionally manipulative?

✓ Have I fact-checked using multiple methods?

📌 Example:

☞ A viral post claims a political figure was arrested. Instead of sharing immediately, you check official police reports, fact-checking websites, and news agencies—finding it was completely false.

Conclusion

✓ **Step 1**: Identify the Source – Check website credibility.

✓ **Step 2:** Reverse Search Images/Videos – Find out if they are old or misused.

✓ **Step 3**: Verify Timestamps & Locations – Check metadata and maps.

✓ **Step 4**: Cross-Reference with Official Sources – Use fact-checking & government sites.

✓ **Step 5**: Analyze Language & Bias – Look for emotionally charged content.

✓ **Step 6:** Identify Repeated Fake News Tactics – Compare with past hoaxes.

✓ **Step 7**: Stay Objective & Avoid Spreading Falsehoods – Think before sharing.

💡 Final Thought:

"A well-informed person is not the one who believes everything, but the one who questions everything." 🚀

12.4 Tracking an Email Address Using OSINT Methods

Email addresses are a key piece of digital identity. Whether investigating fraud, phishing, cyber threats, or background checks, OSINT (Open-Source Intelligence) techniques can help uncover information linked to an email.

🔍 Why Track an Email Address?

✅ Identify the owner (real or fake)

✓ Check for breaches or leaks

✓ Find connected social media accounts

✓ Analyze for fraud or phishing risks

This guide will cover step-by-step OSINT techniques to track an email address legally and ethically.

Step 1: Basic Email Analysis

◆ Examine the Email Format

Look at the structure of the email:

📌 **Example**: john.doe1985@gmail.com

- "john.doe" – Could indicate a full name
- "1985" – Might be a birth year
- "gmail.com" – A free email service (less likely to be corporate)

📌 **Example**: support@bank-secure-login.com

- Suspicious domain (official banks use @bank.com, not "bank-secure-login.com")
- Could be a phishing attempt

☐ **Tool to check email structure:**

🔍 **MailTester** – Tests if an email address exists

Step 2: Check for Data Breaches

♦ If an email has been in a data breach, it may expose passwords, locations, or linked accounts.

☐ **Email breach checkers:**

🔍 **Have I Been Pwned** – Checks breach databases
🔍 **DeHashed** – Searches leaked credentials (requires login)

📌 **Example:**

☞ Searching "johndoe1985@gmail.com" shows it was leaked in a LinkedIn data breach. This suggests the person had a LinkedIn account.

Step 3: Find Social Media Accounts Linked to the Email

◆ Many people use the same email for Facebook, Twitter, LinkedIn, Instagram, and other accounts.

☐ **Social Media Search Tools:**

🔍 **WhatsMyName** – Finds usernames linked to an email
🔍 **Sherlock** – OSINT tool for finding social accounts
🔍 **Namechk** – Checks email-linked usernames

📌 **Example:**

☞ You search "johndoe1985@gmail.com" on WhatsMyName and find a LinkedIn profile for John Doe, revealing his job and company.

Step 4: Perform a Google Search with Advanced Operators

◆ Google can reveal hidden mentions of an email in forums, blogs, and public databases.

🔍 **Useful Google Dorks:**

- "johndoe1985@gmail.com"
- site:linkedin.com "johndoe1985@gmail.com"
- site:pastebin.com "johndoe1985@gmail.com"

📌 **Example:**

☞ Searching "johndoe1985@gmail.com" site:pastebin.com reveals that the email was exposed in a leaked database dump.

☐ **Other Search Engines:**

🔍 **Yandex** – Finds email mentions in Russian databases

🔍 **DuckDuckGo** – More privacy-friendly than Google

Step 5: Reverse Lookup with Email Search Engines

◆ Some people search engines aggregate email data.

🔲 **People Search Tools:**

🔍 **Pipl** – Deep web email searches (paid)

🔍 **Spokeo** – Finds social links & phone numbers

🔍 **EmailSherlock** – Checks public records

📌 **Example:**

☞ Searching "johndoe1985@gmail.com" on Pipl reveals a Facebook and LinkedIn profile.

Step 6: Check for Associated Domains & IP Addresses

◆ If the email uses a custom domain (@company.com), you can investigate further.

🔲 **Domain Lookup Tools:**

🔍 **Whois Lookup** – Checks who registered a domain

🔍 **Hunter.io** – Finds company emails

🔍 **EmailRep** – Assesses email reputation

📌 **Example:**

☞ You search "admin@cybersecurityfirm.com" on Whois and find the registrant's name, location, and IP address.

Step 7: Investigate the Email Header for IP Address Tracking

◆ Email headers contain technical details like the sender's IP address and mail server.

How to Find Email Headers:

✉@ **Gmail: Open the email** → Click More (three dots) → Select Show Original

✉@ **Outlook: Open email** → Click File → Select Properties

🔍 **Extract Key Info from the Header:**

- **Return-Path**: Sender's original email
- **Received**: Shows the IP address of the sender
- **Message-ID**: Can reveal the mail server

☐ **Header Analysis Tools:**

🔍 **MXToolbox** – Analyzes email headers
🔍 **IPinfo.io** – Checks sender's IP location

📌 **Example:**

☞ The email "fraud-alert@paypal-support.com" claims to be from PayPal. Checking the email header reveals it was sent from a server in Russia—a clear phishing attempt.

Step 8: Check for Disposable or Temporary Emails

◆ Scammers often use throwaway email addresses to avoid tracking.

☐ **Temporary Email Checkers:**

🔍 **Scam-Detector** – Flags fake domains
🔍 **Disposable Email Checker** – Detects temporary emails

📌 **Example:**

☞ You receive an email from "support@amazon-secure-login.com", but a domain check shows it was created only 2 days ago, suggesting fraud.

Step 9: Conduct Dark Web Email Searches

◆ Some emails appear in underground hacker forums.

□ Dark Web Search Tools:

🔍 **DarkWeb ID** – Enterprise-level search
🔍 **Onion Search Engine** – Searches Tor hidden services

📌 **Example:**

☞ An email search on DarkWeb ID reveals it was involved in a ransomware attack.

Step 10: Legal & Ethical Considerations

◆ DO NOT hack, phish, or engage in illegal activities.
◆ Only use publicly available data.
◆ Respect privacy laws (GDPR, CCPA, etc.) when investigating.

Conclusion

✅ **Step 1**: Check email format for clues
✅ **Step 2**: Search for breaches & leaks
✅ **Step 3**: Find social media links
✅ **Step 4**: Use Google dorks for deep search
✅ **Step 5:** Look up the email in people search engines
✅ **Step 6:** Investigate domains and IP addresses
✅ **Step 7**: Analyze email headers for sender details
✅ **Step 8**: Identify disposable emails
✅ **Step 9:** Search the dark web
✅ **Step 10**: Stay ethical & legal

Final Thought:

"In OSINT, an email is never just an email—it's a digital fingerprint waiting to be uncovered." 🚀

12.5 Conducting a Simple Website & Domain Investigation

Every website and domain leaves a digital footprint that can reveal ownership, history, hosting details, security weaknesses, and more. Conducting an OSINT (Open-Source Intelligence) investigation on a website can help in:

✅ Identifying the owner of a website

✅ Checking for malicious activity or fraud

✅ Investigating historical changes of a website

✅ Discovering hidden connections between domains

✅ Finding open directories and exposed files

This guide will walk through step-by-step techniques to investigate a website or domain using free OSINT tools.

Step 1: Identify the Website's Owner (WHOIS Lookup)

A WHOIS lookup provides details about the domain registrant, creation date, expiration date, and registrar.

🔲 **WHOIS Lookup Tools:**

🔍 **Who.is** – Basic WHOIS lookup
🔍 **ICANN WHOIS** – Official domain registry lookup
🔍 **DomainTools** – Advanced domain research

📌 **Example:**

☞ Investigating example.com shows:

- **Registered by**: GoDaddy
- **Creation Date**: 2015-06-10
- **Exirationp Date**: 2025-06-10
- **Registrant Email**: privacy-protected (some domains hide owner details)

◆ **If WHOIS info is private:**

- The site owner is using privacy protection services
- You may need to investigate other domain connections (Step 4)

Step 2: Check the Website's Hosting & IP Address

Finding the hosting provider and server location can give clues about a website's origin.

☐ **Hosting & IP Check Tools:**

🔍 **IPinfo.io** – Shows IP address and hosting provider
🔍 **ViewDNS.info** – Multiple domain tools in one
🔍 **Hosting Checker** – Identifies hosting company

📌 **Example:**

☞ Investigating suspicious-site.com shows it is hosted on a server in Russia, despite claiming to be a U.S.-based company. This is a red flag for fraud.

Step 3: Analyze the Website's Historical Changes (Wayback Machine)

Websites evolve over time. Tracking past versions can reveal:

✅ Removed content

✅ Old owner details

✅ Changes in branding & purpose

☐ **Historical Snapshot Tools:**

🔍 **Wayback Machine** – Captures old versions of websites
🔍 **OldWeb.today** – Browse websites using historical browsers

📌 **Example:**

☞ Searching "newsupdates.com" in Wayback Machine shows that it was originally a blog but was later converted into a fake news site.

Step 4: Find Other Websites Owned by the Same Person or Company

If a website is suspicious, it's useful to check if the owner operates other domains.

☐ Reverse WHOIS & Domain Search Tools:

🔍 **SpyOnWeb** – Finds websites sharing the same IP
🔍 **DomainBigData** – Tracks domains by owner
🔍 **SecurityTrails** – Advanced domain intelligence

📌 **Example:**

☞ A WHOIS lookup for fraudulent-store.com shows the same registrant email was used for fake-shop.net and cheapdeals.biz – likely part of a scam network.

Step 5: Check for Open Directories & Exposed Files

Some websites leave sensitive files or directories open to public access. These may contain:

✅ Hidden admin panels

✅ Logs or backups

✅ Exposed customer data

☐ Tools to Find Open Directories:

🔍 Google Dorking (See Step 6)
🔍 Dirbuster – Finds hidden directories
🔍 Pentest-Tools Directory Scanner – Scans for exposed folders

📌 **Example Google Dork:**

site:example.com intitle:"index of /"

☞ This reveals an unprotected directory with PDFs and backups.

Step 6: Use Google Dorking to Uncover Hidden Data

Google dorks use advanced search operators to find hidden website content.

☐ Common Google Dorks for Website OSINT:

site:example.com filetype:pdf
(inurl:admin OR inurl:login) site:example.com
"confidential" site:example.com

📌 **Example:**

☞ Searching "password" site:example.com finds a leaked configuration file!

Step 7: Analyze Website Metadata & Tracking Codes

Websites often use Google Analytics and tracking codes. If two sites share the same tracking ID, they are likely owned by the same entity.

🔲 **Metadata & Tracking Code Tools:**

🔍 **BuiltWith** – Shows website technology stack
🔍 **Google Analytics Reverse Lookup**
🔍 **Wappalyzer** – Browser extension for detecting tracking tools

📌 **Example:**

☞ A scam website shares the same Google Analytics ID as other fraud sites, confirming a connection.

Step 8: Check if the Website is Malicious or Part of Phishing Attacks

Some websites distribute malware or are used for phishing scams.

🔲 **Website Security Checkers:**

🔍 **VirusTotal** – Checks for malware reports
🔍 **URLVoid** – Scans for blacklisted sites
🔍 **PhishTank** – Detects phishing websites

📌 **Example:**

☞ You check "login-paypal-support.com" in VirusTotal and find it flagged as a phishing site.

Step 9: Investigate Website Traffic & Popularity

Checking a website's traffic and ranking can help determine legitimacy.

☐ **Traffic Analysis Tools:**

🔍 **SimilarWeb** – Estimates website traffic
🔍 **Alexa Site Info** – Website ranking & audience data
🔍 **StatShow** – Estimates visitor count

📌 **Example:**

☞ A website claiming to be "a top news platform" gets almost no traffic, suggesting it's a fake or inactive site.

Step 10: Stay Ethical & Legal in Website Investigations

🔏 DO NOT engage in hacking or illegal access.
🔏 DO NOT attempt to bypass login pages.
🔏 DO NOT download private files without permission.

Stick to publicly available information and legal OSINT tools.

Conclusion: Website OSINT Checklist

✅ **Step 1**: WHOIS lookup for domain owner
✅ **Step 2**: Check hosting & IP address
✅ **Step 3**: View historical website changes
✅ **Step 4**: Find related domains by the same owner
✅ **Step 5**: Scan for open directories & exposed files
✅ **Step 6**: Use Google Dorking for hidden data
✅ **Step 7**: Analyze metadata & tracking codes
✅ **Step 8:** Check if the site is malicious
✅ **Step 9**: Investigate traffic & legitimacy
✅ **Step 10**: Stay ethical & legal

🎯 **Final Thought**: A website is never just a webpage—it's a digital fingerprint waiting to be uncovered! 🚀

12.6 OSINT Challenge: Applying Your Skills to a Real Case

Now that you've learned how to conduct OSINT investigations, it's time to apply those skills to a real-world challenge. In this section, you'll follow a step-by-step OSINT investigation, just like a professional analyst.

🎯 **Your Challenge:**

You have been given a suspicious website and a name linked to an online scam. Your goal is to:

✅ Identify the website's owner and hosting details

✅ Find other connected domains

✅ Uncover any social media profiles linked to the scam

✅ Verify if the website is involved in fraud

⚠️ **Disclaimer**: This exercise is for educational purposes only. Do not attempt to hack, access private information, or engage in illegal activities.

Step 1: Investigate the Website's Ownership & Hosting

📌 Given Website: fastmoneyinvestments.com

🔲 **Tools & Techniques:**

1️⃣ **WHOIS Lookup**

- Use Who.is or ICANN WHOIS to check the registrant details, creation date, and expiration date.
- Look for email addresses or company names in the registration.

2️⃣ **Find Hosting & IP Address**

- Use IPinfo.io to check the server location.
- If hosted on a cheap or offshore provider, it could be suspicious.

📌 **Findings:**

- Registered six months ago using a privacy-protected service.
- Hosted in Russia, despite claiming to be a U.S.-based investment firm.
- Registrar email found: johndoeinvest@gmail.com

🔍 **Suspicion Level: HIGH** 🔒

Step 2: Check for Related Websites

🔗 **Objective**: Find if the owner has other fraudulent sites.

🔲 **Tools & Techniques:**

1️⃣ **Reverse WHOIS Lookup**

Use SecurityTrails or DomainBigData to find other websites linked to the same email address or registrant.

2️⃣ **Spy on Shared IPs**

Use SpyOnWeb to check if other domains share the same IP address.

📌 **Findings:**

- fastmoneyinvestments.com is hosted on the same server as quickcashprofits.net and investsmartly.co.
- All three domains have similar website designs and content, suggesting they are part of a fraud network.

🔍 **Suspicion Level: VERY HIGH** 🔒🔒

Step 3: Investigate Social Media Connections

🔲🔲 **Goal**: Find social media profiles linked to the website.

☐ Tools & Techniques:

1☐ Search by Email & Username

Use WhatsMyName to check if johndoeinvest@gmail.com is linked to social media accounts.

2☐ Reverse Image Search on Profile Pictures

Use Google Reverse Image Search or Yandex to see if profile pictures were stolen from elsewhere.

📌 Findings:

- Found a Twitter profile (@JohnInvestPro) promoting "easy money investment schemes."
- Profile picture was stolen from a stock photo website.
- The same username was used on Instagram and Facebook with similar scammy content.

🔍 Suspicion Level: EXTREME 🔍🔍🔍

Step 4: Analyze Website Security & Exposure

☐ Techniques & Tools:

1☐ Google Dorking for Hidden Data

Use queries like:

site:fastmoneyinvestments.com filetype:pdf

Checks if they left internal documents exposed.

2☐ Check for Phishing or Malware

Use VirusTotal to scan the website.

📌 Findings:

- A hidden directory was found containing fake investment reports.
- VirusTotal flagged the site as potential phishing.

🔍 Final Suspicion Level: CONFIRMED SCAM 🚨🚨🚨🚨

Step 5: Responsible Disclosure & Next Steps

Now that we've confirmed the site is fraudulent, here's what to do:

✅ Report to Authorities:

File a report with FTC (Federal Trade Commission) or INTERPOL if it's an international scam.

✅ Warn Potential Victims:

Post findings on scam awareness sites like ScamAdviser.

✅ Share Ethical OSINT Findings:

Avoid publicly posting private details to stay compliant with privacy laws.

Final Challenge Recap: What Did We Learn?

- ✓☐ How to trace website ownership & hosting details
- ✓☐ How to find related scam domains
- ✓☐ How to investigate social media footprints
- ✓☐ How to uncover security flaws & hidden content
- ✓☐ How to ethically report fraudulent websites

◆ Would you have caught the scam before someone lost money? ☐

💡 *Your Turn: Try applying these techniques to a real-world case (legally & ethically) and test your OSINT skills!* 🚀

In an era where information is more valuable than ever, Open-Source Intelligence (OSINT) has emerged as a powerful skill set for professionals across various industries. **OSINT Foundations: The Beginner's Guide to Open-Source Intelligence** is designed as the ultimate entry point for anyone looking to master the art of intelligence gathering from publicly available sources.

This book demystifies OSINT, breaking it down into clear, practical steps that anyone—from cybersecurity professionals to journalists, law enforcement officers, private investigators, and even curious individuals—can apply in real-world scenarios. Whether you're looking to enhance personal security, track down hidden information, or conduct professional investigations, this guide lays the groundwork for becoming an effective OSINT analyst.

What You'll Learn in This Book

- **Understanding OSINT**: Learn the core principles of OSINT and why it's a game-changer in the digital age.
- **Tools & Techniques**: Explore essential OSINT tools, including search engines, metadata analysis, and data scraping.
- **Search Engine Mastery**: Discover advanced Google Dorking techniques to extract hidden information.
- **Social Media Investigations**: Uncover ways to track online activity, analyze profiles, and map social connections.
- **Image & Geolocation Analysis**: Learn how to reverse search images and verify locations through mapping tools.
- **Cybersecurity & Digital Footprints**: Understand how to manage your own digital footprint while investigating others.
- **Ethics & Legal Considerations**: Navigate the fine line between ethical intelligence gathering and legal restrictions.

Through a blend of theory and practical exercises, this book equips you with the foundational knowledge and hands-on experience needed to conduct efficient OSINT investigations. With real-world case studies and step-by-step tutorials, OSINT Foundations is the perfect starting point for those looking to harness the power of open-source intelligence in an ethical and effective manner.

Thank you for embarking on this journey into the fascinating world of Open-Source Intelligence. Your curiosity and dedication to learning are what drive the continued evolution of OSINT, making it a vital tool for truth-seekers, investigators, and digital security enthusiasts.

The digital landscape is constantly shifting, and staying ahead requires not just knowledge, but the willingness to adapt and explore. By reading this book, you've taken an important step in mastering OSINT fundamentals. We hope that the techniques and strategies outlined here empower you to conduct responsible and insightful investigations—whether for personal security, research, professional work, or even just to satisfy your curiosity.

We encourage you to continue your OSINT education by exploring the rest of The OSINT Analyst Series: Intelligence Techniques for the Digital Age. Each book builds upon the knowledge from the previous one, helping you evolve from a beginner to an advanced OSINT practitioner.

If you found value in this book, we would love to hear from you! Your feedback, experiences, and insights help shape future editions and ensure that this knowledge remains relevant in our fast-paced digital world.

Once again, thank you for your time, trust, and passion for learning. Stay curious, stay ethical, and keep uncovering the truth!

Continue Your OSINT Journey

Expand your skills with the rest of The OSINT Analyst Series:

- **The OSINT Search Mastery**: Hacking Search Engines for Intelligence
- **OSINT People Finder**: Advanced Techniques for Online Investigations
- **Social Media OSINT**: Tracking Digital Footprints
- **Image & Geolocation Intelligence**: Reverse Searching and Mapping
- **Domain, Website & Cyber Investigations with OSINT**
- **Email & Dark Web Investigations**: Tracking Leaks & Breaches
- **OSINT Threat Intel**: Investigating Hackers, Breaches, and Cyber Risks
- **Corporate OSINT**: Business Intelligence & Competitive Analysis
- **Investigating Disinformation & Fake News with OSINT**
- **OSINT for Deep & Dark Web**: Techniques for Cybercrime Investigations
- **OSINT Automation**: Python & APIs for Intelligence Gathering
- **OSINT Detective**: Digital Tools & Techniques for Criminal Investigations
- **Advanced OSINT Case Studies**: Real-World Investigations
- **The Ethical OSINT Investigator**: Privacy, Legal Risks & Best Practices

We look forward to seeing you in the next book!

Happy investigating!

www.ingramcontent.com/pod-product-compliance
Lightning Source LLC
LaVergne TN
LVHW060120070326
832902LV00019B/3052